CRIME AND CORRUPTION
IN
INDIA

CONTENTS

INTRODUCTION

What is Corruption? An Overview

The cancerous spread of corruption in India's public life has been a matter of great concern to its citizens in all walks of life. There is a growing literature in the country on the diagnosis of this phenomenon, and the print media, has provided extensive coverage to corruption in high places. But what is corruption, how can it defined in its different facets and is there some remedy for it?

The Oxford English dictionary offers as many as nine meanings of corruption which can be grouped into two main categories:

(a) Corruption may apply to an object (physical decomposition, purification, spoiling of quality, adulteration);

(b) The perversion of language or taste, to morals (to destroy or prevent the integrity or fidelity of a person in his discharge of his duty, to induce to act dishonestly or unfaithfully, to make venal, to bribe);

The last two aspects of the word, based on the Latin word to break, rumour, which implies that something is broken, such as a moral or social code of conduct, or more narrowly, a law or an administrative rule.

Corruption can straddle both the public and private sectors. However given our focus on corruption in the public services, it might be useful to start with a narrow definition that corruption is the 'misuse of public power for private gain.' Other definitions have also been offered citing the misuse of public office, violation of public interest, disapproval of public opinion and the illegal use of public office for private gain. On the other hand, definitions which link corruption narrowly to bribery have been faulted on the ground that they leave out forms of misconduct which can lead to, or result from corruption, such as nepotism, patronage, and a variety of other offences.

India has acquired an unenviable reputation of being among the most corrupt countries of the world. A poll taken among businessmen and financial journalists by Transparency International, the reputed anti-corruption non-governmental organisation, has placed India ninth from the bottom in its 1996 list of 59 countries Why? Look at the record:

(a) In a number of states, the Chief Minister and Ministers have been implicated in major corrupt transactions relating to liquor licences, real estate approvals, large government contracts, allocation of scarce materials, transfers of public servants, and so on.

(b) In both the Centre and the States, there is ample evidence of an increase of corruption in the higher bureaucracy. A sizeable proportion of senior civil servants are believed to be corrupt on their own, and/or to be acting as accomplices, conduits and agents for corrupt Ministers. Equally, a very large number have remained silent to the doings of their Ministers and colleagues.

(c) At the lower levels of the bureaucracy, corruption mostly takes form of speed money for expediting approvals and the demand for bribes for providing or not providing legitimate services (in utilities such as telephones, electricity connections and so on).

(d) Corruption is also rampant in the administration of welfare schemes, the public distribution system, the police, revenue and irrigation departments where the public comes into daily contact with the administration.

(e) Of much greater concern is the interlocking or the vertical integration of corruption at various levels of the government hierarchy—elected politicians, higher and lower bureaucracy. The normal assumption is that the 'principals' at each of the higher levels would act according to standards and norms of probity is no more tenable.

(f) In the public domain corruption has spread to legislatures, the judiciary, media and the independent professions such as lawyers, doctors, chartered accountants and contractors. Through mutual interaction, this horizontal spread of corruption has been strengthened by government policies which has made its prevention and control much more difficult.

(g) Corruption has been politicised—just as politics has been corrupted—in the sense corruption has been used for partisan political purposes rather than with any serious intent to objectively tackle the problem. Sadly, the judicial processes are too slow and dilatory even though in recent times the Supreme Court has intervened to enforce the law in response public interest litigation.

Corruption in India: The Current Context

That corruption in whichever way it is defined is like a cancer which has endangered Indian society, polity and economy can no longer be denied. Consider the following:

(a) There has been a distinct increase—both in terms of numbers and amounts—or scams. Some of these are confined to defence contracts (Bofors, HDW submarines), civil contracts (railways), telecommunication contracts, commodity imports (fertilizer, sugar), privatisation (Bailadilla mines), house allotments, bank scams in the financial sector, violation of Foreign Exchange Regulation and Income Tax Acts.

(b) There are many more smaller scams which if taken together would account for at least Rs.50,000 crores.

(A) CAUSES OF CORRUPTION

The extensive literature on the subject of corruption draws attention to political systems and practices, economic development, economic policies, sociological characteristics and the cultural milieu as the main factors which are relevant for a causal explanation of corruption. For example, it has been argued that democracies and the costly electoral cycles associated with them are fertile grounds for political corruption. While in office, the political leadership and legislators, dependent on external sources of finding for their re-election campaigns, tend to be influenced by pressure groups. In poor developing countries, there is acute competition for the sharing of benefits. At the same time, inequality and expectations are high. Such a situation provides an in-built impetus for corruption. Furthermore, economic policies based on administrative regulations - using devices like permits and licences for the allocation of investment approvals, scarce resources, welfare benefits and subsidies - create powerful incentives for bribery. In terms of sociological factors, it has been argued that caste, kinship and patron-client relationships, especially in predominantly rural societies, generate and reproduce corruption through networks of nepotism, patronage and dependency. Cultural factors that have been relied upon to explain corruption include the custom of 'gift-giving' in traditional societies with the expectation of reciprocal rewards.

While there may be prima facie explanatory rationale in all these factors, none of them can be taken to be definitive or deterministic in explaining corruption in different societies at various times in their histories. Corruption, for instance, has been recorded at very high levels not just in democracies, but also in authoritarian regimes in Latin America, Africa and Asia. Advanced economies, both socialist and market-oriented, are equally prone to corrupt practices.

(B) CONSEQUENCES OF CORRUPTION

There is considerable agreement about the adverse effects of corruption on society, polity and the economy. Corruption corrodes the moral fibre of society. It undermines the legitimacy of Governments because of the widespread cynicism bred on a texture of facts and perceptions concerning the level of corruption. It has been pointed out that general impressions about corruption, circulated in public discussion and gossip, might be unfair and exaggerated but the very fact that such impressions are there causes damage to the social fabric. One result of such deterioration is political instability when one democratic regime after another is outvoted from office on the issue of corruption. More serious is the replacement of democratic Governments with authoritarian or military rule. In a number of countries, such Governments have come to power on the slogan of providing a clean administration but have themselves become highly corrupt in due course.

The adverse effects of corruption on the economy and on public administration are manifold. Government expenditures are inflated and wasteful projects and programs are taken up in order to obtain kickbacks. Standards get diluted in investment (e.g. traffic jams, roads, bridges and buildings) goods (e.g. drugs), and services (e.g. quality of doctors, engineers, teachers) causing hazards to safety, life and health. Government revenues get reduced on account of tax evasion. Subsidies and incentives are abused. The poor are the worst affected since they cannot pay bribes in order to obtain benefits to which they are legitimately entailed. Worse, they are denied basic justice in the hands of corrupt officials, such as the police and village officials. Corruption thus aggravates inequality in an already unequal society.

(C) CHARACTERISTICS OF CORRUPTION

Corruption can assume many forms, cover a wide variety of transactions, and operate at many levels. It can relate to acts of commission, omission or dereliction, involve the exercise of discretion, or the violation of rules, but not necessarily, since illegal gratification can be taken even whilst technically conforming to rules.

Bribery can be in the form of cash, kind, services or other favours. At lower bureaucratic levels, it could take the form of 'speed money' to facilitate or expedite the issue of approvals or the delivery of public services or the fulfilment of rightful entitlement. Corruption may involve a voluntary or collusive relationship between the bribe-giver and the bribe-taker or it may be extortionate for rendering an entitlement, doing an undue favour or desisting from a harmful action.

Corruption can also reside in several policy decisions explicitly or implicitly aimed at benefiting interest groups as well as in a wide gamut of specific transactions public sector contracts for the purchase of goods and services; allocation of scarce materials, permits, licences, exemptions, and waivers; levy and collection of taxes, implementation of projects and programs; delivery of public servants; different stages of the electoral process, conduct of legislators and so on, for no list of this kind can be exhaustive.

In the public sphere, corruption operates at various levels of the political and bureaucratic hierarchies. It can do so indecently among politicians and bureaucrats but, more commonly, there is a nexus between corrupt politicians and bureaucrats who themselves corrupt or who passively collude with their political masters. In such a relationship of complicity, both gain and each protects the other. There is also a vertical integration between layers of the political and bureaucratic echelons: e.g. Minister-legislator-party functionary and Minister-higher bureaucracy - middle and lower bureaucracy. The lower levels operate as agents of the higher levels passing up to them shares in the bribes received at the operating level. Alternatively, the corrupt official may make an up front lump such payment 'commuting' recurring payments of a share in the bribes. In such cases, government posts with lucrative potential for money-making are informally auctioned to the highest bidder from time to time. In this process of collusive corruption, appointments, postings and transfers play a crucial role in aiding and abetting corruption.

1

CRIME AND CORRUPTION

Towards a Definition of Crime and Corruption Indian politics has sunk to abysmal depths of crime, corruption. It has transformed politics of faith and trust by the politics of breach of faith and trust. It is an open secret that some politicians work with an eye only on the vote banks. They put pressure on the police against taking action even in cases of mindless violence: officers who refuse to fall in line are back list. In EMS Namoodriped [1], in an article, "The politician - Criminal nexus", writes :-

The criminalisation of politician of power, to attain which any means are adopted. Policy and society have been so degraded that even those who were selfless and sacrificing in the days of freedom struggle have now become power - hungry. The power they win is used to amass wealth and they engaged themselves in functional quarrels. Such control of the economy, polity and administration of country has spread corruption and other evils, which lead to criminalised politics.

Namoodriped further writes : -

The criminalisation of politics can not be removed by just bringing several individuals before courts and getting them punished. Since it has come to public gaze rather recently, the so-called criminalisation of politics is much talked these days. Unlike the weather-beaten topic of political corruption, which is left to be moaned about occasionally by one moralist or another, criminalisation of politics is on everybody's tongue. Newspaper columns are often filled with facts and figures about criminal antecedents of politics contesting

---

1 EMS Namoodriped, "The Politician - criminal nexus", FRONTLINE, October 3, 1997, pp. 96-97.

elections and getting elected. The best part is even such politicians join the chorus against increasing criminalisation of politics and need to prevent it. It was amusing to hear a Minister known for his Mafia connection philosophically haranguing about politicisation of crime[2].

But what exactly is crime? What do we mean by a criminal background? Who is a criminal - a person suspected of having committed a crime or a person being prosecuted in court for a crime or a person actually convicted and punished by a court? Popular notion about crime and criminals is rather vague and nebulous. Murder of course is a crime, but is prostitution or drunkenness or, for that matter, keeping a country-made gun for self-protection also a crime? One thing is certain. It is something that is bad, evil and sinful. All are evil and sinful, but are all evil and sinful acts crimes? There is no end to questions and doubts once we get about to understand the phenomenon of crime in all its ramifications.

Basically, the view emanates from the perception of good and evil, right and wrong. But the idea of good and evil, right and wrong may vary from society to society, country to country and time to time. Teenage 'dating and even sex between young boys and girls (pre-marital) are considered fairly normal in western societies but regarded as down-right evil in India. Gambling and female nudity are considered bad and sinful in India but not in Las Vegas or Monte Carol. So is the case with drinking and extra -marital sex or homosexuality. Homosexuals have their won associations in America and sometime back there was an international assemblage of homosexuals and lesbians in Australia. No one can imagine such a thing happening in India.

Going back in time, one will be astounded to find even killing not being regarded as crime in some tribal societies which indulged in human head-hunting as a manly sport. In India's north east, some Naga tribes believed in the validity of head-hunting as a sport till

---

2 Shashi B Sahai, Criminalisation of Politics, (1995) p 108.

turn of the century. In mid-seventies, an ex-Governor of Nagaland mentioned in an article about his informal talks with a Naga gentleman who came to see him. The gentleman was all praise for various development activities of the government, but could not appreciate why such a valiant sport as head-hunting was prohibited. He was of the view the ban would erode the valour and manliness of Naga society.

In the middle of the 11th century, a Society of the Assassins appeared in Persia and Syria which believed in righteousness of killing. "The members of this religious political group of Fedawi (Arabic for 'devoted ones') believed that killing bad people on the command of their leader was a sacred duty, which ensured their personal salvation besides getting rid of a corrupt order in this world."** The words assassin and assassination in European languages owe their origin to this Arab cult of the 11th century. Many 16th and 17th century western thinkers were debating whether killing was always murder.

Apart from the judgement about right and wrong being place and time related, it may also differ from individual to individual. Every one would condemn theft or stealing as wrong, but what about stealing of a loaf of bread by a starving child. Victor Hug's classic novel Les Miserables - revolves round the fate of a poor boy who stole a loaf of bread. And the entire story represents the judgement of the boy and against the rigours of a blind law which treated his act as an unforgivable crime. If it left to the subjective judgement of individuals to decide what is right and what is wrong, there may be as many packages of rights and wrongs as the number of individuals.

That brings us back to square one. Merely stating that the idea of crime flows out of our perception of right and wrong, good and bad, does not solve the problem. It does not bring us any nearer to identifying the acts and deeds which constitute crime. It becomes necessary to clearly demarcate the boundaries of what is crime to distinguish it from what is not. A line to be drawn between crime

---

** Terrorism : History And Facets in the World and in India - by N. S. Saxena - 1985.

and non-crime and the line has to be determinate and definitive, and independent of subjective value judgement of individuals. Criminologists have drawn the line but the task is evidently not so easy. A well known criminologist, Hermann Mannheim, has aptly observed : " The frontiers of criminology would not be so difficult to define ... if there would not be so many doubts as to the meaning of its fundamental concept, crime. It is a dilemma confronting probably all scientific disciplines that they are engaged in an unending search for the definition of their basic concepts."

Keeping in mind the limits of any definition, the concept of crime has to be understood in the light of definitions given by criminologists. "Crime and criminal are often loosely used", says Ruth Shonle Cavan, an American criminologist, "to condemn any kind of behaviour that the speaker regards as immortal or anti-social. A more exact use of the term reserves crime for acts that are a violation of criminal laws. These laws explicitly prescribe or prohibit certain types of behaviour under threat of a specific penalty if the law is disobeyed."

According to John Barron Mays, " A crime is an offence against society. It consists in the commission of acts which have been legally prescribed. A criminal is merely a man who has transgressed the legal norms of the society in which he lives. ** Another criminologist, Clarence Darrow, has defined crime as "act forbidden by the law of the land, and one which is considered sufficiently serious to warrant proving penalties for its commission.***

The common denominator in all these definitions is prohibition by the law of the land. All acts are forbidden by the criminal law of a country and for commission of which punishment is prescribed in the penal code come under the category of crime. Accordingly the scope of crime varies from country to country, as an act which is forbidden by law in one country may not be so forbidden in another. For instance, keeping of firearms without licence is a crime because it is prohibited under he Indian Arms Act, but it is not a crime in the

** Crime And The Social Structure by John Barron Mays.

*** Quoted in "Facets of crime in India" by Venugopal Rao. Emphasis ours.

United States of America where no such licence is required by law.

Going by the legal definition, the scope of crime also differs from time to time in the same country. As pointed out by Hurwitz, adultery and homosexuality were once punishable under the Danish criminal law and came under the category of crime in Denmark. But they have been deleted from the Danish penal code and are no longer crime in that country. At the time of the Industrial Revolution in Europe, resorting to strike by industrial workers was a penal offence, but it is an acknowledged right of the workers today. In India, prostitution though considered immoral, was not a crime till about decade after independence because there was no legal bar against it. Prostitutes 'Kothas' flourished in all cities and towns and were openly patronised by people. It is only after the "Suppression of Immoral Traffic in Women And Girls Act" was passed in 1956 and became effective in 1958 that prostitution as such became a crime in India.

Likewise, taking and giving of dowry in marriage was a perfectly valid act and dowry was considered as a status symbol till not very long ago. It was only after it was prohibited by law and made a legally punishable act that taking of dowry became a crime. (it is another matter that anti-dowry legislation has not proved effective in curbing the practice which goes on clandestinely. But that is true, more or less of other acts of crime also. If crimes could be abolished by passing laws against them, there would be no crime in the world).

Defining crime in terms of law seems to make the boundaries of crime and criminality clear and determinate. The legal definition does settle the issue as far as law enforcing agencies and courts of law are concerned, and theoretically for the students of criminology also. But as far as popular notion about crime and criminal act is concerned, doubts persist inspite of the unambiguity of the statute book. In India, unlike in the West, sex outside marriage is considered immoral or bad, and can be valid ground for divorce, but by itself it is not a crime because it is not punishable by law. On the other hand, child marriage has long been banned by law, but the law is largely followed in its breach and, what is more, no one considers it as a crime. The Child Marriage Restraint Act passed as early as 1921, made marriage of a girl below the age of 14 years and a boy below the age of 18 an offence. (The age of consent has since been raised to 18 and 21 for a girl and a boy respectively). But the legislation has largely remained a dead letter because of a wide gap between the laudable objectives of the law and existing traditions and social conditions in India. And that illustrates the limitation of legal definition of crime.

Many instances of such contradiction between social mores and penal code can be found in all societies. What is regarded as evil and immoral by society may not necessarily be forbidden by law and what is legally forbidden may not be regarded as such by society. If tomorrow procreating more than two children is prohibited by law, crossing the limit will become an offence, but who would consider it as crime? Hermann Mannheim had such contradictions in mind when he said there should not be too much gap between law and social morality. Because in that case, Law will lose its strongest support base. For, the value system of a society is the ultimate sanction behind its laws.

The gap between a country's value system and its penal code indicates the limits of legal definition of crime, but does not render it invalid. For that matter, every formulation of social sciences, unlike natural sciences, is subject to limitations because their subject matter, man in relation to society, is not an inanimate object.

But for that reason alone, the laws regarding human behaviour formulated by social sciences cannot be set aside. With proper appreciation of their inherent limitations, the law of social sciences have great validity in analysing and assessing man's social behaviour. That is true of criminology also. In the ultimate analysis, law is only the embodiment of moral code of a society as a whole as distinguished from its sub-cultural groups and individuals.

Having arrived at a workable definition of crime, we have to see where corruption stands in relation to it. Corruption has been dealt with so far both in its narrow meaning of corrupt practices like bribery and broader sense of deviation from norms and decomposition. In dealing with political corruption, its broader connotation is more relevant because politicians not only constitute the ruling class but, in a new nation like India, are also supposed to be the standard-bearers of the nation. Greater emphasis has, therefore been placed thus far on its broader meaning, keeping the legal issues aside, except in case of electoral corruption. That may create an impression that corruption stands as a class apart from other forms of law violation as is popularly believed. It does not.

In its restricted meaning of bribery or abuse of power for illegal gratification, corruption is as much a forbidden act in terms of laws as assault, theft, robbery and murder. The Indian Penal Code, listing primarily the main stream offences and enacted by the British rulers during the 19th century, also enlisted bribery as one of the offences and prescribed punishment for it, vide sections 161 to 165. On the eve of independence, a separate and specific legislation was enacted to deal with corruption more effectively. The prevention of Corruption Act, 1947, covered different facets of corruption that had come to notice, specially in course of large scale supply of defence and other materials to government of India during the Second World War. Needless to say, the provisions of this Act, as well as those of the Indian Penal Code, were aimed at curbing corruption among government servants because there was no question of political corruption before the transfer of power to politicians. But the terms 'Public servant' used in the Act was wide enough to include Ministers in its purview. The Aiyar Commission of 1967 which enquired into allegation against Bihar Ministers recommended for investigation into specific charges of corruption against some of them. The CBI investigated these charges and on finding prima facie evidence filed a charge-sheet in court against three of them, under the Prevention of Corruption Act, 1947. The former Chief Minister was charged for being in possession of assets disproportionate to his declared income and another former Minister for accepting illegal gratification (All the three charge-sheeted Ministers passed away during pendency of the cases in court).

The point of significance is corruption is punishable by law in the same way as any other offence, and is, therefore , basically no different from it. In other words, corruption is crime in every sense of term. It does not even have the saving grace of such 'technical' crimes as child marriage, which is legally forbidden but is not considered as such by society. Corruption is roundly condemned by society, considered in unmitigated evil, and also prescribed by law which provides for punishment for a variety of corrupt acts. What more is needed to designate corruption as crime? The relationship between crime and corruption is one of a genus and species. Crime is the genus of which corruption, like murder, dacoity, theft, assault, rape etc.., is a species.

2

A CANCEROUS CORRUPTION

Corruption is like a virus always around to infect a political system anywhere in the world and make it sick. If it has its full play without any resistance or check, it would eat into the vitals of the system and eventually destroy it . But like the human body, political systems have their own immune systems which automatically fight and resist the virus. The degree if corruption prevailing in any political society depends on the strength or deficiency of its immune system. Corruptibility is inversely related to the efficacy and weakness of the defence mechanism of the system.

In a democratic polity, strong and vigilant public opinion ultimately reflected in electoral verdicts is the in-built immune system which resists and restricts the onslaught of viruses like corruption, criminality etc. The more truly democratic a polity is, the greater the effectiveness of public opinion in saving it from sickness. In modern democratic societies, the media is its most important weapon against corruption. News and views brought out in the print and audio-visual media reflect people's opinions on diverse public issues as much as they help in making it. That is equally, true of public opinion about political parties and the character of their leaders.

In India's tradition, character has always occupied the place of foremost importance. Character has two facets : the one which is personal,, and the other which manifests itself in our relationship with society. Indian culture has always held high the purity of personal character. Indians have never called a personal philosopher who is selfish or given to various vices like wine, woman and gold. The philosopher to an Indian is all a man of absolute purity, integrity and austerity of character. The emphasis of Indian culture is on means. The means an individual adopts to achieve his goals is more important than the ends. Conversely, wrong means will not achieve the desired ends - at least not in the long run.

The scams in the higher ranks of the Indian Society have become common place. Leaders are being charge-sheeted and produced before courts of law almost every day.

An octogenenan Chief Minister had amassed a fortune that would last for his seven generations. His party it is said denied the ticket to him for the general election which gave him such a rude shock that he died the same day. Those were the days when Pandit Nehru as Prime Minister believed in giving a shock treatment but he did not take the matter to the court. Thus the scandals of the party were buried under the carpet. It is also said of a minority leader that wheh he was posted as an ambassador in a foreign country India had purchased explosives from there. The ship which was carrying these explosives was to stop at Karachi harbour . It is said Pakistan some how got the inkling from the Indian embassy and Pakistan confiscated all the gunpowder. Pandit Nehru did not hold a public enquiry but the punishment to the person concerned was given in some form or the other Even his wife disassociated from him.

But now the scams are pouring in daily and they read like a novel. Once the scam is published in the newspaper, it becomes the talk of the town. Elders who are found indulging in these activities are lowered in the eyes of their own children. When Haji Mastan, the notorious smuggler was prosecuted in the court, his daughters who were ignorant about his activities after gaining knowledge about it cried, "Father when it is such a bad work, why do you not leave it". The incident shows that a change of heart is needed to improve the character of a person.[1]

There is an old Indian saying that everything is lost, if character is lost. Today, India has lost it's national character. There was a time when politics was not a means of livelihood for the country. It was a means of service to society. Men of such high integrity and

---

1 "Mould the Character"
The Himachal Times, September 19, 1997, p.3.

character were at the helm of affairs. Today we have lost our identity and national pride.
Our degeneration has started from within. Men of character and vision like Jawaharlal Nehru, Sardar Patel, Rajagopalachari, Subhash Chandra Bose, Acharya Kripalani and many others are no longer there. Today our leaders look upon politics as a means of livelihood. Muscle power, gondanism, falsehoods are justified means to attain power. Criminalisation of politics are merely an extension of this philosophy.

Politicians started taking the help of criminal elements for winning elections and money power is visible every where. The age of rallies, manoeuvring compromises with principles and to get power by any means has became the order of the day. India needs to be saved from the present power hungary politicians..

The Hon'ble Mr. Justice V.V.Kamat,[2] High Court of Kerala, in a lecture delivered on October 6, 1996 said: The aim of educational qualifications and intellectual capacity as observed by John Buskin in his lecture" Sesame and lilies" is acquisition or knowledge and necessary character. The aim of knowledge is in search of truth and life. It is not necessarily for getting into good society or a gratification for the thirst for applause; but striving for eager maintenance of those

conditions of life in which everyone of us would be able to develop the personality to the best. Even according to the father of this nation, Mahatma Gandhi, it must be necessary considerations of humanity; and money too unaccompanied by the corresponding requisite labour.

In my view, any one amongst us venturing to think of independence must dwell on these postulates of independence. Independence gets essentially with individual freedom. "Freedom from Want" and

---

2 Justice V.V. Kamat - Independence of Judiciary. Its Relevance, Responsibilities of the Courts, Status and Duties of Judges". AIR 1997 Journal Section P.67.

"Freedom from Fear" are, in the context basic instincts cherished historically even by the primitive man and his efforts in the process of living. In a society, where wealth outweighs values and principles, justify, balance and equanimity are necessary.

It will be better to recall Henry ward Beeches, who said : A man's character is the reality of himself; his reputation, the opinion others have formed about him; character resides in him, reputation in another people, character is the substance and reputation is the shadow image.

In public mind, the term 'political corruption' throws up extremely unsavoury images. It is the image of liquor barons carrying on their nefarious trade under the benign umbrella of a politician in power; it is the image of under-world dons turning into millionaires by buying favours of other political power centres; it is the image of unscrupulous timber merchants destroying our scarce forest resources under the patronage of yet another politician in power; it is the image of an one-time King of smugglers being hailed as a new messiah warmly wooed by the holiest of the holy political leader for his electoral success; it is the image of a notorious Mafia gangster, with half a dozen murder charges, being unabashedly promoted by one political party and his rivals by the others. The list is inexhaustible and goes on lengthening everyday. The most significant aspect of the above scenario is the perceived linkage between the liquor barons, builders, forest destroyers, smugglers and such widespread corruption and the linkages between politicians and gangsters generates cynicism and reinforces the perception that everything is rotten at the core. And the perception is not unjustified when day-to-day living has become a nightmare - lack of power, water, price rises, pot-holed roads, garbage everywhere. In the public mind, this is merely a manifestation of political corruption.

Perhaps this is an exaggeration because people have not investigated the charges in a proper scientific manner. But the common sense judgement of common people is often more correct than the laboured and hedged-in conclusions, qualified by ifs and buts of professional investigators. In many cases, their gut reaction to the prevailing situation is more reliable than the rationalised reaction of the intellectual fraternity. It is not really a matter of their reacting instantly and jumping to conclusions, but forming some sort of consensus opinions by putting two and two together.

Two factors have facilitated the process of public opinion formation about political corruption. First, corruption is not a simple two-way affair, as is commonly believed between the receiver and dispenser of patronage, or giver and receiver of bribe if you like. It is a multi-dimensional transaction involving not only many intermediate links in the chain but also various sideways fall-outs. The converse becomes much too wide, and even though the principal parties hide their deeds in the a of secrecy, their acts become visible at some point or the other of the wide converse. It is like the corrupt doing business in a house of glass which is opaque inside but largely transparent from outside.

Second and perhaps more import, they do not after all have to be too serious about hiding their act. Even if the harmless and silent others know what they are doing, how does that matter ? Talking of corruption in general, Prof.C.J. Daswani observes : "Today it would seem, corruption has not only become more widespread but it has become more acceptable as a way of life. Acts of corruption are transacted overtly, and corrupt people no longer have to hang their heads in shame or run the risk of social ostracism. Instead of "social ostracism", the corrupt are more acceptable , and in fact in demand, in present day politics in India.

Shashi, B. Sahai[3] , in his book, Politics of Corruption, writes : The nation seems to have lost its horizon and set on the reverse course. Even a state like Bengal where caste divisions had almost disappeared is supposed to identify and list its numerous castes. India's story is like that of a bullockcart man who left his village one evening for the nearby town and slept on the way. Midway in his journey, some have quietly turned the bullockcart-back in the direction

---

3 Shashi B. Sahai, Politics of Corruption, (1995), p.p. 152-154

of the village itself. With the cartoon in deep slumber, the bullocks drove along merrily in the reverse direction taking the cart back to the village from where it had started. The direction of the nation has similarly been reversed and it keeps on marching happily back regardless. While the achieving societies of the world are looking to the future, India keeps on looking to the past. Instead of further modernising and improved upon the political institutions of a modern society, the Indian political class is doing everything to smother them.

Mahatma Gandhi quoted scriptures because he was a religious person, saw visions of the future and raised the moral issue of means and ends, but he remained fully engrossed in the present and future of India, seeking solutions its daunting problems and prescribing his own remedies. He was not unduly enamoured of or interested in India's past. He touched upon the glories' of ancient India only in a vague sort of way occasionally. Nehru wrote and talked about India's past romantically before independence, but not much after that. As the helmsman of India's infant democracy, he described the country's new and emerging industrial complexes as the modern places of pilgrimage for his people. In the hands of successors of Gandhi and Nehru, the nation has not only lost its agenda but also its direction.

The evident incongruity of India's backslide into clannish apart, it has more dangerous potentialities. A number of countries in Africa became independent with the end of imperialism in the post-war period. They started off well with acknowledged nationalist leaders at the helm. The ruling elite were intensely nationalistic and the new states had all the trapping of modern nationalism. But the nationalist veneer started falling off as time passed until they showed up as nothing more than constellations of diverse kinship groups, tribes and feudities - even little territorial societies - without much of a sense of belonging to a nation-wise-society. Even civic associations and political parties in many of these imitation states very often turned out to be sectional and tribal. The only society-wide institution which kept them in one piece was the state, which was taken over by nationalist despots. Strong arms rule by absolutist nationalists kept these societies together as long as they remained on the scene. But once the nationalist Kings, Presidents, Generals etc. went out or were removed, primordial sentiments came to the fore full blast, with the splinters of tribalism, parochialism, communalism etc. tearing these societies as under. This is what happened in countries like Nigeria, Ghana, Ethiopia Eritrea etc. and is happening in Somalia, Rwanda and Burundi.

In India, nationalism is over a century old, nourished and nurtured by a galaxy of great personalities, some of whom lived on to guide its destiny till well past independence. Its strongest, through not the only, pillar remains the Indian state- the most important nation-wide institutions still intact. But it would be a mistake to take too much for granted. The history of human civilisation is the story of emancipation of the individual from the clutches of the group and herd. When a society is on the move forward in time, it produces great individuals, men and women, who join and lead the exciting journey. When India was so on the move ahead, it was blessed with a whole lot of such great men and women to lead it onwards. But when the country's direction has been reversed, it is in the hands of the stragglers and left overs who are leading it back to the age of submergence of the - individual to the group and the herd, symbolising a poverty of leadership matched only by the poverty of the masses. If the march backwards continues unchecked, Somalia cannot be far behind. For the logic of regression and slide-back to tribalism can only lead to a Somalia a Rwanda or Burundi. To eradicate and purge itself from the cancer of corruption, India needs transformation. For the transformation of the kind that the Mother has in mind, human effort alone is not enough. For it's not merely a change in the ways of functioning leaving the system basically as it is. It is the texture of the entire being that has to be radically changed. In other words nature itself is to be changed from the human into the divine. What are taken as the natural functions of the mind, the emotional being, the vital and even the body are seen to be not so natural after all; they are only habits of nature. It is possible, and necessary, to change their very bases of action, direction and place in the general set-up. They need to unlearn many characteristic movements and learn new ones. Older faculties have to yield place to new ones that are formed in the process of this transformation. Not only the centre of the life movement is changed but part of the being is remade.

The cancerous spread of corruption in India's public life, which has been a matter of great concern to its citizens in all walks of life; is a serious problem. No one has so far discovered the scales to measure the dimensions of "the problem". The standard barometer, the report from the head of the instructions, indicates the location of the area of "the problem"—it is omnipresent present and corruption is all prevalent and has global ramifications.

India has acquired the unenviable reputation of being, among the most corrupt countries in the world. A careful poll taken among business interest and financial journalists by Transparency International, the reputed anti-corruption non-Governmental organization, placed India 9th from the bottom in its 1996 list of 59 countries.

In a number of States, Chief Ministers and Ministers have been implicated in major corrupt transactions relating to liquor regulations, real estate approvals, large government contracts, allocation of scarce materials transfers of public servants and so on. Similarly, on the basis of proven cases, well substantiated allegations and reliable internal information, it would appear that corruption among ministers in the States is widespread. This again cannot be the case unless it countenanced by the heads of Government in the States.

Of grave concern is the interlocking or 'vertical integration' of corruption at various levels of the Government hierarchy - elected politicians, higher bureaucracy and lower bureaucracy. The normal assumption is that the 'principals' at each of the higher levels would be committed to ensure that their 'agents' at respective lower levels would act according to standards and norms of probity. In a situation in which the principals and agents collude with each other in corruption, the problem of tackling it becomes much more intractable.

In the public domain, corruption is not confined to the executive Government. It has spread to legislatures, the judiciary, media and the independent professions (such as lawyers, doctors, chartered accountants and contractors). Through mutual interaction, such a horizontal spread of corruption has entrenched it further in Government and made its prevention and control much more difficult.

Mechanisms to prevent, monitor and punish the corrupt are not adequate nor have they proved to be effective to the extent that they exist. At the national level, India still does not have an Ombudsman type, Lok Pal legislation and machinery to deal with corruption among ministers and the higher bureaucracy. In general, Governments at the Centre and in the States have been tardy, at best, and insecure, at worst, in investigating and pursuing corruption. Commissions of Inquiry established for these purposes over the years have been able to effectively prove or punish corruption.

Corruption has been politicized-just as politics has been corrupted - in the sense that cases of corruption have been used for partisan political purposes rather than with any serious intent to objectively tackle the problem. As is to be expected, opposition parties in Parliament and State Legislatures have played a role in agitating issues relating to corruption but by and large, their efforts have not been effective. Judicial processes under normal anti-corruption laws are dilatory although in recent times the Supreme Court, in response to public interest litigation, has intervened to enforce the law. A number of activist groups have taken up local issue of corruption. However, their contributions have varied widely over different parts of the country and have not assumed the critical mass required to generate a popular movement against corruption.

Despite the fact that corruption is pervasive and has gone largely unchecked and indeed, perhaps because of it there is now a strong demand by the public for elective punitive and corrective measures to tackle the problem. That corruption is a national concern in the consciousness of the people has been demonstrated by the fact that it was the most important issue in the general elections to Parliament in 1989, 1996 and in several elections of State legislatures. Essentially, the challenge that concerned citizens face is to translate the widespread public sentiment against corruption into effective public action.

What needs to be taken into account at the outset is that the very scale and spread of corruption has generated helplessness, at best, and violence, at worst. These, in turn, tend to be rationalized in terms of cynicism or in arguments that end to corruption. The first task is to generate the confidence that India is not doomed to live with corruption and that in India - as has in many other countries - it is possible to mobilize public pressure for reforms aimed at containing and rolling it back. As corruption intensifies and spreads it tentacles, it tends to reproduce and perpetuate itself on an increasing scale. No time should, therefore, be lost in undertaking all possible efforts to put a brake on the process. At the same time, there is a need for the sober recognition that it would not be feasible to eliminate corruption altogether. Tackling corruption cannot be achieved in one stroke but through a continuous and cumulative endeavor. In addition, it carries its own costs. All that can be aimed at is to progressively move toward a state of affairs in which corruption is the exception rather than the rule.

It is possible and legitimate to approach the problem of tackling corruption from different angles. Generally speaking, four approaches can be distinguished. One consists of fundamental changes in the Constitution which would, like a Presidential system, insulate executive authority from legislatures and include appropriate checks and balances against the abuse of political power. The second would emphasize thorough deregulation and privatisation of Governmental activities so as to reduce the role of the state as much as possible along with reforms aimed at enhancing efficiency. The third would argue for an extensive decentralization of governance so as to promote accountability and transparency at local levels in order to check corruption. The fourth, would rely on an increased development of moral values among the people at large beginning with youth and focused on politicians and officials in particular.

Each of these approaches is germane to the problem of tackling corruption; they are a necessary but not sufficient condition. They cannot be relied upon as each of it has its limitations. There can be much debate about the pros and cons of fundamental constitutional changes and, in any event, they would not appear to be readily feasible. Nor can there be the assurance that the replacement of parliamentary democracy with an executive Government, with checks and balance be a remedy. Similarly, deregulation and decentralization, for which there is already a wide consensus, could be a penaca. But the state cannot be wished away, nor - can it be expected to wither away. Corruption can continue under different forms in a largely privatized economy. Likewise, it can itself get decentralized, persisting in less visible ways under local authorities.

The upgrading of moral values is of fundamental importance but a moral revolution cannot be expedited on the basis of rhetorical appeals. It can be promoted and sustained only around a series of concrete incremental measures which demonstrate that reform is possible and can cumulate. This is the surest way to strengthen and channel the moral impetus for a more honest policy. There is no easy way out.

While the proposals offered in this book will be useful as an actionable initial agenda for tackling corruption in India. It is clear that no set of proposals, however well conceived, will themselves be able to bring about the necessary changes. They can only provide a basis for action. They will remain a dead letter unless public action is forthcoming at several levels for winning acceptance for the proposed reforms.

3

WELFARE AND CORRUPTION

The word "Welfare" in welfare legislation or the welfare State refers generally to government support for the poor, and particularly to the free or subsidised supply of certain goods or services, for example, health and education. Welfare State is a political system assuming State responsibility for its citizens by universal medical care, insurance against sickness and unemployment, old age pensions, family allowances, public housing, etc., on a "cradle to grave", basis.

In a Welfare state, the concept of common good makes the public employment a mission, as well as a challenge, the entire machinery of the government works and functions for the common public good. The posts are created, filled and held, to achieve the objective of common good. Even the pay and emoluments of any employee are not merely personal to him but bear an element of public good and welfare. As such a welfare State would simply promote the welfare and realisation of collective aims of society carrying the needs of each and every individual. It is imperative for that the State must allow for the just and fullest possible development of the creative self- "free expression for its people, its policies, plans and actions, all must enable the citizens to realise that is within. It is expected ultimately to enrich their happiness, promote spiritual uplift and ensure general welfare-bread, clothing, and shelter and beyond. It is time to make the "rule of law" and "rule of life" run in close approximate, so that fountains of social justice may arise and flourish.

A welfare State is synonymous with welfare society. The concept of welfare State has engaged the minds of social thinkers ever since the dawn of civilisations in both the capitalist and socialist systems. And welfare State is a vast subject occupying an ever-expanding area increasing in complexity as the awakening of man assumes greater and greater penchant for the values of refined, dignified and purposeful living, the sky being the limit for the expansion of man's mental horizon.[1] The concept of a Welfare State has been fully embodied in Indian Constitution.

The founding Fathers of Indian Constitution have bestowed considerable through, time and energy on the concept of Welfare State and after deep deliberations, have incorporated in Part-IV the Directive Principals - the popular, recognised and traditional elements of Welfare State though they were at the time, over-conscious of financial constraints and dearth of economic potential to begin with. Much attention has been paid by the Constitution makers not only to the basic aspirations of the under-privileged but also to the finer aspects and values of refined living[2] with emphases on quality of life. However, as S.K. Ghosh in his book, "INDIAN DEMOCRACY DERAILED", puts it:-

"The constitution safeguards are systematically violated by the rulers, who have "twisted" "bent" the safeguards to their personal or party advantage. The ideals provided in the Constitution are almost a dead letter for the man on the street who has not perceived any change for better. Law enforcement and the entire criminal justice process have vacillated back and forth in response to pressure groups, militant groups and others. The rulers and their party cadres assume they are law, and therefore, openly and will fully violate the law. We are under a constitution but the constitution is what our rulers say that the constitution is left in the cold storage".

A basic factor that can make a difference in the success or failure or failure of a plan for Welfare activity of the State is the administrative machinery which is pressed into action from execution of such a plan keeping in view the basic objective and the strategies

---

1 Justice HG Balkrishna, New Dimensions of Law of Justice, (1992) p 222.

2 S. K. Ghosh, Indian Democracy derailed (1997) p 14.

laid down by the Government for the Welfare of the people. M.V. Pylee,[3] a Constitutional authority has rightly observe:-

It comes to life and begins to grow only when human elements get together and work it."

Similarly Dr. B.R. Ambadkar,[4] while throwing a flood of light on the practical aspect of the Constitution remarked:-

"I feel, however good a Constitution may be, it is sure to turn out bad because, how bad a constitution may be, it may turn out to be good if those who are called to work it, happens to be good lot. The working of the Constitution does not depend wholly upon the nature of the Constitution. The Constitution can provide only the organs of the State such as the Legislature, the Executive and the Judiciary. The factors on which the working of those organs of the State depends are the people, they will set up as their instruments to carry out their wishes and policies".

The first priority of a welfare State ought to be to provide potable water to its citizens. Fifty years after independence, the Election Commissioner of India would have us believe that the biggest failure of Indian democracy is the inability of eleven successive Parliaments to provide something so basic as clear drinking water to every citizen. Some suggest a ;switch over from parliamentary form to presidential form of Government. But the defect is not in the constitution but in the people who work at it "for forms of government befouls contest, whenever is best administered is the best." Bharat Jhunjhunwala,[5] a known jurist in an article, "Corruption and Welfare State" meaningfully writes:

"There seems to exist a consensus that we must have an honest welfare state., the two cannot go together. Welfare state is the

---

3 M. V. Pylee, Constitutional Government in India, (1960) p 700.

4 CAD XI P 975, also see Dr. P. L. Mehta, Constitutional Protection to scheduled Tribes in India, (1991) p 369.

5 Bharat Jhunjhunwala, "Corruption and Welfare State, The Tribune, September, 7, 1997, p. 10.

justification for many taxes being impose and expenditures made by the government. And these provide a gateway to bureaucrats and politicians to indulge in corruption. Welfare state is really the high altar behind which many a suitcase changes hands. The Delhi and Haryana governments initiated a scheme to supply biscuits to children and pregnant mothers through anganwadis. Tenders were floated. The officials joined hand with traders, and or nurseries supplies of biscuits were made. The government officials gave receipts of the biscuits they did not receive, and the traders "supplied" what was never produced. They split the booty fifty-fifty. All in the name of welfare State.

Or take the drought relief work under the Indira Voice Yojna in Orissa. 'A' Poor' beneficiary, it was reported, had, to pay commission to the following persons to avail himself of the assistance to the gram sevak for recommending his name, to the block officer for getting a house allotted to the cashier for collecting the payment and lastly to the junior engineer to provide a utilisation certificate. All in the name of the welfare of the poor. Among the long list of allegations against her government were kickbacks on the purchase of TV sets for villages, funds siphoned off in the schemes of providing free saris and footwear to the poor, and fraud in the Indira Voice Yojana.

The NGOs are no better, The Standing Committee of Parliament has said that nearly 50 percent of the moneys given by CAPART to selected NGOs had been misused the ministry is reported to have initiated CBI enquires against 61 such NGOs. The latest fad is for Secretaries to the Government to set up NGOs so that the party can continue after retirement. The list can go on and on. Needless to say, the infamous fodder scam was but a "Welfare Scheme". Government money breeds corruption twice. Firstly in the collection of taxes and secondly in the expenditures. It is virtually impossible to have 'Honest' government officers. Kautilya has put the problem thus : "the money misappropriated by government officials from state funds is as hard to ascertain as it is to find out how much water has been drank by the fish in the pond. In other words, larger the pond and greater the number of fish, so also inevitably the amount of water drank by them."

The Welfare state is but a justification for making the pond bigger. The UF government is the epitome of "social justice", that too of the tax-and spend variety. Just to name a few of its wonder scheme. In February this year it came out with a plan to spend Rs. 450 crore to "eliminate manual scavenging", Recently, mighty liberal that he is, Mr. Gujarat is all set to launch a Rs. 1500 crore scheme child in society. "No one now-a-days talk about the massive amounts spent on the National Adult Education Programme. The unending procession goes on and on. The welfare state is predicated on a bloated financial involvement of the state, which in turn fuels corruption. Thus, where there is a welfare state there is corruption of course, this is not say that corruption does not prevail in other non-welfare activities of the government. Bofors and HDW deals, Telecom scam would be clear examples. After all, the fish will continue to drink water irrespective of whether it is sweet water of a pond or salty water of a sea. But lesser the water and smaller the number of fish, proportionately smaller is likely to be the water that they drink away. Neither is this problem a new one.

Gandhi was perturbed about the reports of corruption among the ministers. In the six months that he lived in Independent India it was a Herculean job to secure honesty even in a "clean" government which mainly discharged the essential functions of law and order, justice defence, currency, communications and external affairs.

This is not to advocate that the poor should be abandoned. the alternative to the welfare state is charity. Meals are run in the temples. Widows are provided a place to rest in many a ashrams. India has a vigorous tradition of building charitable institutions like schools and hospitals. Any knowledgeable person will verify that the level of corruption is low and that of efficiency high in these institutions. The reason is simple. The money from the rich to the poor is transferred directly without the mediation of the state. The ITO does not collect that money, nor the District Education Officer spend it: yet the rich "gives" and the poor "gets". That is precisely why the politicians and bureaucrats denigrate our traditions of charity. They keep on harping at the welfare State.

In fact some of the most serious difficulties which are encountered by the State are, due to the fact that we are trying to create a Welfare State without a Welfare Society. Welfare State is what the Parliament declares and decrees and the Government administers but the Welfare Society is what the members of society actually do, actually think and actually feel on matters which influence or affect the general welfare. There is often a wide gulf between social attitudes and public policy. The fulfilment of the objectives of the Welfare State depends upon how far the people generally respond to the policies and assumptions of the Welfare State in their mental attitude, social behaves and actions.

The Directive principles of State Policy embodied in Part IV of the Constitution of India are aimed at building a Welfare State. The principles are not justifiable and are not mandatory though these principles are intended to be followed by the States in the matter of administration and in the matter of enacting laws. The directives assure equality of men and women in the right to adequate means of livelihood, assure the distribution of ownership and control of the material resources of the community to subserve the common good. Gender equality, welfare of children, legal aid to the poor and so on have been enshrined in the Directive Principles.

But the standard of life in a Welfare State can be assessed in terms of the quality of environment, the benefits provided by the social services, the level of incomes, the distribution of wealth, job-satisfaction, leisure and recreation, health and education, housing and similar criteria. One of the basic needs of a Welfare State is a sense of fellowship and public sprit throughout society.

Fifty years ago when India became independent on in, 15,1947, those at the helm of affairs under the leadership of Jawaharlal Nehru, the first Prime Minister, of free India, had envisaged a crime and corruption free India and pattern of political, economic and administrative system which was enshrined in India's constitution. India accepted the Westminster model of parliamentary democracy. The government is quasi-federal as well as it is unitary form of government with centripetal tendencies as most suited to India's experience in the last few decades of British rule. India also accepted the concept of federal policy with division of functions and finances between the centre and the states. Afraid of the fissiparous tendencies endangering the unity and the integrity of the country, the Constitution provided for a strong Centre. the Constitution did not provide for Gandhi a concept of Grammar though as an afterthought Article 40 in the Directive Principles of the Constitution stated that villages shall be promoted as institutions of self government.

P.R. Dubhashi[9] in an article "India Today - Time To Restructure The Systems", writes :- India steered clear of totalitarian communism on one side and unbridled capitalism on the other side and decided to follow the third way of the 'mixed economy" and "democratic planning", otherwise known as "socialist pattern of society". The mixed economy would consist of three sectors- the public, the private and the co-operative with the public sector gaining the commanding heights of the economy. The mixed economy and state directed development did not deliver the goods. More specifically, the rate of growth was not up to the mark- it was below 5 percent and not nearly 10 percent as in the case of Japan, South Korea and other eastern Asian Countries.

Mass poverty was not abolished among the disadvantaged sections of society. Even basic amenities like potable water and approach roads could not be provided to village communities. Programmes of rural development suffered from inefficiency and could not attain the objective of abolition of poverty and unemployment. thanks to the green revolution, food production increased but stagnation has set in. Planned MEd economy and the attendant controls led to the licence permit raj and black money. The parallel black economy has played havoc with the lives of the people. Public sector enterprises did not come up to expectation. Many suffered from losses and became a drag on the public exchequer. Populist economic policies led to measures which proved to be ill-conveyed.

---

9 P. R. Dubhashi, "India Today Time to Restructure The System", The System", The Statesman, September 22, 1997, p8.

Nationalisation of banks and textile mills was taken up more for political reasons rather than on the basis of sound economic considerations. "Get rid of poverty" became a mere political slogan leading to unsound but populist anti-poverty programmes. As a result, the economy was caught in a severe debt crisis in 1991, leading to a U-turn in the economic policy and ushering in an era of, liberalisation and privatisation.

But the economic reforms have been adversely affected by political uncertainties. It was expected that with the rolling back of the licence-permit raj, corruption will be controlled. But the liberalisation era has seen mega scams and scandals in India: Sadly the political landscape has became chaotic. National parties have became fragmented. Regional parties have emerged and become well entrenched. They have formed a federal front and have an effective say in the formation and functioning of the central government which is a coalition of 13 parties. But the Central government has no stability and runs at the mercy of outside support, do not have a clear-cut ideology and there is a great deal of opportunism[10] Without stability, the government has become weak and is unable to give a sense of direction and decisive action. Political leadership of national stature has become scarce.

Ministers lack experience and competence to deal with national issues. Instead of dealing with national issues they dabble in local politics. A sense of idealism has disappeared from public life. Ministers and others holding political power tend to make a fast buck. Ideals of service and sacrifice for a healthy public life have given way to the naked pursuit of self-interest. Arbitrary misuse of public power has become a rule rather than an exception. Criminalisation of politics has tarnished the political process. Elections are fought through the use of money and muscle power and misuse of the machinery of government, Seshan used strong measures to curb electoral malpractice but with his departure they have started raising their ugly head.

---

[10] Ilnd.

4

CRIME AND CORRUPTION: THE CIVIL SERVICES

In the 50 years after Independence the quality of the Civil Services has declined beyond recognition. The ICS which was maligned as "neither Indian, nor civil nor service" has been replaced by a nondescript Indian Administrative Services that is apologetic ("I am sorry) and weak - kneed. The definition of a bureaucrat in the Oxford Dictionary as "one who Follows rules", should be changed to one who follows the dictates of politicians rather than rules.

On the midnight of 14-15 August, 1947, Pandit Nehru spoke on the floor of Parliament, "India will awake to freedom". He said several things all of which I am not going to quote and make life difficult for you and for myself. Among many things, he said that "we are a free and sovereign people. I am the first servant of the people". Gandhi has shown us the true principles on which to work. Always keep the suffering masses in your mind. Industry must progress, but it should not progress at the cost of increasing inequalities by the concentration of wealth in the hands of a few to the detriment of many. All of us owe a common allegiance to that which is called India.

Between 1947 and today, what has happened? Have we not progressed? From a cantonment which was the home of all retired, and people of retiring disposition, has not Pune become a bustling industrial city, where all kinds of things are made and sent to the rest of the country, and the world? Has not the rest of the country progressed? Before Independence we did not know how to make a pin, but today we can make not only planes, but rockets, satellites. Anybody who says we have not progressed in the last 46 years is guilty of unnecessary pessimism, guilty of unnecessarily trying to weaken the minds and hearts of the younger people. And that is certainly not my intention.

The world has developed in an extraordinarily dynamic fashion. Twenty years ago if somebody had said that you will see several channels on television either by cable or by dish antenna you would have considered him crazy. Several other things have happened. Even India's telephones have started working. In the world, a country which was considered, if not the first, at least between the first two, is now bitterly involved in tearing itself apart through its entrails. Other parts of the world which are tearing themselves apart are from Azerbaijan to Abkhasia to Georgia to Uzbekistan, in Central Asia, to much of tormented Africa, from Somalia to Ethiopia to Namibia. In different parts of the world, different people are pulling each other's entrails out. Now, have we adjusted ourselves in this country to this dynamic atmosphere of change? T.N Seshan, the former Chief Election Commissioner in his book, "A Heart Full of Burden", writes:

"I shall pick up a few things which Nehru said on that fateful night and say a few words which have relevance to the screen in front of which you have to judge a question about what kind of elections are we running, what type of democracy are we running. Nehru spoke of the political people who would be servants. He spoke of the industrial people, who would be servants, or at least trustees on behalf of the poor. He spoke of a civil service. He spoke of the judicial service. Now, starting in 1947, we survived for a few years on the basis of mutual confidence and harmony where issues were settled sometimes with arguments, sometimes with acrimony, rarely ever with a loss of the sense of confidence or an accumulating sense of despair. But, today when someone comes and talks to me of his optimism at lunch break, I have reasons to pinch my shirt and say I dare not say anything against him. But, in the deepest recesses of my mind, I ask, is he not an eccentric? From being honest servants, every category has become self-seekers and self-servers without exception. You make a quick fix, you make a quick buck. It matters not." Gandhi told us means are as important as ends. Today means mean nothing, ends alone matter. They spoke of our being free and sovereign. Free for whom, sovereign for whom and the answer is, there has been a steadfast and steady erosion of all the institutions and all things which go to make up for freedom. All that we built to enshrine freedom has been eroded by a plethora of decrees, laws, rules, ordinances which serve a few; it serves the State, but not the citizens. Today, it has become desperately difficult for the citizens to defend themselves against the onslaught of laws, rules and ordinances, and against the overpowering destruction of individual freedom and dignity.

Indians have suffered oppression and discrimination for thousands of years and there is a yawing gap between "the sophisticated and poor sections of the society. The gap is to be filled by the State and its instrumenties for the freedom of dignity of its people. But the progress is retarded by crime, corruption and a mad race for consumerism. The rampant corruption among the civil servants cannot be seen in its isolation. It is a manifestation of the general malaise in the society. It is rather difficult to imagine what poverty and deprivation is all about, especially the background of depleting standards levels in the society. In such a situation bureaucracy needs analysis and study, because they are required to implement technical, social and political policies.

Bureaucracy inclusive of police services seeks the best brains. On joining the government civil servants, more particularly the officers of the police force, soon become like that unbridled horses can win any Derby race provided the jockey is imaginative, competent and capable of giving proper direction. Peter F Druker refers to the bureaucrats as of sheepish mentality and clannish in attitude. The changes in clan-based social organisation have upward mobility. But Drucker's opinion may be true partly but most of the India bureaucrats are full of vigour and even today have the capacity capability of safely navigating the shop. Sardar Patel was justified when he said, "I have tested them and they are worth their weight in gold." There is no dearth of such bureaucrats, provided some one like Sardar Patel, Govind Vallabh Pant emerges to navigate. T.N Seshan, M.S. Gill, Krishnamurthy, are the shining examples of the Indian bureaucracy.

If civil service was one of the earliest casualty of political corruption, police is perhaps the worst casualty. While civil services have some how kept the show going, police has almost been destroyed. The three cardinal pillars on which a sound police structure rests are its own hierarchy, discipline and strict adherence to law. Each of these pillars has been demolished bit by bit by rampaging politicians. Police has been the special target of the political class because it is the most visible symbol of power.

It can be traced back to nepotism—the most primitive form of corruption—which was reflected in the appointment, placement, transfer, punishment, promotion of police personnel. What it did was to shatter public confidence on the one hand and the morale of honest police officers on the other. So the question to ask is :

It is all started with nepotism primitive form of corruption—in the appointment, placement, transfer, punishment, promotion etc. of police personnel. With nepotism is disturbed the even tempo of life of the community Does it lead to disturbance of the current life of the community so as to amount to the disturbance of the public order or does it affect merrily an individual leaving the tranquillity of the society undisturbed?

If society, and not only an individual, suffers on account of the questionable activities of a person, then those activities are prejudicial to the maintenance of "Public Order" and are not merely prejudicial to the maintenance of "Law and Order. Crime is a revolt against society and an attack on the civilisation of the day. Order is a basic need of any organised civilised society and any attempt to disturb that order affects society and the community. The distinction between breach of "Law and Order" and disturbance of "Public Order" is one of degree and the extent of reach of the activity in question upon society. In their essential quality, the activities which affect "Law and Order" and those which disturb "public order" may not be different but in their potentiality and effect upon even tempo of society and public tranquillity there is a vast difference. In each case, it is for the courts to see the length, magnitude and intensity of the questionable activities of a person to find out whether his activities are prejudicial to maintenance of "public order" or only Law & Order."

It is a matter of concern that the last time decades have witnessed a careerist approach by bureaucrats who make their way to the top in every conceivable field of national activity. Their achievements in the fields primarily assigned to them have remained questionable. The problems of antiquity like poverty, illiteracy and unemployment have only been aggravated with nobody accountable for them. But bureaucrats have sneaked into the fields of academicians, public-undertakings, hotels, airlines, defence services, legislatures, judiciary and media, as the nation braces up for a new breed of problems – terrorism, communal tension, illegal migrants, scams and scandals. The executive has emerged as the strongest of the wing of the State stronger than the legislature and the judiciary.

- Though the first 5 Year Plan in India was introduced in 1952, yet some of the critics like P.H Patwardhan asked in 1966 "why had the actual progress of the country not been commensurate with the high purpose and vision with which Pundit Jawaharlal Nehru worked so strenuously? Why on the eve of the Fourth Plan was there so much disappointment and confusion all round? Why was there so much indiscipline, inefficiency and corruption?" And the one answer given to these intriguing questions is not that the vision was merely a vision and far beyond the capacity of the people nor that Indians as a whole are at fault, nor event that the stars in their courses have been against India. It is that Jawahar Lal Nehru ultimately depended on the bureaucracy or steel frame created by the British to maintain a Police State to enable it to carry on the economic exploitation of India.' It is as simple as that.

That the British bequeathed to India an apparently irremovable Police State no more than a convenient belief to the national ego. But there is a large body of evidence to the contrary which, neglected though it is in contemporary India, I likely to carry weight with future historians.

Unfortunately, the feeling all-around is that the rulers want, the executive—the back-bone of the administration—"committed", as also the committed judiciary; whereas the judiciary on its part treat the institution of bureaucracy as its subordinate. One may readily concede that courts' interference in the administrative decisions has not always been for the better and that it has on occasions caused more difficulties than found solutions for the problem.

The solution, however, may lie in the independence of legislature, judiciary and the bureaucracy. But that is dependent on the political will and its resolution to push through the reforms.

With the decline of norms and standards and galloping corruption in the post-Nehru era, naked corruption was added to nepotism in police personnel management. At the cutting edge level of police station, police has always been known to be more or less corrupt. The upper echelons in the hierarchy are meant to keep a check and reduce, if not altogether abolish, the incidence of corruption at the Police Station level. A stage has been reached where direct nexus exists between the politicians in power—Ministers and other power brokers—and the corrupt functionaries at the P.S. (Private Secretary) level have almost paralysed the state machinery.

Appointment to police stations are "priced" according to their capacity to "learn" money from the public. For instance, if a civil engineer "buys" a worth while post for Rs.5 lacks, similarly the SHO (the Station House Officer) "buys" a lucrative posting where public dealings would recover his "investment" in little time.

Depending upon the degree of corruptibility of a Minister or a Chief Minister, this business of 'selling' positions in police hierarchy may go to unbelievable lengths. In 1987, a senior Police officer of a state on refresher course at National Police Academy, starred his colleagues when the alleged that the top post in his state had been 'sold' at a fabulous 'price'. Everyone heard in stunned silence, there were murmurs and whispers but none could do anything about it. It was after all a 'political' decision of the political executive?

Hierarchy and discipline having thus been destroyed, the only other pillar which could keep the police going is strict adherence to law. The modern police system in democratic societies is a creation of law. All its powers are rooted in the law of the land and upholding 'the rule of law' is its very raison deter. Even in common parlance, police is called upon to maintain "law and order"—an expression in which "law" comes first and "order" after that. It only highlights the priority of enforcement of 'law' in maintenance of 'order'.

The expression "Law and Order" is wider in scope in as much as contravention of law always affects order, while "public order" has a narrower amulet and the public order would be affected by only such contravention which affects the Community or the public at large. Public order is the even tempo of life of Community taking the country as a whole or even a specified locality. The distinction between the areas of "Law and order" and "Public order" is one which can be traced back to the days of provincial Autonomy of 1937-39. It started with a fresh momentum after independence.

Initially it was confined to preferential treatment in appointments, postings etc. to kith and kin, friends and relations of politicians in power. With the advent and growth of casteism in politics preference and privilege started being extended to whole caste groups, depending upon the caste of the Chief Minister or the Minister in charge or otherwise powerful politicians. In a sensitive force like the police, nepotism tends to weaken and destroy hierarchy and discipline. Growing nepotism and extended nepotism in the shape of casteism has played havoc with the discipline and hierarchy of the force making it progressively less and less effective in its role performance.

This vital pillar of undiluted commitment to law has suffered even worse devastation and is on the verge of collapse. Police investigation of crimes is a purely judicial process, the bedrock of the entire criminal justice system. It has to be carried out in accordance with the procedure laid down by law to identify persons behind crimes and put them on trial before law courts. Police can perform its basic duty of detecting and preventing crimes only if it is allowed to go about its task of crime investigation without any exterior consideration of money or politics. The supervisory levels of the police system are meant to correct any aberrations on the part of the ground level investigating staff. But that has become a thing of the past. Crimes have now to be investigated in the political interests of the political masters. The implication is obvious. If the persons committing crimes have the support of ruling politicians for considerations of money or electoral interests, the arm of law cannot reach them. Political interference in police investigation has become the norm rather than exception. In one state, the ruling party cadres decide and dictate who should be charge-sheeted in a criminal case and who should be not. In others, even minor peddlers in politics deem in their right' to interfere and influence police investigation.

And that brings us to the most lethal blow to the institution of police—Criminalisation of politics. Corruption was bad enough, but Criminalisation had demolished the entire police structure. 'Rule of Law' cannot with rule by lawbreakers. The Rule of Law begins with self-engineering and self-management precedes social engineering. If we have faith in human dignity, the spirit of liberty and the spirit of man, there is no alternative to Rule of law. Justice H.G Balakrishna, in his book "NEW DIMENSIONS OF LAW AND JUSTICE" gives three recognised interpretations to the concept of "Rule of Law", namely;

One : The rule of law neglects the performance of citizens for law and order within the state rather than anarchy, civil strike or warfare;

Two : The rule of law postulates that the government must be conducted according to law and that the machinery of government should operate through law. The concept of government according to law also means that the citizen can challenge governmental action before the courts an

Three : The rule of law must reflect the changing social values and implies the legal system exists within a wider social and economic framework.

However, the rule of law must incorporate those current social values which extend a far beyond those typically held by the legal profession itself. The rule of law should be extended to uphold the social & economic values of modern welfare state. And under the Rule of Law, the governmental powers can only be conferred on executive and administrative authorities by the legislature. The rule of law contemplates that the public authorities their officials are subject to effective legal sanctions if they infringe or depart from the law which they administer.

The rule of law means the authority of the law courts to test all administrative actions by the standard of loyalty. The administrative executive action that does not meet the standard will be set aside. The aggrieved person brings the appropriation action in the Competent Court.

Even when a leader of the stature of Jayaprakash Narayan embarked on the rehabilitation of Chambal dacoits, K.F Rustomjee, the Police Chief of Madhya Pradesh, raised his voice of protest to the move on professional grounds. We have travelled far on the path of 'rehabilitation' of hardened criminal since then, or the criminals are fast 'rehabilitating' themselves into politics, courtesy our later-day political gods.

Above all other things, criminalisation of politics has rendered the entire criminal record system of police infructuous. The system is built on some basic assumptions as follows:

(a) A majority of criminals repeat their crimes.
(b) Individual criminals or set of criminals have their own peculiarities in organising crimes and they stick to their
(c) Special modes of operation or modus operandi in commission of crimes.
(d) By repeating his crime, a criminal becomes professional with the passage of time and attains proficiency in his art'.

These time-honoured assumptions about criminals behaviour have been derived from empirical studies of crimes and criminals across the world. The point to the great utility of crime and criminals record system in the investigation and detection of crimes. The system envisages the creation and maintenance of records ranging from history-sheets and dossiers of individual criminals to gang histories, finger prints and a centralised criminals records organisation. A well-managed records system is of immense help in tracing unknown professional crimes to known criminals, many crimes to one criminal or set of criminals and otherwise chasing criminals through documents.

But what happens to the system if the history-sheeters and dossier-holders whose modus operandi fill the meticulously maintained crime records enter politics of power? What happens if some of them become Ministers and, who knows, Ministers in charge of Home or Police Department in some states? Once they are cordially accepted in the citadel of political power, what prevents them from exercising power to subvert the police system? Which police official will dare making adverse entries in their history sheets and keeping their dossiers alive? Which investigating officer will have the guts to refer to their existing criminal records in solving crimes in the first place? If a recorded bank robber becomes a political big-wig, who will check up on him to solve a case of bank robbery next door? These are not hypothetical questions but tragically relevant to the situation obtaining on the ground.

The Civil Servant is covered with an anonymity clause and the public have, therefore no access to what transpires in their deliberations and what sort of "note" they put up for consideration of the political leader in the Government. There is also no knowing whether the "note" that is put up is not put up after a considerable arm twisting by the political boss on promise of reward. The lacking or hiding of the information depends upon the bureaucratic interest and bureaucrats exercise discretion in such matters. Consequently, the bureaucratic arbitrariness results in damaging the system. However, there may be sound reasons for maintaining secrecy in Government. There are numerous grounds necessary in the interests of national security in withholding information and maintaining secrecy. Secrecy may be necessary in the interest of defence, national security, foreign relations criminal law, personal privacy, trade secrets, and perhaps, anonymity of Civil Servants in a parliamentary system and frankness in departmental communications and budget proposals. Thus a proper balance has to be drawn between openness and secrecy.

The most successful man is he who has the best information. Information is a must for progress of man and the society. Just like noble thoughts, information should also come to us from all corners of the world. However, information not the misinformation, is welcome. To find out whether it is information or misinformation, independent thinking is a prerequisite. Thinking and information are co-related.

However, all type of information cannot be shared with everyone. Certain communications are strictly prohibited and are to be kept as a guarded secret, such as certain privileged communications between husband and wife. The information which is vital for the security of the State cannot be shared. may be perhaps, with a view to not making the present miserable. Only a limited information to the concerned persons need to be given and shared.

But unfortunately the present generation wants animal freedom. The freedom with animal instincts cannot be extended and imparted to human beings because after all we are human beings. But the bureaucrats who try to be secretive may do so with a view to shielding their misdeeds. Withholding of the information cannot be permitted as a lever for hiding one's misdeeds.

The basic question is the right of the people to information vis-a-vis the right of the government to secrecy in the larger public interest. It can be argued that in a democracy the people have the right of information but this right has to be exercised with a sense of restraint, and if this restraint is not shown then the government has the legitimate right to withhold the information in public interest.

But what about the press and the media which are the main source of news? How much should be kept back by the government and how much should be released to the public? There are no hard and fast rules but one of the handicaps of democracy is that quite often matters that should remain suppressed at a particular moment is often leaked to the press. A sense of balance that should be exercised is often lost in the hunt for news.

With history sheeters and known criminals entering politics all these niceties of democratic politics have been redundant and irrelevant. All information is available, even State secrets, for money and power. After all, mafia leaders, bank robbers and their ilk have no other consideration except money—everything is up for sale.

Undoubtedly, law is a great regulator of human conduct as the jurists say, but no law can effectively work unless there is an element of acceptance by the people. No law works out smoothly unless the interaction is voluntary. In order that human conduct may be in accordance with the prescription of law it is necessary that there should be appropriate awareness about what the law requires and that there is an element of acceptance that the requirement of law is grounded upon a philosophy which should be followed. This would be possible only when steps are taken in an adequate measure to make the people aware of the indispensable necessity of their conduct being orientated in accordance with the requirement of law.

The law, the administration of justice as a whole and the issue of public accountability, which are key concept in the rule of law, warrants a collective approach from the perspective of public litigants and the society at large. The centre of gravity of the law lies in the society itself. But in our society we have even after five decades of independence, a large number of persons who are hungry, illiterate, ignorant, with no food to eat, with no house to stay in, and in many places, not even good water to drink. The hungry people are looking to the democracy and asking, "what has the arrival of political freedom and law meant for us".

Alred Russel Wallance said: "I have lived with communities of savages in South America and in the East who have no law or law courts but the public opinion of the village freely expressed. Each man scrupulously respected the rights of his fellows, and any infraction of those rights rarely or never takes place. In such a community all are nearly equal". We like eagles were born to be free, yet we are obliged, in order to live at all, to make the cage of laws for ourselves and to stand on a perch.

Ancient civilization particularly that of India, conceived a legal order based on compendious Sanskrit expression 'Dharma'. In India it was history of Dharma, which signified duties. It was the highest law. Everybody was under it. Nobody was above it. Event the king was under the law, laid down by Dharma. Who can punish the king, if he violates the law? 'Dharmasya Dandasya', Law is the king of kings'. This mighty king is the Jagannath of law. The law which is Dharma, 'not in the sense of performance of rituals, but Dharma in the sense of 'rule of law' which sustains Dharma or law, which in turn sustains social structure and endures spiritual progress. Law is more rigid and powerful than the kings. Nothing is higher than the law – By its prowess the weak shall prevail over the strong, and social democracy will succeed.

So the question that would be asked repeatedly is: What is to be Done when the criminalisation of politics has gone to such an extent? Or, conversely, what is to be done when all values have been debased and everything is up for grabs? Slowly but steadily, even the civil services which had provided a modicum of law and order in society has also been corrupted? The quality of men and women joining the services despite the recent hike their emoluments has gone done. More money is clearly not the answer because there will never be enough. Only the enforcement of the law against corruption or some kind of judicial activism will provide the necessary impetus for reform from below.

Corruption - Political Process

The provisions of law as to election expenses should be put back fully to their pristine position and should be along the lines of UK provisions in this respect. As in the UK, periodical review of the ceilings of election expenses must be undertaken by the Election

Commission and its recommendations in that behalf should be made binding.

There should be a complete ban on contributions to political parties by business houses and companies. In the alternative, the contributions could strictly be regulated by taking remedial measures; as regards state funding of elections. The items chosen should be such as may easily eliminate or contain wasteful election expenditure; the state subsidy should be in the form of kind only and not in cash (in items,) cost, one round of parliamentary elections would be about $25000/- for a bigger constituency and about $20,000 for a smaller constituency; only candidates of recognized political parties should be made eligible with the provision for later reimbursement if any other candidate is elected to raise necessary funds (about $ 10 million in total for parliamentary elections); and graded amounts should be laid down in the Indian income tax law as in the USA which may be deducted from specified income tax payers. Except Election Commission, no other authority should have any control over the funds and their distribution. Similarly State Funding for State assemblies elections, deductions should be made from sales tax payers and necessary funds raised; if a ceiling on expenses is still required after the scheme of the state funding of elections is put into operation, it should be kept low.

While the foregoing is a summary of the mainstream view of corruption, there is also a revisionist standpoint that holds that corruption may be justified or actually be beneficial under certain circumstances. A bribe offered to escape from an unjust or a repressive act, for instance, may not be morally reprehensible. If economic regulations are dysfunctional, corruption, by evading them can result in greater efficiency. Speed-money can expedite decisions. Corruption may provide an opportunity for disadvantaged or minority groups to obtain benefits from which they might otherwise get excluded. Should the gains from corruption accrue to those who are able to invest them efficiently, the economy can benefit.

A numbers of reasons can be advanced in these arguments relating to these 'benefits' of corruption. The first is the normative position that corruption is morally unacceptable regardless of any instrumental advantages it might bring. The second is the practical argument that it is not feasible to confine corruption to those areas or activities in which it might be marginally beneficial. And the third, the 'benefits' from corruption are argued on the assumption that corruption provides a safety-valve from repressive regimes, over-regulated economies, administrative delays, and discriminatory practices. There is no reason for taking this set of evils for granted. They also need to be tackled as part of the overall reforms for curbing corruption. Although, therefore, one should include that the costs of corruption are bound to overwhelm the benefits which might be associated with it on a superficial reckoning.

India has not been free of corruption whether in ancient times, the immediate pre-colonial period, British rule or the decades following Independence. But it is a fact that corruption has increased many times since Independence. It is not an exaggeration today to talk about corruption in terms of a crises or a cancer endangering India's society, polity and economy. Considering following:

There has been a distinct increase - in terms of the number and amounts in transaction in which the presence of corruption has been substantiated. At the Center, these he included, but have not been confined to, defence contracts (e.g. Bofors, HDW submarines), civil contracts (e.g. railways), telecommunication contracts, commodity imports (e.g. fertilizer and sugar), privatization (e.g. Bailadilla mine), house allotments, the financial sector (e.g. the Bank scam) and violations of the Foreign Exchange Regulation and Income Tax Acts (Hawala cases).

A number of Ministers and Governments of States have had to resign on account of being legally charged with corrupt transactions. In more than one instance Prime Ministers have been tainted with suspicion though investigations against them do not seem to have been expeditiously or effectively pursued.

There should be separate judicial agency i.e. Ombudsman, to enquire into the conduct of civil and public officers at the time of elections on the basis of complaint by any of the political parties or public men.

A Code of conduct should be laid down by law and a Conduct Committee under the head of the Speaker or Chairman and consisting of members of the House drawn from the parties represented in the House concerned should be formed and punishment should be given for violators. An appeal should lie to the Supreme Court to finally decide the issue and with powers to give interim orders including stay of the adverse decision by the Speaker.

Elected representative should also file their accounts of assets every year. The proposed Committee should be allowed to scrutinize members' annual return of assets, etc.

A law in the Parliament should be made to cover not only all the Ministers but also the PM, CMs and the elected members. This law in this respect should be made without any delay.

Corruption, Political Interference and the Civil Service

The primary responsibility of the Government, is to uphold the rule of law and the political neutrality is the cornerstone of the edifice of the civil service.

A number of issues pertaining to the All India Services need to be examined afresh. These include the future in-take in the services, age of recruitment, number of chances to be permitted to a candidate to appear for the competitive examinations, weight age to be given to the preferences of candidates in making allotments to States within the quota to fifty per cent earmarked for the "outsiders", emphasising a value system and moral foundations in the training programs, compulsory service in both the State of their allotment and the Center, a review of procedures and laying down of clear criteria for selection of officers at every stage of promotion, and the introduction of a system of weeding out officers through early retirement schemes.

Special problems of the cadres in small States such as Jammu and Kashmir and those in the north-east need to be reviewed to ensure that the role of All India Services is not diluted in any way and their effectiveness is increased to cope with the serious problems of insurgency, alienation, corruption and slow pace of development.

The Center and the States should lay down rules and regulations concerning the transfer of officers to ensure a reasonable term of three years in a post to any incumbent. The reasons for any departure from the prescribed rules must be recorded in writing and conveyed to the effected officer.

The powers of suspension which are being used indiscriminately by the State Governments should be withdrawn so that the Center and the UPS would have to say in it. No extension or re-employment should be allowed to any officer beyond the prescribed age of retirement.

The role of the civil service associations needs to be redefined. Apart from raising their voice against policies and actions which lead to self-realization of the officers, the associations will have to set standards of conduct and safeguard the image, prestige and position of the service they represent.

Statutory Civil Service Boards should be established in the Centre and the States to oversee all matters pertaining to the services. Their recommendations must be binding on the concerned Government. Any departure there from must be for reasons to be recorded in writing and open to review by the Civil Service Tribunals will be presented before the CATISAT.

The right to information must be guaranteed to all citizens and a comprehensive Central legislature enacted for the purpose, Simultaneously, the Official Secrets Act should be repealed and a new legislation enacted to confine its ambit on to safeguarding Nation Security and defence concerns.

Steps should be initiated to bring in greater accountability and transparency in the functioning of the Government. A legislation should be enacted to give protection to those officers who expose corruption, wrong-doing and mismanagement of Government.

The investigating agencies in the Center and the States, charged with the responsibility to investigate cases of corruption, excess and misuse of power and position should be placed under statutory created authorities with appropriate safeguards against politicians.

5

URBAN CRIME

Cities have multiplied crime. They have also made it more visible. And the all too visible strains of daily existence in a city have prompted many to consider urbanisation itself as some kind of disease. Sivaramakrishan[1] , in his book, "Indian Urban Scene", writes :-

"Often it is said India is only one fifth urban, but a fifth of 950 million is a lot. Large city growth is a significant feature of this urbanisation. India now has about 150 mega cities with more than 100,000 people in each. In another twenty years there will be 300 mega cities. Every patch of Indian cities have become rotten and infected with the bracelet of crime.

Urbanisation is closely associated with the economic development of a country. It would not be an exaggeration to say that the test of development lies in the shift of population to the urban areas. During the early part of 20th century there was economic stagnation in India and so urbanisation was limited. Urban population which accounted for 11 percent in 1941 and in 1951 rose to 17.2 percent.

The pace of urbanisation has been quicker during the recent years. But none can deny that urbanisation is a recent development. But all cities can not be called areas; according to 1971 census the urban areas mean those places which have a municipality, corporation or cantonment or notified town area. Apart from it the places which have a minimum population of 5,000 and if 75 percent of a male working population is not that of agriculturists and the density of population is at least 400 per sq. km. are also urban areas. The definition of urban areas adopted in earlier censuses was some what different.

---

1 Sivaramakrishan, Indian Urban Scene, (1978)

In Europe and North America urbanisation was the direct consequence of industrialisation. In India industrialisation started very late and so urbanisation was also a later phenomenon. Up to 1941, urbanisation was not so rapid and only 43.81 million people lived in the cities. The figures rose to 108.80 millions in 1971. Even now the urban population of India is only 19.87 percent of the total population of the country. In all other countries the urban population is comparatively higher. For example in U. K., it is 78.87 percent of its total population, in Japan 68.09 percent, in the former Soviet Union 57.85 percent and in the U. S. A. about 95 percent. But none can deny that there is a tendency towards urbanisation in India.

T. V. Chaudhry has given a large number of the reasons for the migration of rural population to urban centres. According to him they generally come to find work and employment. There are no continuous work opportunities in the villages due to the seasonal nature of agricultural operation. Industrialisation in the urban areas can provide better employment opportunities. Sometimes the villagers gravitate to urban centres to enjoy the comforts of the life.

In recent years the elaborate economic planning has created new townships in the project areas and new industrial towns like Sindri, Bhokaro etc. the mining centres like Neyveli. and Mr. Bale Subramaniam mentions three sets of factors which are responsible for urbanisation in this country. He describes them as "Pull, Push, and Neutral factors". According to him 'Pull' factors are the opportunities of better employment, growth of new business and education facilities and availability of cultural and social amenities. The 'Push' factors are unemployment, insufficient income, family disputes, class tensions, indebtedness and insolvency. The 'Neutral factors which Subramaniam mentions are the commitments of the operation of the natural laws of life marriage and dependency.

Mumbai, is the state capital of Maharashtra, is the industrial heart of India, Maharashtrians are not renowned as business people. They are better known as social reformers, politicians, statesmen, artists, educators, scientists, administrators, writes, journalists, freedom fighters and soldiers. They have contributed immensely to Indian music, culture, theatre and cinema. But now fifty percent of its population lives in slums. In Olga Tellies, Y. V. Chandrachud, the then Chief Justice of the Supreme Court of India, portrays the plague of lakhs of persons who live on pavements of Mumbai:

In the pre-industrial cities the pattern of urbanisation was somewhat different. The cities were mostly unplanned and the population seemed to concentrate in or around the centre of the city. Here most of the facilities were available. That is why the cities were not big in size. Another feature of the towns in ancient India was that there were no separate residential localities each having its own shopping centre and other facilities. Entire business was concentrated within the bazaars, and the distribution of population was on community lines. With the coming of the Europeans new pattern of urbanisation was introduced. They built administrative offices and residential areas outside the old cities. They were planned in a manner that there should be no congestion. The pattern of segregation was also introduced by them. That means they started having separate colonies for class I officers, class II officers and so on.

The social consequences of urbanisation are many. It creates the problem of housing because of the labourers and other people who come from the villages. Labour disputes and the pressure on the schools are the other direct consequences of civilisation. They start following a different pattern of life. In the cities, "there is physical proximity but social distance." The hotel life has a great attraction for the younger generations. The urban slums start growing. Economic hardship and poverty lead to tensions between different groups. The criminal tendencies like illegal gambling, prostitution, unwed mothers, intimidation of witnesses, election frauds start increase. Moreover, it has created overcrowded houses, and result in slums., traffic-jams and many other problems.

There is a general concern over the rapid increase in the population of major cities. This had not only put an additional burden on civic amenities but also led to chaotic traffic conditions. Almost all the important roads in major cities are choked all the time and some concrete strategy would have to be prepared to grapple with the situation.

The million-plus cities, as per the 1991 census are : Ahmedabad, Bangalore, Bhopal, Calcutta, Chennai, Cochin, Coimbatore, Delhi, Hyderabad, Indore, Jaipur, Kanpur, Lucknow, Ludhiana, Madurai, Mumbai, Nagpur, Patna, Pune, Surat, Vadodara, Varanasi and Visakhapatnam.

Unplanned urbanisation affects both the individual and the environment. Researcher says that "the great danger to morality and good government is that the individual is lost in the multitude of atoms - the condition that may abolish the sense of duty and make the great cities as insecure as the wilds". The insecurity in turn would breed apathy and indifference along with a feeling of importance.

But it is the effect on the family that urbanization that needs to be considered. It leads to the nuclear family breaking up old family ties and sooner and later even the nuclear family breaks up, as is happening in the West. Inadequate housing, water supply, sewage, lack of creational facilities create enormous pressures on the individual and the family which disrupts community life.

Even in rural areas the rapid growth of urban centres has had its effect on community living. While some villages have shown a tendency towards integration with the cities, many have been reduced to become suppliers of raw materials and dependent upon the city for market, credit and even employment. These villages have become suburban towns in the long run.

India is no longer a land of villages, but of growing urban centres, of mushrooming slums in cities whose burgeoning population pressures the entire urban infrastructure. Rural-urban migration following the collapse of the rural economy, is the root cause. But the past few decades have witnessed a radical changes-transformation in the scene of an Indian village - in some ways for the better, in other ways for the worse. The main catalyst responsible for this change has been the fast and speedy advent of modern technology in our country. Today, modern technology holds an important place in India in all the development fields, viz., scientific industrial and, of course, agricultural. When we speak of agricultural field, it pertains to Indian villages on the whole. The effect of modern technology on Indian villages has been felt in a very remarkable manner in different spheres of life. Let us see how.

First and foremost, farming is the backbone of India villages. Because of modern technology, the methods of farming have been revolutionised. Outdated and obsolete methods of farming have been discarded and new and innovative methods are being widely adopted. The use of tractors and other modern agricultural implements has perfected the art of farming and, in the process, commercialised it to a large extent. The standard of living of an average Indian farmer has risen, and as more and more machines are taking the place of manual work, farmers are encouraged to take up subsidiary occupations, like cattle-breeding, poultry-farming, etc., which are an additional source of income for them. Extensive and intensive cultivation of crops, hybridisation of crops, rotation of crops and the greatly successful "Green Revolution" have presented a better picture of Indian villages to the world.

Previously, sowing seeds and reaping harvests used to be a laborious task for the Indian farmer. He was entirely at the mercy of nature for rain for the crops. But today modern technology has discovered artificial irrigation methods like tube wells, canals, dams, etc., which prove a boon to the farmers in times of crises. Also better quality seeds and fertilisers are yet another result of modern technology which have successfully led India on the path of self-sufficiency in foodgrains. India today is proud exporter of foodgrains in contrast to

being an importer country when she attained freedom in 1947. These seeds and fertilisers yield crops in greater quantity and government sees to it that they are produced on mass scale and are sold at reasonable rates so that a majority of villagers can be the beneficiaries and can procure them to obtain a good harvest income.

Darkness ruled supreme in villages until a few decades ago. But with modern inventions and low production costs, electricity has been provided to many villages. Electronic goods were a far-off dream in Indian villages. Today some of the Indian villages have Television Transmission Relay Centres. Communication too, has touched new height in Indian villages. Roadways have improved many villages. Most of them are now linked directly with cities and towns by means of railways. In olden times, and Indian villager was satisfied with bullock-cart as the sole means of transport, like buses, trucks and even cars, plying on village roads. Post and Telegraph system too has, acquired new dimensions in villages.

But there are certain aspects of modern technology which have had adverse effects on the life of people in Indian villages. Modern technology has given birth to machine operated jobs in cities which offer attractive remuneration and other facilities. So most of the male population of villages has fast increased in cities and their family ties with members of their families back in the villages are fast losing ground. A typical Indian village is no longer a self-sufficient unit. This is largely due to modern inventions, and innovations and production of modern sophisticated machines which manufacture from the smallest sewing needle to the giant-size fighter-aeroplane in India. As a result, the craftsmen and artisans in villages are thrown out of employment. Also in some villages, modern implements of farming are beyond the reach of many poor farmers, which leads to an inequitable distribution of wealth, even in villages.

Nevertheless, when we weigh the pros and cons of influence of modern technology on Indian villages, we find that it has definitely transformed life in Indian villages. Greater and diverse horizons of modern technology have helped to put Indian villages on a strong footing—economically, socially and politically. An Indian villager today has greater hopes and aspirations in life, as he is more educated than his counterpart in older generations. Literacy has taken roots in many villages which makes them eager to experiment with new and contemporary methods of farming and other occupations.

India is a land of villages, and she is proud to be one because no stone has been left unturned to herald and usher in new realms of modern technology in Indian villages to transform rural life for betterment and upliftment of masses. No doubt, the Indian villager of the 20th century is much better-off than his counterpart in the 17th or the 18th centuries.

Crime grows as the city grows.

JAWAHARLAL NEHRU rightly said that the future of India does not depend upon her numbers or even her past, except in so far as the future grows out of the present, and the present grows out of the past. India has a large number of people of mediocre quality. Worse, the majority of the villagers are illiterate. The rate of illiteracy is particularly high among women, who not only runt he homes in villages but also work in the fields. Since the spread of education among them is slow, and since their general outlook has not been materially affected by the progress of science and technology in urban India, they are likely to continue the traditional patterns all round, except in areas of activity where young men dominate. These young people are naturally affected by the new yearn for change and detest the culture of the elders.

The attraction of the city is seductive. Socrates said that nothing of interest happened outside the city walls, and their was two thousand years ago. But city life is a soup opera that never ends. It reinforces and strengthens the heresy of humanism, that narcissistic belief - that nothing important happens that is not a human interest.

Socrates in, Earth Conference One; Sharing a vision for Out Plant, (1989) p. 16, by Anuradha Vittachi City living corrupts. It gives a false sense of priority over environmental hazards. We become inordinately obsessed about personal mortality, especially about death from cancer. Most citizens, when asked list nuclear radiation and Ozone depletion as the most serious environmental hazards. They tend to ignore the consequences of green house gas accumulation, agricultural excess, and forest clearance. Yet in fact these less personal hazards can kill just as certainly.

Cynics and pessimists go to the extent to saying that the increasing mechanisation of agriculture, and of other village occupations, including handicrafts and cottage industries, will increase the existing economic disparities. Such disparities are likely to mean that the sorry condition of those in distress will get worse. The bigger landlords, who are becoming more and more influential and prosperous, may buy and gobble up the small farms which are becoming uneconomical, and whose owners are almost perpetually in debt. So the small holdings may gradually disappear, or at any rate, their number may become smaller in the coming decades. The gobbling up of the smaller fry by the giants may even reach its culmination in the 21st century.

Cattle dung is still being used as fuel. It comes free because most villagers own cattle. The progress of installation of boogies plants is slow, and only the comparatively better placed farmers opt for them with the assistance of Agriculture development officers. Consequently, cattle dung will continue to be used for cooking food in most village homes. The villagers have been told time and again that use of cow dung as manure would increase agricultural production many times over, but the question of finding an alternative fuel remains unsolved, especially because fuelled is getting scarce. The reckless felling of trees for utilising timber in urban areas has created a problem for villagers, and this problem is likely to get accentuated as the years pass.

Again, poverty is traditional, and evidence of it is to be found in most of the countryside. Poverty, in fact, is a basic reality in this country, and is deep-rooted. It is not likely to be eliminated in the next 25 years or so; even a notable dent into the malaise may not be possible despite all the anti-poverty drives and officially sponsored programmes. We are deeply moved when we see half-starved, half-naked children roaming the streets and playing amidst dirt, stink and squalor. These conditions may take a long time to improve materially, though there need be no doubt that there will be some progress in sanitation, water supply, general living conditions and the standards of life, by the turn of the century. Every village will have electricity and every home will consequently have a brighter look. The kerosene lamps may still flicker in huts and hovels, but by and large, the countryside will have electricity. The supply of power may, however, be erratic and far from cheap.

Twenty five years hence, poverty may not so crushing and destructive of human values as it is today. It is also possible that the existing spirit of resignation, and the fatalistic attitude may give way to a more rational approach, and a determination to shed the legacies of the past. This process will certainly be expedited by the spread of education, the enlightenment that the radio and the fast-expanding television network brings.

Moreover, with the gradual passing away of the elders, and their replacement by the better-placed and more educated younger generation, many traditional practices will be discarded and new attitudes will develop. While the new generation will be more conscious of its rights, and demand more attention to their growing needs, it is far from certain whether they will simultaneously develop a higher sense of responsibility. In fact, if the current trends are any indication, dishonesty, selfishness, lack of respect for elders and many other negative aspects of human character will become more evident. Verily, human greed knows no limits, and only incorrigible optimists bank on a notable change in the character of the Indian people, in the next quarter of a century.

The increasing sham and hypocrisy, so characteristic of urban life, are likely to affect the countryside also. There might be greater intrusion of anti-social elements, cliques and "dadas" (local bosses). Of course the masses should try to forget the tensions, bickering and inter-group rivalries, but who can assert with confidence that, with the rapidly changing scenario, the life of the average villager would be happier, and more enjoyable in the 21st century?

One reason why very little dent is made in the wide extent of this problem is, that anti-poverty programmes are all official. In this regard the Prime Minister recently sought the co-operation of voluntary bodies, which can play a crucial role. These bodies are now asked to monitor the progress of programmes. He has also sought the co-operation of all political parties in achieving the national task of reducing the percentage of the poor to only 5 per cent by the turn of the century. When officials alone are entrusted with the task of selecting the prospective beneficiaries of government programmes, many deserving people are left out. It is true that the suggested selective approach for identifying beneficiaries would help in reducing the absolute levels of destitution of people in urgent need of assistance. If locally elected representatives of the villages are associated with the anti-poverty plans, the errors and aberrations noticed in the identification of beneficiaries would be eliminated, at any rate by 2010.

Unfortunately, the women have so far benefited much less than men from the series of anti-poverty programmes. It is far from certain whether the coverage of village women for accrual of benefits will equal that of men. On many occasions, despite Ministers' assurances of assistance the poor in backward areas live in state of fear, and they are ruthlessly exploited by landlords with such fear and exploitation end?

6

ELECTIONS : MAFIA AND CRIME

Mafia and guns have been an integral part of the battle of the ballot over the years. A parallel government of militants has been conducting a parallel process of polling in almost every State. Worse, even ministers in State identified with pre-poll and poll violence and supported, if not instigated, the mafia gangs in action.

The subversion of the electoral process began as early as in 1962 with the silent intimidation of voters. This was followed by impersonation and interference with the work of polling personnel as witnesses in 1967; these means were used more blatantly in 1969 along with threats and violence. If one party showed the way, another followed and when one party introduced a new technique others were not slow to master it they often improved upon it.

Free and fair elections are an exercise central to a democratic system. But political parties do not want a free and fair elections. The lessons drawn from the last five elections show that even after massive deployment of security forces, framing of code of conduct for political parties by the Election Commission and special security arrangements at and near the polling booths, no human effort or mechanical device could ensure a free and fair election if the politicians and political parties themselves really do not want it. The result of such an election is not likely to have stability, but an era of uncertainty and further political upheavals. The law and procedure are comprehensive and all possible contingencies are thought of an appropriate steps laid down. But the law in enforceable only in a society which respects the law.

But can a law be enforced if the atmosphere is surcharged with fear and vitiated by ruthless campaigns and organised gangsters.

The poll violence consists of booth capturing, forcible removal of ballot papers and ballot boxes, burning of vehicles, man-handling of voters, election staff and police and even killing of candidates and polling officers in which firearms and explosives are used in a large scale. Nalini Singh's T.V. Programme "Booth Capturing" is remarkable for its interviews with professional booth captures mostly, gangsters of the underworld hired during elections. The film shows that the entire election machinery is controlled by them, the pressure being one of bribe or terror unleashed on the presiding officials, polling agents and the police on duty.

What happened in the prime minister's own constituency of Amethi in the Ninth Lok Sabha election in 1989 is without a doubt a national disgrace. The local mafia hierarchy went berserk in their bid to influence the electoral verdict. If this is the example set in the prime minister's own constituency he was left without moral authority to control the mafia hierarchy who made a mockery of the democratic process in other parts of the country.

It is also necessary to note the inability of those voicing the nation's conscience to rise to the occasion. Not only Amethi, there had been gross perversions of the electoral process in other parts of the country. For instance, 402 of the 587 booths spread over seven States where repoll had been ordered. Furtyer, rigging was reported from Haryana, on a staggering scale in three constituencies namely, Faridabad, Bhiwani and Hissar where the Congress(I) candidates posed a serious challenge to the State's ruling party. The incidents in this opposition ruled State was not qualitatively comparable to those in Amethi but that only underlines the magnitude of the attempt to subvert democracy.

There was rigging and large scale violence in the Amethi constituency on 22 November 1989 where Janata Dal candidate, Sanjay Singh, close to Janata Dal leader V.P. Singh, was pitted against a powerful Congress nominee. There was exchange of fire in village Bhusiaon and Munshiganj - Musafarkhan road crossing in the afternoon of the polling day. It was alleged that armed men were waiting in ambush for those who were either proceeding to the polling booths. Many burnt motor vehicles were found in a number of places. The murderous attack on Sanjay Singh showed the length to which subversion of democracy by unscrupulous politicians, supported by mafia hierarchy could go.

In 1989 elections Om Prakash Chautala's son, Ajay Singh terrorised the whole population in Meham, Haryana, in front of the national press and police. Hundreds of Green Brigade volunteers were enlisted in the police and got licensed firearms. While the firearms were freely used the law enforcement officials watched helplessly when the rigging was in progress. The superintendent of police was seen moving about with Ajay Singh in the same vehicle.

In Vishnupur Bhagnagri, north Bihar, the day after May 20, 1989 Ninth Lok Sabha poll, hundreds of armed musclemen surrounded the Harijan basti, set fire to their huts, reducing them to ashes. One of the most active groups fighting on behalf of the Harijans was the Indian People's Front (IPF). It had a strong base in Central Bihar. Harijans constituted 14 per cent of Bihar's population and a section of them realised the importance of their votes. Oppression of Harijans had spawned numerous movements under the C.P.I., the C.P.I. (M) and Naxalite groups to organise Harijans and gave them greater awareness of their rights.

In Bhojpur's Danwar - Bihita area, in Bihar, in 1989 Rajpur landlord Jawala Singh was responsible for the murder of 23 Harijans in their sleep, with the help of his private army. It was a massacre. When Jawala Singh was given anticipatory bail, police force was sent to protect not the Harijans but Jwala Singh. No attempt was made by the police to arrest him and his armed private army personnel after the massacre. At Bhojpur, on the day of polling in 1989 about a dozen armed men of the private army attacked hundreds of Harijans and forced them out of their hutments, molested their womenfolk, captured booths and rigged Harijan votes.

Imagine the involvement of Union Minister of State, home affairs, Subodh Kant Sahay in booth capturing on 20 May 1991. Sahay was himself contesting from Ranchi Lok Sabha Constituency. He was moving from both to booth in HEC area with his armed bodyguards and armed partymen in vehicles. The police seized four of his vehicles and arrested 157 armed men belonging to Janata Dal, the ruling party at the centre which had fielded Sahay. The Deputy Commissioner of Ranchi, Sudhir Prasad, who was also the returning-cum-election officer for the constituency lodged a complaint against Sahay to the Election Commission (The Statesman, 21 May 1991).

The Indian People's Front (IPF) a militant Naxalite group alleged that Laloo Prasad Yadav in 1989 Assembly elections visited several booths in his Chapra Constituency and himself supervised booth capturing by his armed Green Brigade. Laloo won the election. Congress(I) supporters working for the party candidate Mahendra Prasad, invaded a Harijan colony, shot and wounded three residents including two women and a girl aged about 10 years as they had defied the party directive to stay away from polling. They had to be rushed to Patna Medical College Hospital for treatment. Countless harijans in Bihar, Uttar Pradesh, Andhra Pradesh and Gujarat have not seen the inside of a polling booth.

The Bihar government resorted to every dirt trick to defeat George Fernandes in the Banka by-elections. Workers and voters were terrorised to stay away from polling booths. When Fernandes' supporters complained to the police they were themselves arrested.

Bishnu Mahato, leader of the IPF contesting from Hatia Constituency, Bihar as an independent candidate was shot dead. His wife and family members alleged that the victim had been offered money by some Congress(I) leaders to withdraw from the contest before he was killed for failing to oblige them. In Nalanda, Bihar's crime capital, notorious for manufacture of illicit guns, an independent candidate, Mahendra Prasad was gunned down in his house a day before the polling. In Masauri, Bihar Congress(I) candidate Janeshwar Prasad Singh was shot dead in the election office, his supporters said that DMKP was responsible for his murder. Banwari Ram, an independent candidate who contested from Bokaro

Constituency in Bihar died in his sleep allegedly in mysterious circumstances; some said he was poisoned because he had a fair chance to win.

Dhanbad MLA Suraj Deo Singh with a number of criminal cases pending against him, had been manipulating his victory, election after, election, with the help of mafia gang. So powerful had been Suraj Deo that he never paid road taxes of large number of vehicles he owned, nor paid entertainment tax for the cinema houses owned by him. He was in a possession of number of licensed and unlicensed firearms. He dictated postings and transfers of law enforcement officials in Dhanbad Prime Minister Chandrasekhar accepted Suraj Deo's invitation to a breakfast in his house. Chief Minister Bhagwat Jha Azad of Bihar was allegedly lost his chair when he tried messing up with him.

In Uttar Pradesh, during the tenth-general elections, the first day's polling on 20 May 1991 accounted for 198 deaths (Pre-poll 110 and 88 poll and post poll violence). In the Moradabad Constituency, when Chandrapal Singh, a minister in Uttar Pradesh went to file his nomination papers, a pitched battle reportedly took place in which 18 persons were injured while the minister was forced to hide in a room. The Janata Dal office was ransacked. In Meerut, 17 persons were killed and army had to patrol the area and so was Bulandshahr where the army had to be called out against several bomb explosions and gun attacks.

Central to the use of violence has been the conflict between the upper castes and backward castes including Harijans. Harijans are prevented from voting and their votes are rigged by the powerful upper caste landlords with the help of their private armies.

As Chief Minister, Mulayam Singh Yadav had been accused of issuing gun licenses, in a large scale, to Yadavs in Etawah from where he fought elections. In Bihar, there is no dearth of firearms which are manufactured illicitly in hundreds of gun manufacturing units funded by politician-criminals. A few months before elections these units are flooded with orders for supply of guns not only from different parts of Bihar but also from other States. Ironically, the

Bihar government has taken no steps to ban these illegal units flourishing as a cottage industry.

Violence during elections is not confined to the Hindi speaking belt, particularly, Bihar, Madhya Pradesh, Uttar Pradesh and Gujarat but also in the south. In Andhra Pradesh, political parties fighting elections take the help of criminals and gangsters. There were reports from Bihar, Gujarat and Andhra Pradesh about convicts released on parole to fight elections on behalf of the ruling party candidates.

In Mumbai, the powerful underworld plays a very important role during elections. It not only provide finance to the candidate and parties fighting elections but also provide muscle power and guns. Successive chief ministers of Maharashtra and political parties have been accused of their close nexus with powerful gangsters of the underworld.

Apart from the overtly criminal gangs, there are other political criminal gangs who operate under cover and work for the candidates of the ruling party. They are above the law. The private armies viciously polarised on caste politics of Bihar are also at work.

Before every election, hundreds of thousands of criminals and anti-socials are arrested and detained under the NSA; hundreds of thousands of illicit weapons are seized; illegal gun manufacturing factories are closed down and the Election Commission identifies thousands of booths "sensitive" or "extra-sensitive" for enforcing special security measures and shoot at sight order is issued. Identity cards have been introduced to prevent rigging. As far as possible, polling stations are run by officers from outside to prevent local influence and par-military forces and even the army have been used to keep the politicised and partisan local police outside the electoral process. Number of poll observers has been increased. Code of conduct laid down by the Election Commission for the political parties and polling officers has been enforced as far as possible. Nevertheless, poll violence is reported. Every political party in power has blatantly misused the official machinery to rig the polls ever since 1969 elections. Guidelines provided by the Election Commission has been able to solve the problem till recently after T.N. Seshan took over.

While he has been able to enforce free and fair polls conforming to the strict electoral guidelines laid down by him, he is distressed at the performance of the Bihar government. He recently said "Bihar needs that little extra attention because at the end of the day it should not be said it was bright everywhere else, but in Bihar we failed".

In a confidential, strongly worded note sent on February 23, 1996 the Chief Election Commissioner virtually accused the Bihar government of trying to side track the issues that he had raised, the highlights of which are : (India Today, March 15, 1995: Law & Order-Damaging Dossier).

1. As many as 8,719 persons were reported to have been involved in cases of electoral offences in the previous elections and 950 criminal cases relating to electoral offences were registered. But not a single conviction has been achieved.

2. As on date, 10,600 warrants and challans are lying unexecuted/unserved at different police stations in the State. The preventive action taken so far is negligible considering the size of the State, law and order conditions and the number of assembly constituencies, districts and polling stations. Only 1,322 illegal weapons, 581 bombs and 1,246 cartridges were seized while only 8,290 preventive detention were made.

3. In the 100 per cent scrutiny of arms licence-holders as directed by the Election Commission in September 1994, as many as 11,124 licence-holders still remain unverified. While 50,935 persons were directed to deposit their firearms only 35,527 have actually done so.

4. Only 17,150 out of the total 82,692 polling booths in the State have been identified as "sensitive" by the State government. This figure, the Commission believes is unreliable. Also, as per the Commission's orders, the State government was supposed to prepare and forward a comprehensive list of sensitive polling stations by 30

September 1994 with constant updating. Till now, no list has been sent to the Commission.

5. On 17 February 1995 the State government was directed to monitor, compile and forward to the Election Commission everyday at 20.00 hours the law and order situation in the State in a prescribed format. The reports being received till now are incomplete, incorrect and irregular. The State was warned that these reports were critical inputs for the Election Commission for assessing the possibility of holding free and fair elections and that not sending them in or sending incomplete reports would be gross failure.

6. The Commission funds "most unbelievable" the statement by the Bihar government that no middle-level officers have been transferred in violation of Election Commission's directives. The report of the Director General of Police (DGP) which was routed through the Chief Electoral Officer (CEO) himself, stated that hundreds of inspectors of police have been transferred in violation of his and the Election Commission's directives.

7. Top-secret security-related information, statistics and communications are being leaked out every day from all the districts. The Election Commission was especially alarmed when communications regarding critical statistical information - particularly a correspondence between the DGP and the chief secretary regarding the acute shortage of revolvers and bodyguards and messages sent by the district magistrates of Katihar, Giridih and Palaman, regarding a similar shortfall - appeared in a news item in Janasatta dated February 19th.

8. The security of contesting candidates has not been viewed by the government with the seriousness it deserves. In the case of the murder of a candidate contesting from Gopalganj it is clear from the government's reply that it only gives instructions to the police authorities concerned that it does not check to ensure that the police authorities have adequately assessed security assessments requirements in proportion with threat perceptions, it does not periodically check whether the required security has been provided

and it does not investigate the causes of security lapses when they occur.

9. The district magistrates of Bettiah, Buxar, Goda, Muzaffarpur, Nalanda and Samastipur have sent a message to the Commission that almost all the candidates in their districts are without bodyguards, since there are not enough bodyguards and those available do not have a sufficient number of arms anyway.

10. The Commission is concerned about the unsystematic creation of units of administration. For example, five districts continue to be manned by part-time district magistrates; and the number of assembly constituencies contained in each revenue district is widely varying subsequent to the creation of new units. This has rendered co-ordination and supervision difficult in some districts and superficial in others.

> "These allegations highlighted by the Election Commission seem to be substantial" comments India Today, March 15, 1995. Earlier this month, in a confidential letter informing V.D. Ram, DIG, HQ Patna, of the Maoist Communist Centre's (MCC) threat to boycott the poll by unleashing violence in his district K.P. Ramaiah, the district election officer-cum-deputy commissioner of Palaman stated: "I expect there will be large scale violence, bloodshed and poll boycott, to the extent of 50 per cent. I have already reported this several times earlier to the departments concerned but the response to my signals or reports is insufficient. Hence, I request you to give me sufficient forces to deal with the abnormal situation".

An intelligence Bureau report, submitted to the Election Commission last week stated that the MCC and CPM-L(PU) have been continuing their campaign for poll boycott through public meetings and wall-writing in Jehanabad, Gaya, Aurangabad, Giridih, Dhanbad and Hazaribagh districts. On February 10 at a meeting in Narsingpur in Gaya district, Pramod Misra, an MCC candidate openly directed party cadres to loot poll boxes and attack police parties with explosives.

Coupled with reports of a deteriorating law and order situation, The Election Commission had also found cases of serious violations of its standing orders. The commission found "highly unsatisfactory" the knowledge of election rules and procedures among some of the returning officers. In 50 cases of allotment of symbols in 43 constituencies, the Commission had to revise the decision of the Returning Officers. This did not include the 10 cases in which the Returning Officers had themselves, without any authority under law, changed their orders on receipt of queries from the Commission. The Bihar elections witnesses several tussles between Laloo's government and Seshan.

Seshan, the Chief Election Commissioner (CEC) came in conflict with political parties when he took stern measures to purify the electoral process. His predecessors in office had full knowledge of the systematic sabotage of the democratic process but they regarded their duty done with the submission of statutory reports to the government. Seshan was too conscientious to leave things at that - he stretched the powers given to him by the Constitution to their limits to stop the unfair practices of political parties and candidates against which has predecessors had considered themselves helpless. He draw upon the unused power of the GEC to insist on a photo identity card for each of the 600 million voters of the country to present rigging and on the candidates and their sponsoring parties keeping the election expenses strictly under the enhanced ceilings fixed by government.

The enhanced ceilings are even now inadequate, but the government had turned down the Election Commission's suggestion for further increase to make the ceilings realistic. Candidates and parties accustomed to spending millions or even crores of rupees to win a Lok Sabha seat were naturally outraged, for they realised that if the ceilings were enforced, that would be the end of elections financed almost wholly by black money. The patrons of political parties would not like that either, and while money would not be available in that abundance. At a modest estimate Rs.1000 crore, the bulk of it in black money, is spent on every election. Money is power, black money is black power, and wielders of this power are understandably reluctant to accept any curtailment of this power which gives enormous clout to the government and political parties.

Seshan's other obsession, the insistence on photo identity cards for each of the 600 million voters came as a bombshell on political parties, particularly, the ruling parties who are prone to rigging, in large scale, with the help and connivance of the government machinery. On grounds of stupendous administrative and financial problems the implementation of photo identity cards was strongly opposed by the ruling parties. Seshan said the administrative and financial problems were for the government to sort out. But, as CEC, he finds that photo identity cards are essential for free and fair elections. To coax the Centre and State governments he announced "no identity card, no election", and declared that without identity cards, there would be no elections after 1995.

All political parties were up in arms against Seshan saying that the business of the GEC is to hold elections, not stop them. They were right, but Seshan had a point too. The ultimatum was meant to intimidate the political parties and the government into taking up the forbidding task of preparing the photo identity cards. No political party really wanted the photo identity cards to be introduced for that would cut into their votes considerably. Every partly practised false voting, each according to its own capacity. They would not give up the privilege simply because Seshan wished it.

So, simultaneously with the preparation of the photo identity cards, they tried to cut down Seshan to size. Tempting offers of alternative jobs were made to him to induce him to resign as GEC. He would not. Threats to remove him from office through parliamentary censure as provided for in the Constitution were held out but Seshan would not give in. Political parties and their leaders let loose volleys of abuses at him to reduce him in public esteem. Jyoti Basu called him made. If Seshan was really made, there would have been no difficult in getting rid of him, for mad men are fit for no posts, still less for the post of CEC. Basu would never have called a judge of the Supreme Court made. That would have exposed him to the charge of contempt of Court. Seshan could have sued Basu for libel, but he refrained from taking any action. He refused to react as long as he had the freedom to pursue his constitutional job of ensuring free and fair polls.

Ultimately, the Narasimha Rao government set up hurriedly three-member Election Commission through promulgation of Ordinances to amend the Constitution and the Representation of Peoples Act so that Seshan may always be under the threat of being overruled. The half finished work of providing photo identity cards to all voters seems to have been abandoned. Even Seshan does not talk of it any more. The GEC will continue to preside over Election Commission's meetings, but last that should create an impression of superiority of the CEC over other two commissioners, it has been provided that in the event of differences of opinion in the Commission, the issue will be decided by voting. This has taken away from the CEC his power of decision making on his own. The CEO is now chief in name only. A constitutional watchdog has been put to sleep by an unholy league of political parties.

Seshan's reforms have clearly put a fright into the nation's politicians and brought the beginnings of orders to a process that had drifted from the hubbub of democracy to ranchos anarchy. Seshan had employed a varied arsenal from the expenditure audit scheme, which regulated campaign spending to the identity card for voter eligibility to prevent widespread impersonation. His true canon has been the moral code of conduct, the gentleman's agreement that supposedly prevails in electoral contests. Seshan sought to give the code the force of law by censuring those who violated it, including cabinet ministers. And without doubt, he has laid the foundations for better politics by making our polls a little less of by prospective MLAs by Election Commission auditors, fear of rigging, booth capturing and electoral roll tampering. The 1996 State elections in Andhra Pradesh and Karnataka witnesses a voter turnout of 65 per cent.

Seshan has become the darling of the Harijans and down-trodden who had not seen inside of a plying booth in the previous elections. He has won for himself a substantial following in the countryside. He had, however, found himself facing an unprecedented attack from Congress(I) and the CPM(M) in 1994. Never before had Parliament resorted to a special session nor the Government sought to amend the Constitution, just to curtail the powers of one person, as they did in June 1994. His outspoken remarks on the judiciary earned him a warning from the Supreme Court.

His scheme to issue identity cards to all voters provoked considerable outrage after the Bombay police questioned the eligibility and the nationality of thousands of Muslim voters. But it prevailed all the same.

Another area which needs clearing up is to prevent criminal history sheeters from entering legislatures. More and more criminal history sheeters are contesting elections and becoming MPs and MLAs. One reason why criminals are joining politics is that there has been close nexus between politicians and criminals. If the trend is not checked Parliament and State Assemblies will be dens of criminals in the next 20 years, if not earlier, and they will rule the country. Despite the issue being discussed in Parliament and completely ignoring their stand on criminalisation of politics, all parties have fielded criminal history sheeters in 1996 Assembly elections.

Legal experts feel that Section 8 of the Representation of Peoples Act 1951 may be amended to debar persons against whom criminal cases are subjudice, from contesting elections. In 1995 a Committee headed by Justice H.R. Khanna and eminent jurists Justice Lentin, N.A. Palkhiwala and persons of eminence like R. Venkataraman, C. Subramanian and S.L. Shakdhar as members, discussed the problem but no solution could be reached so far.

CONCLUSION

Free and fair elections are in exercise central to a democratic system. The subversion of the electoral system began since 1962. It kept on escalating from elections to elections. Mafia gangs and bullets have become an integral part of the battle of the ballot. The lessons learnt from the past elections show that even after massive deployment of security forces, framing of code of conduct for political parties by the Election Commission and special arrangements at an near the potting booths and comprehensive law and procure, no human efforts can ensure free and fair elections unless the political parties shun violent organised gangsters. The largest democracy in the world has come to such a sorry pass that only bullets can ensure that the battle of ballots is not hijacked by the gun runners of the underworld. The proliferation of gangsters in the election process has been the major problem that is subverting free and fair elections. The solution to the problem lies in stricter measures by the Election Commission. The task is difficult but no impossible.

The Statesman editorial came to mind when T.N. Seshan retired recently as Chief Election Commissioner of India. It must be admitted even by the vehement detractors of Seshan that he did succeed in 1996 general elections to curb the role of money and muscle power in hindering free and fair poll. He could not claim complete success in this endeavour but even the limited success that he achieved made him many powerful enemies who tried their utmost to restrain him by means, both lawful and unlawful.

Everyone in the country knew that the ceilings on election expenses were very low and they were not being honoured by any candidate who does not hope to returned unopposed. Seshan persuaded the government to raise the ceilings and then tried to ensure that the ceilings were adhered to. He did not succeed wholly, for the ceilings are still unrealistic and below the level suggested by Seshan and there are other lacunae in the electoral laws permitting candidates to spend much more than the prescribed limits. Yet he succeeded in making the 1996 general elections a comparatively austere how, an exercise shorn of much of the vulgar competition among the candidates to influence the voters in various ways.

The other major electoral reforms that Seshan had set his heart on was to provide every voter in the country with a photo identity card so that no one could vote for another person. All political parties and State governments were up in arms against him for this proposal and invented all manners of excuses to frustrate the move. They said that providing photo identity cards to billions of voters would be administratively and financially unfeasible and would meet with social and religious resistance, especially in the rural areas. Seshan was undeterred. He threatened to stop all elections till the voters have been provided with photo identity cards. "No identity cards, no election" was the slogan he raised. For this he was reprimanded by the Supreme Court which reminded him that the duty of the Chief Election Commissioner was to hold elections and not stop it. Seshan could have restored that his duty was to hold free and fair elections and he had threatened to postpone elections only to ensure that they were free and fair. Seshan did not persist in his effort. He gave up.

The political parties - all of them, with their nannies unclean, did not forget and forgive the endeavours of Seshan to cleanse the election process. Free and fair elections did not suit any political party. They all combined to promulgate an ordinance to make the Chief Election Commissioner one of the three equals to introduce a set up in which the chief was not the chief. No ordinance was necessary to make the one-man Election Commission, a multi-member commission. The Constitution provides for that. The real purpose of the Ordinance was to make the two newly-appointed members of the Commission equals of Seshan and to rob him of his vetoing right. Seshan went to the Supreme Court for redress which he did not get. The validity of the ordinance was upheld by the Supreme Court.

The Ordinance has altered the structure of the Election Commission and, may be, made free and fair elections more difficult. Seshan's humiliation was a disgrace to the democratise pretensions of the country and a tribute to his commitment to the responsibility that the Constitution had conferred upon him.

Seshan has shown everyone that free and fair elections can be held. He has paved the way for a cleanser election process. It is now up to the electorate to ensure that things stay this way. A sad man, certainly not a mad man, as Jyoti Basu called him, or a bad man, goes unhonoured and unsung.

7

SCAMOPAEDIA INDIA

Since independence, have scams and scandals have occurred without pause. Some of them have been highlighted and many suppressed. Business India in its August 11-24, 1997 issue has given a Scämopaedia[1] .

CORRUPTION was made a big election issue by politicians, during 1996 General Elections. To use mix metaphors the pots called the kettles black even as no cupboards were short of skeletons. Unlike the developed world, until quite recently corruption operated mostly at relatively low levels in India. With economic progress, corruption too made rapid strides to catch up with the standards of the West. Since power and money are convertible, almost like the famous mass-energy equation of Einstein, it was only natural that politicians led the bandwagon. A surprising spirit of comradeship was displayed by politicians of all colours to cover each other's tracks. As the tracks multiplied, so did the spirit of camaraderie. It came to be widely believed that no one of any importance would ever get punished for economic offences.[2]

CORRUPTION : Corruption is the single most important factor undermining the efficiency of any enterprise.

Corruption has become epidemic and seeped into every facet of government activity. This makes it imperative for us to defeat the diabolical and dubious design of the government by our prompt and principled reaction and response. If equality of opportunity and equal

---

1 "50 years of Scams and Scandals"
BUSINESS INDIA, August 11-24, 1997.

2 Sharat Kumar : "Pains of Growth", Mainstream, June 1, 1996.

access to material resources of the country have any meaning combating and containing corruption must become the fighting faith in the democratic struggle of promoting republicanism and constitutionalism so that the anomie pursuit of power and politics can be effectively rebuffed.[3]

In the next century skills in interfacing with computers and networks would be an elementary requirement. This will be as important as learning the three Rs. Everyone will have access to the same information. Analytical skills an intellect will lead to superior performance of the individuals. We are moving to a knowledge - based economy. Even in social sectors, the time for citizens initiatives has arrived. Non-governmental organisations have begun to play a dynamic role. These organisations are close to the people and can channels their constructive impulses for a noble cause. In efficient delivery of education, health care, cleanliness, water supply, beautification of environment and relief to the needy, voluntary group of citizens can be many times more effective as compared to bureaucracy. An enlightened and active citizenry are back bones of a healthy society.[4]

Every time we brought goods abroad it was under the shadow of corruption-submarines, jeeps, big guns, ammunition, pistols, sugar, medicines, airbuses, locomotives and now urea. These were cases where a fuss was made in Parliament. Many others may have passed by unnoticed. Hawala recently was covered up for years, buffaloes shone much in Bihar, Jayalalitha-she certainly needs a refill of honesty - and banks seem to be made for looting. What shameful record : This cold decay will go on forever unless we make up our minds to stop it. It is to our shame and disgrace that the deals have steadily become more murky, with more losses, more brazen support from the Ministers, even the Prime Minister, and the whole system has got so subverted that we have come to accept

---

3 Vijay Kumar : "Rebuff Attempts to subvert the democratic Struggle against Corruption". Mainstream, October 19, 1996, p34

4 Mukesh Abani : "Challenges in the New Millennium, The Mainstream, November 16, 1996, p 34.

graft as the attractive mistress of democracy[5]. We must find ways to save the state, this nation of the poor, from being defrauded by its trusted men. Politicians may not want to stop it. Bureaucrats and police may not want to hurt their masters, or lose their cuts by protesting. All our methods of preventing and spotting corruption have become useless. We just thrive on dishonesty and corruption.

A lament increasingly heard throughout the country is the poverty of the national leadership. The jockeying for power, pelf and self, is what passes for democracy in India. We have new governments, new Prime Ministers, the promise of a new broom to clean up the acres of mire in which our institutions have systematically been dragged down over the past five decades. Leadership is busy in advancing its own petty vested interests which have no relationship with the good of the nation or country's economy.[6]

The most disastrous effect of all the corruption has been on the education of children who are the guardians of tomorrow. Men of character and outstanding ability have now vanished or subdued into doing nothing. Horse trading and corruption in various forms have sapped the morale of honest, idealistic secular leaders who see little point in asserting their authority against the forces which are arrayed against them.

Education is a social process. It is growth. It does not simply prepare one for life, but it is life itself. The Gandhi, education is to draw out the best in a child-in body, mind and spirit. According to Herbert Spencer, "Education is training for completeness of life". With the advent of East India Company in the country, the concept of education underwent a drastic change. The pattern of education was however, directed to serve the cause of British rule. The purpose and object of education to Lord Maculay was to produce educated young men knowing English who could serve as clerks in the service of the Company. During their rule the British administration could not resolve

---

5 K. F. Rustamji.

6 S. K. Ghost, Indian Democracy Derailed : Politics & Politicians, (1997) p 113.

the spread, and the medium. Macaulay's hard line concerning the triple question of content, spread and medium echoed in the education programme of British throughout their stay in the sub-continent. Maculay recommended a policy of imparting Western knowledge through Western tongue and then only to the minority : "We must at present do best to form a class who may be interpreters between us and the millions whom we govern - a class of persons Indian in blood and colour, but English in tastes, in opinions, in morals and in intellect. To that class, we may leave it to refine the vernacular dialects of the country, to enrich those dialects with terms of science borrowed from the western nomenclature, and render them by degrees fit vehicles for conveying knowledge to the great mass of population. " Although education is the most potent means for social regeneration and true development, the poor rule India have been largely deprived of it. That is why even after 50 years of Independence, almost half the population continues to be illiterate and poor. The largest chunk of population lives in village, but thrusts of our schemes, plan after plan, is on the urban people. In this dismal scenario, education of the poor is ignored.

Many endeavours have been made in India to reform and reconstruct the system of education. Several Communities and panels were formed from time to time for this purposes. To mention a few for them : the University Education Commission (1948 - 49) under Dr. S. Radhakrishnan; the Secondary Education Commission (1952) under Dr. Laxmanswamy Mudaliar; the Education Commission (1964-66) under the Leadership of Dr. D. S. Kothari; a committee of members of Parliament Constituted in 1967 to prepare the draft of national policy on education (1968). Draft National Policy on Education (1978), National Policy on Education (1986), its Review (1990-91) by the Acharya Ramamurti Committee; and the subsequent Review Committee Report (1992) by the Janardhan Reddy Panel.[7] All this clearly indicates a deep rooted national awareness, a welcome keenness to evolve a viable system of education. Education is the most potent instrument for social regeneration and true development, the poor in rural India Have

7 Almala, Education For the Poor (1997) p 106.

largely remained deprived of it. The biggest chunk of population lives in villages, but thrusts of schemes, plan after plan, in on the urban regions.

The analyses of various issues on education indicate clearly what the system and its managers at present lack, and strongly favour pragmatic approaches and alternatives to arrange for and upgrade education of the many. All this underlines the need of realistic, down to earth, new and at times unconventional strategies to impart good education, the most potent weapon of human resource development. This is urgently required at the juncture in the history of the country if education is to be geared towards all round progress, democratic patterns, communal harmony, mutual understanding, and preservation of human rights. Eradication of corruption.

CORRUPTION, CRIMINALISATION OF POLITICS

Sir Douglas Young,[4] Chief Justice Punjab at the High Court of Judicature at Lahore, explained the wide-spread corruption at the village level and emphasised. The accumulated wisdom of the centuries with regard to children is summed up by this ancient saying. "Bring up a child in the way should go and in his old age he will not depart from it". A more modern one is : "Give me a child till he is seven and you can do what you like with him for the rest of his life". These three sentences emphasise the necessity of developing the character of children at the earliest possible period of their lives. The influences surrounding an Indian child are bound to have a decisive effect both on him and India. A large proportion of the children in India live under such conditions that it is almost impossible to expect that many should become useful citizens. They are brought up, for instance, to look upon corruption as normal and even proper. An intelligent child, if he is born in a village will see that his father, if he wishes to have a peaceful life, has to bribe in one way or another

---

4 Sir, Douglas Young for Necessary Action, pp 28-30, Indian Cases, Ltd. Publishers.

every petty official in the village. He will be told that it has existed for centuries and that no one will assist him to resist extortion. He will, to a large extent, be uneducated. He will not be taught anything which makes for character. He will see that it he wished to be moderately comfortable in life he must try to be a petty official himself. He will try to become a patwari a canal patwari for preference a policeman, ahlmad, process-server of bailiff in the Judicial department, a clerk in the Railway, or any one of the other petty officials. If he is fortunate enough to obtain one of these position he will be able to oppress the great body of peasants from whom he has sprung and he will then be able to act on the principle pungently expressed in a Punjabi proverb: "Honey cannot be poured from one pot into another without some of it sticking". If the boy is of a higher class, or manages to be educated, he will have many greater opportunities. He may become a Municipal Councillor or a Director of a public company. Many of these personages have a very high sense of their duty to themselves and their relations and a very elementary idea of their duty to their constituents. Infect, whatever position of life he may be in, he will find that to be corrupt or to corrupt is considered at the worst but an amiable weakness. If a corrupt official is discovered he is generally safe as his dismissal becomes a communal matter. Our boy will find that there is a lamentable lack of public opinion of this matter, that his parents, however, eminent, wealthy and distinguished they may be , will suffer in silence. He will be told as, I have been told, that he has only to live long enough in this country to find out that it is better and easier to acquiesce in what after all has been the experience of India and Indians for centuries. If he is well read of travelled, he will know that corruption exists in Great Britain is that in that country there is a strong and healthy public opinion which results in the elimination of the corrupt.

If the present position is maintained, India, in existing circumstances, will march blindly to destruction. If it is altered, no country has a brighter future. There are only two alternatives. There can be no

[1] Sir, Douglas Young for Necessary Action, pp 28-30, Indian Cases, Ltd. Publishers.

doubt as to the choice.[2] The assertion then made about the dismal position in India, was a case for consideration according to the prevalent conditions. There seems an exaggeration in saying that corruption was rampant everywhere during those days but it has not been remedied in type, quantum and form. Now this practice is not considered as draw back of selected few but a quality of character of those who have the desire to earn more through fair and foul means. Scams are now an ordinary news to hear very often. We however, are aware that man is not corrupt, by nature and there are people in every society who can hardly be corrupted. They are the real gems of mankind and there can be no disregard to their services towards the society to which they belong. Yet, when we talk of corruption, we have those in mind who accept gratification and aware wealth by unfair means and out of the way obligations to undesirable elements who pay them off in lieu of such favours in cash and kind.

Rampant corruption has seeped at every step of the government structure, and what is more depressing is that the woes of the common man to get ordinary and routine things done in normal ways, and without loss of much time, have remained unremedied, and his sufferings will go on unabated. The vagaries of officialdom at the lower of "grassroots" levels, and public life is cleansed of the huge accumulated and mounting silt and slush. Those guilty of corrupt practices should not merely be punished to undergo imprisonment or pay fine or both but must also be made to forfeit the ill-gotten wealth that they have grabbed.[3] It may interest many to know that as early as September 1934, Mahatma Gandhi, in his letter to Sardar Vallabhbhai Patel in which he conveyed his decision "to sever all official and physical connections with the congress, including the original membership", gave the reason that it was the menace of corruption "that has crept into the organisation" which has impelled him to do so.[4] Perhaps at that time the stream of corruption was quite narrow and small, but even that disturbed the Mahatma'

---

2 Ibid., pp. 34-35.

3 D. P. Verma, "The Roots of Corruption", The Tribune, March 12, 1996, p. 8.

4 D. G. Tendulkar, Mahatma, Vol. III, p. 317.

unfaltering conscience, and he decided to sever his formal links with the organisation "which I have worshipped since my youth". Now, of course, that "stream" has assumed threatening width and proportions and has almost flooded every nook and corner of the country, doing incalculable harm and destruction.

Prof. Z.A. Nizami,[5] of Jamia Millia Islamia University eloquently sums up the turmoil our country is going through at the moment when he says. "There is no single party in country which is trustworthy. All the old values are sacrificed once they come to power". National leaders from almost all major political parties are allegedly involved in the scam in one way or the other. Rampant corruption has almost become synonymous with our political system and threatens to erode the very fabric of society.

Dalip MacCune,[6] asserts : Hawala may prove to be a blessing in disguise for India' body politic. On one hand it has been responsible for denting the image of politicians wearing the garb of honesty, on the other it has turned out to be a crucible in churning out the nectar of new hope to the people of India. The episode is fraught with potential of filtering out corrupt politicians and sifting upright ones. Many a time, the electorate has acted intelligently to punish those who have attempted to rip apart the socio-political fabric of the country. But, the same electorate accepted back the leader with open arms when they though him/her worthy.

No region of the world can claim any form of moral superiority when it comes to corruption. Indonesia, China, Thailand, India, The Philipines and Pakistan were among the last ten which also included Mexico, Italy, Italy, Brazil and Venezuela. Whereas New Zealand, Denmark and Singapore in that order, are the three least corrupt

---

5 Prof. Z. A. Nizami, "All About Hawala", Rashtriya Sahara, March 1996, P. 4.

6 Dalip Mac Cune, "Rao will be the PM Again", Rashtriya Sahara, March 1996, pp. 17 - 23.

places in the world to do business.[7]

No Country is free from the vice of corruption. Corruption travels from one end of a country to another in the company of those who know how to buy what they want with the power of money, whether it is a business deal or a lucrative job they wish to grab. It spirals downward. The principal agents of proliferation of corruption are politicians who need vast sums of money to fight elections, dictators who regard the public exchequer as a storehouse of their private assets, bureaucrats who wield limitless power over ordinary citizens because the latter's needs are their permanent hostages and the business community that is every busy in the odious exercise of counting and accumulating currency notes together with allies and co-shares of the national loot. The eclipse of moral values in the age of materialism saying goodbye to time-honoured concepts of simple living and high thinking, and the emergence of a consumer society attracted by the gadgetry of technological breakthrough of modern science have created a fertile soil in the minds of people for corruption to take firm roots, breed and thrive. Corruption scandals are cleverly capped and allowed to be erased from public memory with the passage of time. The face of corruption is scientifically marked with the damage-control material of lies and unsound reasoning. If corruption is to be eradicated or atleast reasonably controlled the man at the top must change. The breeding ground of corruption in the society of upper class. From them it seeps into lower circles of ordinary citizen like rainwater from the sky above entering into subterranean layers of the earth through pores in its surface.

Way back in 2000 B. C. Kautilya meticulously described 40 different kinds of corruption in his Arthashastra. He remarked : "Just as it is impossible not to taste honey or poison when it is at the tip of the tongue, so it is impossible for a government servant not to eat up a bit of revenue. And just as it can not be found out whether a fish swimming through water drinks or not so also govt. servants can

[7] Corruption Index (1995) Published by Berlin Based Transparency International and the University of Goettingen.

not be found out while taking many for themselves. Thus the problem is of a serious nature. What is needed is a sustained, methodical weeding-out of [5] corrupt officials, reforming the administration so as not to generate corruption and carrying out economic policies that eventually ensure its people a reasonable standard of living. Corruption threatens to infest society so long in the foreseeable future as to necessitate repeated talking and writing to keep the future governments awake and alive to the paramount need to eradicate it. Mr. Thankur Sen Negi, Former Speaker, Himachal Vidhan Sabha on the issue of Corruption elaborates. In the words of T. S. Negi, corruption is "Moral deterioration, especially wide spread. Use of corrupt practices especially bribery or fraud". (concise Oxford Dictionary 1994).

He adds further. "This write up adheres to the above definition, especially the "WIDE-SPREAD" aspect.

If the question were to be begged then just two short sentences would do. "The very kiln is stinking. The brick-builder himself is gone morbid and morbid." The kiln" is the society as a whole. The brick builder is the teacher at the bottom, at the root, and the ruler at the top, the flower-cum-seed pod.

What follows now is but to substantiate, for double conviction, the obvious begged at the very outset. "SO MEIN ASSI BEIMAN, PHIR BHI BHARAT DESH MAHAN" (In every hundred, eighty corrupt in India. Nevertheless a country the great is India)" is no poetic flight of fancy, nor philosophic premise, but the common man's common-sense experience boiling over into words of desperation. The first time I read this tell-tale quip was as one of those crisp saying that vie for space with number-plates and like at the back of the public carriers like trucks. One day, when terrorism was at the Worst in the Punjab, the back of a truck warned " BURI NAZAR WALE TUJHE ANTAKWADI TAKRE" (O, you with the evil eye, may terrorist set upon thy). That, I felt, was more pithy than a whole column condemning terrorism, like the former quip becoming

University of Goettingen.

corruption. The eloquent back of a truck is Vox populi. After all it took a Prime Minister of this land, where the Ganges flows, to plead, "Corruption is a global phenomenon". The tragedy is not that she lied. No, she did not lie. It is just that she was defensive, what she uttered was an argument of the lawyer defending a criminal, the largest democracy of the world. As for fact, the malaise has grown today so virulent, world-wide, that any pioneering specimen of human society, if transplanted on any other planet, might carry the virus there too, scandals threaten to grow stale as news. There is that adage attributed to a newspaper baron of England, "Dog bit man is no news, man bit dog is". Corruption may, at this rate, cease altogether to be news, yielding place, as "NEWS" to the stupidity of honesty. Actually newspapers have already started quoting stray instances of honesty as box items of news. Heads of even Prime Ministers and President have been rolling more and more under the guillotine of corruption. America has enriched the English vocabulary by contributing "WATERGATE" and "WHITE WATER (GATE)". We have already subscribed "AYA RAM AND GAY RAM", and are well on the way to adding "HAWALA". Halve (The Concise Oxford Dictionary, defines it as "A seat confection of sesame flour and honey") is already there at the head of the reception Committee of Hindustani words assimilated into English.

"Sir, if you don't mind my plain speaking, the rot in a stale fish starts, I have heard, at the head and leakage, as is well known, begins from the higher stories and travels down to the lower ones and not vice versa. If the Minister is himself honest, then integrity and, if he is dishonest, corruption seeps and percolates all the way down to a peon. "I was deposing before a team of the Administrative Reforms Commission visiting Shimla. As I remember it was headed by Mr. Hanumanthia. He did jot down something on a paper before him. I do no know exactly, what in the wings was a bunch of Government of India officials. I had been introduced as a former Chief Secretary freshly turned a politician after recently retiring from Government services as Chief Secretary to H. P. Government.

That bunch of official and myself exchanged not just glances but smiles also. To be sure, corruption obtained even under the British Government and much more in the princely state. As a collegiate at Lyallpur (now Faisalabad in Pakistan), I heard of Reader of Third Class magistrate, who used to accept bribes from clients as parties to cases, under the very nose of boss presiding over the court. Of course, the share holding superior looked the other way, but the facade was so thin that once the Reader returned a coin then and there as it was false. Nevertheless, there always hung over the heads of corrupt underlings the Damocles sword of the possibility of detection and punishment at least from the levels of the Deputy Commissioners, if not the lower echelons.

More than once, when cornered by concrete instances of corruption, Congress (I) friends have retorted to me. "O. K. O. K. Negi, granted for argument that Congress (I) is corruption ridden so much as you think. But, the Congress waited at least for twenty years. What about your B. J. P. ? Haven't your Partymen been found corrupt during the very first spell of power ?"

I have vivid recollection of the suddenly and very perceptibly changed atmosphere with the very advent of the "INTERIM" National Government of Pandit Jawaharlal Nehru. The word went round and the general feeling abroad that those with the spiritual purity, born of sacrifices and sufferings for the freedom of the mother land, had now taken the helm in hand and sin will no longer flourish. From the class IV employees to the class I category there was a noticeable change. This did not wholly last for twenty years but it is indeed a fact that the first three Congress governments or so were, on the whole, inspiring examples of Ministers with lofty standards of integrity, devotion to duty and selfless public service. I remember having read a news item in the Press that some persons approached Mahatma to intervene and prevent some of the ministers from killing themselves by overwork and Mahatma pleaded helplessness. The Proverbial corrupting influence of power, for much too long of an unchallenged Congress rule, set in, and slowly, silently but steadily the process advanced and then came the period of that Prime Minister, when along with certain historical achievements to be proud of, corruption of almost all hues reached levels of national grief. And, there was no "LOOKING BACK". The outcome is INDIA TODAY - not the magazine but the Society.

Corruption has poisoned the very source of the spring of democracy, the voter whose overwhelming tendency to fall for the lure of lucre and a sundry assortment of promised favours generated and fanned by unscrupulous "Leader" has gained run away proportions and is the taproots of mounting electoral expenses.

The teacher, the other brick builder, in fact theoretically the senior one of the pair, no longer, with rare exception, deserves the honorific "GURU". Campus politics has come to stay as an almost incurable headache. These "Educationists" are supposed not only to inculcate values and build character but also to create values. And in human history, wars have been waged and won for some values and revolutions have shaken and re-shaped whole societies and entire systems. What about today's teachers? They mostly speaking, though still with some shining exceptions, know only one value, the value of money.

Religion? Show me a single religion worth that sacred name that preaches or teaches or tolerates corruption even on paper or by word of month. The test is living up to the lofty spiritual heights enjoined by every religion. No use quoting saints or scripture. Modern Gurus, so called in the religious text, whether Jet Gurus or the pedestrians, and their Ashrams, again I emphasise with high relief of exceptions, figure in the papers, besides what passes unpublicised or hushed up or not even discovered or disclosed, for corruption not only financial but also sexual.

One day in early 1993, I was one of a bunch of 5 or so sitting at the feet of Satya Sahibaba at Prashanti Niliyan. This topic came up and hooted up. He concluded by flourish of his hand, "Just a passing phase". The late Mr. Swami Yukteshwar Giri of sacred memory worked out a far shorter view of the time cycle of Satyug, Treta, Dwapar and Kali. According to that time scale, the next century should mark an improvement. Anyway the bottom is that starting point back of every ascent. Let us cross our fingers and hope for the best.

Meanwhile, of course, we cannot just sit back at that.

Unless an organism is dead and gone, there lingers, even at the height of a disease, the inborn element of self cure, recuperation and rejuvenation. Human society, for all this "PASSING PHASE" of degradation, is never going to be dead and gone before the Atlantic Parlay, Absolute Dissolution of creation. And the Indian Society has behind it repeated ages of revived spiritualism and civilisation.

There has already come into being some kind of a body of intellectuals and reformers in the country. That organisation, especially its Chairman and General-Secretary, may integrate the outfit into a regular think tank of the nation comprising the still living morally inspired and imbued individuals and institutions of all walks of life, motivated not by any scheming mentally with ulterior ends but solely by a selfless mission of guiding and propelling the society on wholesome lines. The youth of the generation, though not a patch on the generation of the fight for freedom and alarmingly oriented towards valueless politics in the making, is still not without its natural talent of dynamic and instinctive urges and capabilities of healthy reaction. But, it has to be guided by seasoned leadership to lasting fruition. Witness the youthful stir in Gujarat - Rajasthan, that provided such a push to Lok Nayak Jai Prakash Narayan' move for "TOTAL REVOLUTION". The youth of those days had coined "TOTREV" as their own "Short for Total Revolution. The A.G.P. was born as a Youth Movement. Many a historic revolution of the world would be traceable to the hot blooded "barricades", processions, gatherings, orations, other activities, sufferings and sacrifices of the youth. Unfortunately for human nature, its innate proneness to err and to deteriorate sooner or later asserts itself. The fact to be put together is to ward this off as long and as much as possible.

Scandals have been mushrooming up, the fresh ones tending to rise higher and higher than the beach mark. Each scandal has its peculiarities apart from the common curse of Satan.

Taking up the latest (still) Hawala earthquake, there are the following salient of the sordid spectacle :-

1. Hawala Proper : The characteristic feature is the violation of F.E.R.A. and other laws governing foreign exchange. The income, private or public, for own pocket or party funds, originated on foreign soil. If it is brought to Indian soil for party or other public purpose of recognised social good, the corruption would consist only in transgression of laws. If the lining is to be of a private pocket, the crime is double and has the magnitude of sin.

2. Hawala, So Called : Since the Jain Brothers have got integrally, so to say, bound with Hawala proper as the dominating transaction, a bribe or a genuine donation even out of local Indian income of the Jains has come to be wrongly called Hawala. Here too, a genuine donation to a political party would be a measure of accepted practice. The very system is to blame, if blame does come to be apportioned. The donation becomes a bribe because it is an investment for favour and is also within the stride of the system, call it corruption or whatever you like. Again, the so called donation meant AB in to, ultimately usurped, as personal gain would compound the clandestine transaction into a crime for mundane terminology and a sin for religious vocabulary.

The long and short, the sum total and the moral of the whole tale is that the conscience of this great land of ours has to be awakened into a blaze of solid action far more than fireworks of the tongue and the pen.

The pensioners and other (Van Prasthas) of the Ashram system too have a role to play. I am a pensioner.

Rohit Kansal,[8] in a published article "Corruption the enemy within" writes : A society gets the leaders it deserves, in fact

---

[8] Rohit Kansal, "Corruption: The Enemy within", The Indian Express May 1996, p.8.

> the leadership of a country like ours represents the middle class morality of our nation - a value system where everything is fair as long as it's in cash. Corruption, let there be no mistake, is a matter of opportunity. The businessman who evades income tax is as corrupt as the politician who accepts bribes; each falls prey where he finds an opportunity. The solution to such a state is not in casting righteous stones at the political establishment; the enemy is within. Unless we have a shared value system that despises dishonesty., that pays as much attention to the means as to the ends, we as a nation shall continue to slide into despair and oblivion. The only way to build that value system is mass action at our agenda of the nation. Let us not look up to any dictator to clean our Augean stables. Let us purge our own lives of the hundreds of corrupt acts that we commit, sometimes without so much as a thought. The right persons to begin this change are we - the middle classes. The right place to begin is our own backyard. Let us first gain that moral authority to ask for change. For a beginning let us start paying our taxes. Of Indian business men who fudge their accounts to evade taxes, of Indian lawyers who fight cases of blatant corruption for penury gains, of Indian teachers who miss their teaching to charge for private tuition, of Indian managers who connive with their Indian or foreign owners to corrupt those in positions of authority .... The list could go on and on. The roots of our country's malaise lie neither in the deviousness of our political class, nor in their seemingly unsuitable desire for money. The answer lies in a much more fundamental human truth. Human beings everywhere behave in manner that depends besides their upbringing and their genetics on the shared value systems of a society.

Crooks and criminals will never be brought to book in our life-time. In the last decade far too many crimes have gone unpunished and the common man in the street can not be blamed that this is a veritable Kalyug where adharma reign supreme. One is sick and tired of reading about scams and Hawala rackets and how much ministers and politicians have taken as bribes on the pretext of collecting funds to fight elections, how many civil servants have done the same to sanction funds for inflated deals with foreign firms and how many honest men (unfortunately very few) who stood against the corrupt and the powerful paid the price by losing their jobs and even their lives. It wasn't always so. Pandit Nehru never forgave the corrupt. Amongst the many he fired were close colleagues like hare Krishna Mehtab, K. D. Malaviya, T. T. Krishnamachari and Pratap Singh Kairon. The slide to iniquity began with Indira Gandhi. She shielded corrupt ministers and civil servants and knocked down the three pillars of democracy - the legislature, the judiciary and bureaucracy. We have been downhill ever since. Now the Jain Hawala scandal. The Disturbing feature of this case is that they had been doing so for many years with absolute impunity. Even the first expose of their criminal activities by Sanjay Kapoor of Blitz in August 1991 hardly attracted any attention. Blitz was known to make mountains out of mole hills.

The murder Mafioso was also reported but the perpetrators of the crime remain untracked. The first one gets aware of the magnitude of the Jain hawala racket was when one saw Vineet Narain's Kal Chakra on T. V. with Ram Jethmalani showing a Photostat copy of pages of Jain's diaries listing names of 115 recipients of slush funds. On this list were may one could never believe could be bought with many. This was confirmed by a story carried by Jansatta. Immediate reaction was t say "It is not true, it can not be true. It turned out to be true. One can read all about it in Bad Money, Bad politics, the Untold Hawala story by Sanjay Kapoor. It is an absorbing story of how the Jain family starting as small-time contractors in Bhilai were able to amass thousands if cores by getting huge contracts for foreign firms with commissions for themselves, how they were able to bride ex-Presidents, Prime Ministers, Cabinet Ministers, top civil servants to do their bidding. They also ran a fancy house near Mehrauli where they entertained lavishly providing their guests with premium brand Scotch whisky, French wines, bimbos, call-girls and swinging socialites. Knowing the fate of previous scams, one is inclined to think this will also fade out of public memory. As is men accused of accepting bribes are fighting elections and promising voters that they will root our corruption from the country. "In the absence of Gandhi to guide us out of this moral labyrinth we can draw lessons from his teachings. For Gandhi the means for attaining a goal was as important as the ends. "We may as well remind Sri Krishna to fulfil his undertaking to return as an Avatar to redeem the world of wickedness.[9] Khushwant Singh[10] suggest, "perhaps the best we can do is t o read the Gita and forget Hawala."

The difference between the levels of corruption in developed countries and developing societies is that in the developed countries an average citizen can afford to live a life of relative anonymity but with dignity without bothering over much about corruption in high places. In India, it is the grassroots level corruption which needs to be fought by involving the common citizen in a relentless campaign against corruption at the macro-level. In this respect an organisation in Rajasthan called Mazdoor Kishan Shakti Sangathana has shown the way by organising "Jan sunwais" (people's hearings) for fighting corruption at the village and tehsil level. Chief Minister Bhairon Singh Shekhawat has promised freedom of information to the people of Rajasthan. In simple terms, anyone would be entitled to procure a copy of any official documents by paying the prescribed fee. If the Rajasthan experiment is allowed to take roots, then in the long run it may be possible to put the beaks on even major scams."[11] To bank on the promises of political parties alone as far as fighting corruption is allow the cancer to grow.

Piara Singh Ghumman,[12] President Forum of India Nationals Abroad Virginia (USA) in a write up said : Matter of fact, corruption is a very essential phase of economic growth under a democratic system. It has been the way with all democracies. In western democracies they say that if your want to destroy a business, entrust it to the government. Unless there are reforms on the pattern of the USA, Germany etc., to fund the election process partly with the state funds, this evil is likely to continue, no matter which party is at the helm of affairs. And even then it can only be reduced , not completely eradicated. But there are definitely ways and means to get some

---

9 "The Hawala Story",The Tribune, May ,8 1996.

10 Ibid.

11 Combating Corruption, The Tribune, May 8,1996.

12 Piara Singh Ghumman, Privatisation Can Cut Corruption", The Tribune, may 15, 1996,p1 13.

relief from this curse. One of the most effective may is to privatise most of the business and industry operations that the government has taken over. There is another very popular saying. "Government is the best that governs the least". Government is there to make laws and implement them; to make rules and regulations and to enforce them; not to indulge in trade and industry. If someone does adulteration or tries to cheat, he or she should be promptly brought to book. All the laws to deal with the crimes of bribery etc., are there in the Indian Penal Code. We have only to enforce them. And if the police or any other agency is unwilling or incompetent to investigate the crime and to bring the culprit to book; those police officers should be promptly punished or removed from their jobs. There should be a police to police the police like the CBI and its performance should be closely watched by Parliament. Privatisation of business and industries will not cut into corruption and deposit alone; it will also reduce the burden of bureaucracy and top heavy administration an thereby provide lots of savings in the government budget and consequently big relief to the tax payers. It will increase productivity and raise the standard of living of the people.

Satya Pal Dang, a renowned Communist leader, in a lead article "The taste of Fighting Corruption" writes : those who want to find solutions with in the present system seem to be on the right track. Radical electoral reforms no doubt will help and these must be pressed for. At the same time it must be realised that more State funding of elections fully or in part will not do away with money power and muscle power. State funding whatever its extent and form can help not-so-well-off candidates to fight elections on a less unequal footing. As regards those who use money power to win elections, to the extent their election expenses are met by the state, they will have more money their disposal to buy votes and also those who are supposed to prevent such illegal practices. State funding of elections to be useful must be in kind and certain specific respects. That will do good but will not give blow to corruption. Various other types of radical electoral reforms will not doubt help and are, therefore, urgently called for. But besides these, many other steps are urgently needed.

1 Anti-corruption forums to expose and fight corruption manned by men and women of undoubted integrity and not interested in election;

2 Laws making is obligatory for all ministers, M. P. MLAs and Class-I Officers to lay annual statements of their assets and liabilities on the tables of their respective Houses as also of the assets and liabilities of their family members;

3 Lok Pal manned by the best from the judiciary with powers to entertain complaints from citizens and to award deterrent punishments to those proved corrupt.

4 Laws must be enacted power to probe foreign accounts of Indians.

5 CBI must have unfettered power to probe foreign accounts of Indians.

6 CBI should be independent agency answerable only to the Supreme Court

7 Laws must be enacted making obligatory punishments for those proved guilty whatever the level.

8 Definition of corrupt must cover attempts to hush up corruption and failure to do duty in relation to complaints of corruption.

II People must be mobilised to throw up new leaders of integrity. Upright persons - specially, young persons keen to serve the country and the people, must not shun politics but must join it with a determination to fight a ruthless battle against corruption.

III Black money must be curbed to the maximum possible extent. Without transparent economy , we cannot have a fully transparent political system. There must be agencies which are properly trained to deal with economic offences.

There are no short-cuts to a clean moral public life. An all right is needed.

K. Madhavan in an article writes : The prevention of Corruption Act, 1988 came into force with effect from September 9, 1988, replacing the Prevention of Corruption Act, 1947, Section 2 of the Act defines 12 categories of public servants which include Minister, Judges, Government officials, of public sector undertaking and so on. It appears, as per judicial interpretation that MPs and MLAs are also public servants on accounts of the following provision:"2(Viii) any person who holds an office by virtue of which he is authorised or required to perform any public duty". Any public servant who take any gratification whatever, other than legal remuneration" (popularly referred to as a bribe) for doing, of forbearing to do, any official act is guilty under Section 7 of the Act. Any public servant, who by corrupt or illegal means or abusing his position as a public servant obtains for himself or for any other person any valuable thing or pecuniary advantage, commits an offence under Sections 13(1)(d)(I) and (ii) of the Act. Similarly, any public servant who, while holding office as a L.M. Public servant for any person any valuable thing or pecuniary advantage without any public interest, is guilty under Section 13(1)(d)(iii) of the Act. It is relevant to note that the term "any person" in this sub-section includes the concerned public servant himself. Generally, in prosecution under Section 13(1)(d) of the Act, the act of quid pro quo by the public servant will be part of the charge made by the prosecution with supporting documentary and oral evidence. However, and extremely relevant and interesting provision is Section 20 which lays down a rule of presumption. Under this section if it is proved that any public servant obtained any gratification other than legal remuneration, it shall be presumed that he did so far doing, or for-bearing to do, an official act, namely, to do a favour. In other words, once the payment to and receipt by the public servant of the illegal gratification is proved, in order to make out the offence of bribery, no further proof is generally necessary of any act of quid pro quo b the public servant. However, it is the normal practice of the CBI to collect and adduce evidence of quid pro quo before the Court to make the case stronger. In the event of conviction for the various offences under the Act, imprisonment ranging from six months to seven years is proved for along with fines.

In order to reduce the vicious impact of the black-money on our electoral process, N. S. Gehlot,[14] Assistant Professor, University of Ajmer, suggests that a law to this effect should be made providing that :

(a) All kinds of expenditure incurred by the political parties, friends and well-wishers in the furtherance of the prospects of the prospects of party or a candidate in a constituent should be brought within the ceiling of election expenses. Donations received by the parities from the private companies should be overtly made, accounting and auditing being obligatory on them. There must be a ban on unauthorised expenditures by any club association or company, etc. with penalty for contravention. They should be made to submit audited accounts regularly to the Govt. and the Election Commission.

(b) Each political party should be required to maintain detailed accounts of their books, in which each item of receipt of money obtained by way of subscription, donation, subsidy, etc. and each item of expenditure should be recorded and the accounts be subject to periodic audit. The Election Commission should be empowered to examine these election returns on merit to satisfy itself that they are accurate and correct in all respects.

(c) The entire election expenditures be met by the Government. The Centre and the States should bear this expenditure on the Parliamentary and Assemble elections respectively.

(d) As far as practicable, the holding of the elections to the Lok Sabha and Legislative Assemblies should be

---

14 N.S. Gehlot,"Election and Electoral Administration of India(1992),pp 329-30.

simultaneous. This would enable the parties and the candidates to save a huge expenditure incurred in the elections as well as the huge administrative cost which can be profitably diverted towards the development activities.

(e) Making of false returns of election expenses and failure to lodge accounts of election expenses should also entail qualification at least for five years as against 3 years at present.

(f) The use of electronic voting machines should be introduced in our electoral system, because the device has successfully worked in the elections held in Kerala and Delhi, and it would considerably cut down the election expenses. Therefore, and adequate provision in the budget be made for the purchases of these machines with a view of covering up the entire country within a short period.

Chief Election Commissioner T. N. Seshan,[15] has said the main problems plaguing election in India were M's money power, muscle power and minister power, Indian elections still contained" an unacceptably large amount of money in sense of cash, criminality and corruption". There were far too many wrong-doers who were getting into legislatures and were people who "ought to be jail are not in jail but elsewhere". While there was corruption in every part of the world" Indian corruption owes a great deal to political corruption related to elections".

It is very well known that the big industrial and business houses donate generously to all the major political parties and individual candidates belonging to the various parties. Even before the elections are over, a major portion of the funds is siphoned off to the pockets of the important members of political parties and individual candidates, bureaucrats working in important positions in the economic Ministries also receive ideally from those seeking their favour. A corrupt Minister will find it difficult to catch a corrupt

---

15 "Three M8s Plaguing Elections: Seshan", The Indian Express, April 22, 1996, p.9.

bureaucrat. A Corrupt bureaucrat can not have the guts to accuse his corrupt subordinates. The vicious circle goes on an results in all round corruption. Reverting to the judicial system, it is not enough if the judge selected are just brilliant but they should be men of personal integrity who must maintain utmost honesty in private and public life as only then they can have public. Bar concern over graft in judiciary, is too general when the all India bar Association[16] expressed its concern over growing corruption in the judiciary and suggested that the institutional mechanism should be evolved to look into complaints of corruption against judges of the Supreme Court and High Courts. "The rising corruption in the judiciary and overstepping of the jurisdiction by the Supreme Court in several matters has created serious problems to the litigants which have to be addressed by the legislatures", Mr. Rajiv Khosla, co-ordinator of the association said in a statement. He also suggested that Article 142 of the Constitutions, which gives over riding powers to the apex court to buy pass the procedure in certain circumstances, should be regulated and defined. Similarly, the contempt of court act should also amended by which the truth must be made defence. Only the poor quality of human material has failed the otherwise honest political system. Unless the lawyers and judges are noble, high-minded and compassionate and on judicial appointments political bias, personal likes and dislikes are avoided, the legal system would not be living and vibrant. It is not going to be an easy task to root out corruption in the judiciary, public services and other spheres of governmental activities. The intensity of corruption is so bad that, out of every rupee sanctioned for any welfare programme or developmental activity, hardly 15 paise reach the intended beneficiaries and the rest get absorbed in the pipeline by corrupt elements. Answer to the problem may lie in the teachings of the Gurus. It would be worth while to remember, "Dharam di Kirt" - Honest earning is only hard earned money which is sweet like honey. Wealth collected through corruption and unfair means makes the mind dirty and evil. Those who become dependent upon other people's earnings, usually become their mental slaves. Such economic

---

16 "Bar Concern Over Graft In Judiciary",
The Hindustan Times, April 27, 1996, p.10.

dependence limits their independent thinking and speaking.

Crime arbitrates political differences when organisation of debate and socialisation becomes ineffective. There are two faces of all political organisations - the public and private. The public faces works to enter representative bodies and capture power. This is a very legitimate end. This end is believed by many to be achieved through illegitimate means. This is reflected in the quality of workers, their methods of mobilisation through intimidation, use of arms - legal and illegal - for coercing allegiance, trying to manipulate the course of justice, and thus establish a tainted power base. This is the private face. No wonder splitting of political organisations has been the destiny of this country since we won freedom. Integrative political process as also social and political consolidation has remained a mirage. The claim to leadership in more parties than not rests not on the progressive rise in an organisation with inner-party democracy and settled convictions and commitment but on the capacity of a leader to deliver votes by means fair or foul. Crimes of all description become a welcome qualification become a welcome qualification in the bargain.[17]

Serious consequences follow as fruits of politicisation. The public law enforcing authority is eroded. The respectable citizen goes to a police station under duress. Harassment of citizens has become the hallmark of police administration. Senior officers feel helpless because of the attachments of their subordinates. Investigation discloses clear bias in a large number of cases and is the cause of declining convictions. Time was when Chief Ministers would rarely contact the Superintendent of Police. Now the contact with the Police officers is a regular feature. The Head of the department is legally authorised to undertake transfer and posting of officers at this level but large-scale interface is common. This harmed the command structure of the organisation. Political patronage has a price. Crime is beyond control. Complaints are not registered and how figures are displayed. Politically sensitive cases are weakened

---

[17] Kamala Prasad, Interface of Politics & crime, Mainstream, September 13, 1997, p 15.

and the means are many. There is some resistance in the urban areas. Media proximity also helps. But the rural areas hardly have such means at their command. There are people's organisations which take up larger causes. They hardly have political recognition. They are suppressed ruthlessly. Insurrectionary activity is the result. It is a tragic commentary on the working of our democratic institutions that such movements have to face not political dialogue but police and the courts of law. Agarian movements in the Naxal areas are only one such manifestation. The Local administration has made peace with such movements in many areas; the organised political parties have not.

Herein lies a fundamental problem, about the legal remedies to what is an issue for political reform. Rajiv Gandhi was perhaps the only recent administration should be reduced, if not eliminated. This has increased further in the last ten years. The simple measure of reform suggested for Civil Service Boards in the meeting of Chief Ministers of Chief Ministers in May 1997 did not find favour with them! Will more litigation help? After all, the state pays for the forced litigation. There are also withdrawal of criminal cases involving the politically attached. In the reverse opponents are roped in many cases and great ingenuity is shown in applying the various provisions of the laws. Is there a will to surmount this deficiency in the rue of law? The Answer has to be in the negative. Has the administration of justice reduced the scope of misuse of law? The answer again is in the negative. This is really the charge of our legislatures. They have failed.[18]

This is the answer to critics who single out the performance of administration for the " jungle raj". There is a counter-demand presently that the administration needs a new identity. There is a feeling that some change in the mind set of the past will follow only if it is insulated from partisan politics. This will still work within a new basis for politics alone. And this will require a reversal of the trends of the past.

---

[18] IInd, p 16.

Centralised party machines are dependent on centralised mobilisation of funds. The bulk of such funds is either from the immense black money in circulation or from the operation of official discretion in the transaction of work. This has given space for power-brokers within the parties. They wield immense clout with the party leadership. A leadership beholden to such attachments has no escape from supporting criminal activities. Money requirement has kept on increasing for running the party machine, for keeping the supporters' loyalty, for enlisting cheer leaders and' of course for fighting elections. All these factors work together. Targeting election is relevant for the Election Commission. But election is part of a larger political process of the organising parties, their activities, electorate education, and administration protection as a mean of safeguarding the public and democratic process. A corrupt and criminal party machine cannot be excepted to promote a clean electoral process or expected to promise a clean electoral process or candidate choice free from the taint of crime and corruption. The Lok Sabha has done well, therefore to focus on the comprehensive political dimensions of the problem.

Why is Criminalisation of politics so much is focus. Electoral malpractice's have been attacked for some time. It is claimed that some advance has been made in making elections fairer. Bur it is becoming a security operation rather than a purely politics process. It is surprising that those who attack the police for violating people's rights are now claiming greater purity under heavy police surveillance! The great concern now is on the entry of convicted criminals in the law-making institutions. A member of the Commission publicised the fact of 40 Members of Parliament and about 700 of State Legislatures having criminal records. What a criminal record implies has not been clarified. It is not clear if they have convictions and for what crimes. On the other hand, Subhash Kashyap, the former Secretary-General of the Lok Sabha, has stated that of about 169 cases of this nature only three ended in convictions. There are other risks in bestowing power of rejection of nomination papers on imprecise legal grounds to a large band of Returning Officers. They are subject to local and other political influences and the parameter of surveillance must be clear beyond doubt. That does not seem to be the case of present . The Election Commission's commitment to the cause in unquestionable. What is questionable is the efficacy of the legal course without relevant changes in the environment in which the institutions involved work.

The use of criminal elements in elections is well known. They are engaged in campaigning and in managing the voting at the polling booths. They are known from the records of the Police Stations as also reputations in the local areas. One MP told me once how such management was facilitated by the way the scheduling of polls in different constituencies is planned. One-day polls do neutralise such factors. During the 1991 elections in Bihar a large number of criminals, even those on ball, were rounded up and the areas cordoned off for the polling days. But this requires equal treatment for all since there are considerable chances of miscarriage of justice. The administrative agenda has to anticipate the candidate's agenda and act. The candidates are rarely helpful. One advantage in the use of criminals is that they do not demand money. They seek protection on a continuing basis though, to pursue their profession under police protection. This patronage the politician provides. This patronage is needed for manipulation of the charge-sheet, for help in securing bail, for privileges in jail and for freedom from police pursuit for as long as possible.

Why has the incidence of Criminalisation increased? The gains of official positions are many . In the era of monopoly of power by one party the monopoly of fireman was with its supporters. As politics became unstable and struggle for changing the social bases of politics intensified, fragmentation of politics also appeared. The cult of the gun became its accompaniment. It was the application of its principle of balance of terror as the determinant of the electoral outcome. This was behind the growth of illegal and crude arms. A villager once told me confidently that country-made weapons did not require licence! The state power provides the means of getting legal arms now. Socially, a leader with criminal records is accepted as he/she shows capability in delivering the personal favours promised. Excessive electoral promise without later fulfilment have increased the attractions of the feared ones. They may use unfair means but they are effective within their limited areas.

The general impression of some benefiting from more criminals than others is misplaced. During the 1995 Assembly elections the opponents of Laloo Prasad thought so. A compilation by one of them showed that other parties had more candidates with criminal records than the then JD. The gang warfare in UP and the political attachments of parties is no secret. Maharashtra knows the power of the Shiv Sena over the criminal elements and accepts it for protection from the underworld. The clout of Veerapan is coming to the fore gradually. And yet the dacoits of MP could hardly make it to the elected bodies in strength. The picture elsewhere is no different. A wholesale take-over of the political process is hardly a near possibility. It is the change in the character of the emerging leaders and parties that is frightening to the sophisticated accustomed to the old ways of politics. There is a change in the character of politics and the standards of judgement must change. The system has to contend with this change.

Criminalisation, so understood, has to be seen in the total context. Criminalisation of politics has to made unattractive for the parties.[19] The current public outcry may itself make some difference. However, it should not be presented in a way as to mean a censure of the emerging power structure in the country in replacement of the old. That will be counterproductive. What is legally prevented may become a more serious problem politically and socially. As it is there is flight of industry and commerce from State like Bihar, Vulnerable people avoid residence in crime-infested locations. The faith of the common people for their peaceful existence is a precondition for eliminating criminals from politics.

Politics an art of possible - Politician says;

Politics an art of ruling - public feels;

Politics an art of fooling - Poet's experience (K. C. Verma)

Politics an art of healing - Statesman Pre-supposes.

---

[19] Ilud pp 16-17.

It is not that our politicians & political leaders do not have the ambition or the hunger for power. The problem is & they know it that not all of them have that self - belief in their ability to govern. But they are not honest enough to admit that he is not quite competent & being a minister yet. The tragedy is that no Gandhi dominates the Indian political scene.

8

NON-VIOLENCE: A WAY OF LIFE

Non-Violence is the way of life devoid of all extremes of passions like anger, enmity, pleasure and pain. True peace emanates from non-violence. Non-Violence is a rational and mighty force. The practice of non-violence is life - affirming which contribute to the human unity, progress and peace. However today violence, aggression and cruelty have become a way of life, if one were is analyse contemporaneous incidents of rape, arson, bomb explosions and terrorism reported daily in media. What reaches our eyes and ears is far less than what takes place, and goes unreported. And it shows desensitisation of human feeling for whatever reason - profit, greed, hatred, political or racial fanaticism. Undoubtedly, the very air is heavy with this desensitised element.

Recently, Mallia Sarabhai's activity theatre staged a performance, "V for...."showing the surfeit of violence that has desensitised people to sights and incidents they should be appalled at but are not. The performance was not meant to project any political ideology. It was staged with express aim of provoking the audience out of its flaccid complacency. In an interview Sarabhai maintained that "violence in us all" and it is not only the "hooligans" but even we, "the so-called educated, cultured people" who are guilty of violence. Usha Bande,, in an article. "Can violence be way of life?" writes: The quantum of aggression has brought about a sense of insecurity in the ordinary citizen's life. This is particularly alarming for a country given to the ideal of non-violence to seek solutions to problems through, violence.

According to Dr. Bande,[6] violence is a complex phenomenon and it has many faced. We see around us its external manifestations -

[6] Dr. Usha Bamde, "Can violence be way of life?" The Tribune, June 7, 1997.

violence against women, the neglect of children and so on. Apparent physical violence leads to killings, loot, arson and frenzy which destroys the harmony of society. Latent and structural violence leads to more harm and cuts into the vitals of the country. Under this we have exploitation of children, cruelty to girl child and down trodden.

His Holiness The Dalai Lama elaborates: Violence is not good. People might be attracted to something more because of violence, but as a basic human being, one will not admire violence deep down. People don't like situations where people are killed, beaten or tortured. The basic human instinct will disagree with violence. Therefore, it is important to pay more attention to those activities which are non-violent. They involve reason, respect for human life, human compassion and human understanding. The Buddha Shakyamuni taught non-violence. Mahavir, the Jain teacher, also taught non-violence. Many other Indian masters also taught non-violence or animas. In the modern era, during the 20th century, Mahatama Gandhi implemented this new and noble idea in politics2. Gandhian philosophy of peace depends upon his method of non-violence. On the contrary violence evokes counter violence and resentment. Wars escalate, brutalises and make the people more callous. Wars breed evils such as hatred and enmity. However, non-violence and that the violence that can be relied on to establish peace.

India today is nowhere in peace because of the inability of the existing Indian polity to mobilise itself for the noble cause of peace and non-violence and has misdirected its genuine anger into rebellious mood. The people take country liquor, beat up their wives and children. Some of the politicians, bureaucrats and educationists take to drugs, chase women and gather in the city's red light areas. If given a chance, they decide to rape, loot and murder. A bureaucrat's dictionary invents the term 'criminality' to describe their violent actions, aggressive moods and angry gestures. While they are sent to jail, the culture misses another opportunity to look at its brutal insanity.

What makes the situation more ironical is the doctrine of non-violence, the politicians often utter without understanding its meaning and origin. For Mahatma Gandhi, it was not merely lofty talk. Being essentially a social philosopher with deep insights, he realised that non-violence would be meaningful only in a society with decentralised polity, small industry and human technology.

The society that Mahatma Gandhi liked to dream of, post-independent India chose to forget. The culture India is passing through proves its absurdity, when the representatives of the modern State - an institution that Gandhi dislike from the core of his heart - talk of 'peace' and 'non-violence'. When they learn that Gandhian non-violence is an impossible proposition in a non-Gandhian culture.

The path of non-violence is more superior and lasting than the means of violence and dictatorship. 'Non-violence' is often taken to be the 'be-all and end-all' of Buddha's teachings and showed that it is much more than that 'Non-violence' is in fact that most useful aspect of Buddhism; useful for India's ruling classes/castes. Taking the cue from Gandhi, the champion of the ruling orthodoxy, non-violence was projected as an end in itself . To answer distortions in India, Dr. Ambedkar quoted the Buddha's reply to Sinha Senapati, the commander in chief of Vaisali, on the question of practising Non-violence: Buddha replied ! "you have wrongly understood what I have been preaching. An offender must be punished and an innocent man must be freed. It is not the fault of the Magistrate if he punishes an offender. The Magistrate who inflicts the punishment is only carrying out the law. He does not become stained with Non-violence. A man who fights for justice and safety cannot be accused of violence. If all the means of maintaining peace have failed then the responsibility for Violence falls on him who started war. One must never surrender to evil power. War there may be. But it must not be for selfish ends[7] . Buddha's Non-violence was not as absolute. Ambedkar justified the use of force when he said: "Millions of people

---

7 "Buddha or Karl Marx", Dr. Babaseheb Ambedkar - Writing and Speeches, Vol. 3, Government of Maharashtra (1987), P451.

are killed. It his no violence? If a murderer can be killed in war because he belongs to a hostile nation why cannot a property owner be killed if his ownership leads to misery for the rest of the community? There is no reason to make an exception in favour of the property owner; why one should regard private property as sacrosanct".

Non-violence, prime Dharma is an extreme doctrine. It is a Jaina doctrine. It is not a Buddhist doctrine. Buddha make a distinction between Principle and Rule. He did not make non-violence a matter of Rule. He enunciated it as a matter of Principle or way of life. A principle leaves you freedom to act. A rule does not. Rule either breaks you or you break the rule. The law should be non-violence wherever possible; violence wherever necessary[8]. The path of non violence as more superior and lasting than the means of violence and dictatorship[9]. Hindu society had only adopted such innocuous domas like non-violence' from Buddha while rejecting the essence of his philosophy of 'equality'. Non-violence in a social structure based on inequality and enslavement of the 'Shudra' and the women,[10] amounted to 'Violence' and this was sought to be camouflaged by the Hindu adoption of Buddha's Non-violence?.

Ambedkar loved the principle of absolute non-violence as an end and believed in relative violence as a means. He was of the opinion that Gandhi's non-violence as a means. He was of the opinion that Gandhi's non-violence was derived from Jainism and not from Buddha, who never stretched it to the extreme view of Jainism. Ambedkar observed that he had love for the principle of non-violence, but he differentiated non-violence from abject surrender. He told the volunteers that it did not befit a man to live a life of surrender, servitude and helplessness. He declared that he believed with saint Tukaram that destruction of the wicked was also a form

---

8 D.C. Ahir, The Legacy of Ambedkar (Bharat Ratna) (1990), p285.

9 Thomas Mathew, Ambedkar: Reform or Revolution (1991),P.142.

of non-violence. Although love and kindness towards all creatures was a part of the principle of non-violence, to destroy all evidencc was the principle element in the doctrine of non-violence. Without that, non-violence was an empty shell, a beatitude. Shakti (strength) and (character) should be their ideal.

Russell was against war; but not for quietist. According to Russell activity led to growth; quietist was another name for death. Force was energy which must be used constructively to achieve anything and not destructively as violence. Ambedkar was afraid that Indians might read in Russell's book a justification for their philosophic bias for the doctrine of non-violence. In the end Ambedkar added that Russell deserved full credit for having emphasized the psychic basis of social life. Social reconstruction depended upon the right understanding of the relations of individuals in Society a problem which had eluded the grasp of many sociologists"

Jesus Christ had to encounter with Jews, Hebrews, scribes and Pharisees. No doubt these people were religious leaders but the morality was at the lowest level during those days. Jesus scolded them and thus many turned out to be His enemies. In his teachings he preached the message of repentance and non-violence. Jesus Christ once said: "All they take the sword shall perished with sword"[11]

Fight, whether violent or non-violent, was just if the end sought was good. If the end sought was just, the insistence on its achievement and the fight for it must be equally just. But the justness of an end did not change: the means here also to be just.

Ends and means are convertible terms. Two are inseparable. The purity of one affects the purity of the other. Criticising those who do not give due importance to means Gandhi said: "They say means are after all means. I would say means are after all everything. As the means are so the end. Violent means will give violent Swaraj. That would be a menace to the world and to India itself... there is

---

11 M.M. Man ad the Universe of Faiths, P.157, Also see Mathew5:17

no wall of separation between means and ends. Indeed, the creator has given us control (and that too every limited) over means, none over means, none over the end. Realization of goal is in exact proportion to that means. This is the proposition that admits of no exception. Holding such a belief, I have been endeavouring to keep the country to means that are purely peaceful and legitimate".

"The man who comes to kill you, or to outrage the modesty of a woman, or sets fire to anther house, or commits theft and is killed while struggling to escape", observed Ambedkar, "dies by his own sins as well as aggressors and wicked men do if wounding one's feelings is violence", He said, Gandhi's fast "is also based on violence:. "Truly speaking", he concluded the law should be non-violent wherever possible, violent wherever necessary.

The Mahabharata contains the Krishna legends and the famous poem, the Gita. Even apart from the philosophy of the Gita, it lays stress on ethical and moral principles in stagecraft and in life generally. Without this foundation of dharma there is no true happiness and society cannot hold together. The aim is social welfare, not the welfare of a particular group only but of the whole world, for 'the entire world of mortals is a self-dependent organism'.

Yet dharma itself is relative and depends on the times and the conditions prevailing, apart from some basic principles, such as adherence to truth, non-violence etc. These principles endure and do not change, but otherwise dharma, that amalgam of duties and responsibilities, changes with the changing age. The emphasis on non-violence, here and elsewhere, is interesting, for no obvious contradiction appears to be noticed between this and fighting for a righteous cause. The whole epic centres round a great war. Evidently the conception of non-violence, non-violence, had a great deal to do with the motive, the absence of the violent mental approach, self-discipline and control of anger and hatred rather than the physical abstention from violent action, when this because necessary and inevitable.[12]

---

[12] Jawahaar Lal Nehru, The Discovery of India,(1981) PP.107-108.

Mr. J.L. Nehru, in his Discovery of India, elaborating on Dharma, Sanatan, Sanatan dharma, Buddhism, Janism and Hinduism, writes: Hinduism, embraces many beliefs and practices, from the highest to the lowest, often opposed to or contradicting each other. Its essential spirit seems to be to live and let live. Mahatma Gandhi has attempted to define it: 'If I were asked to define the Hindu creed, I should simply say : Search after truth through non-violent means. A man may not believe in God and still can himself a Hindu. Hinduism is a relentless pursuit after truth.... Hinduism is the religion of truth. Truth is God. Denial of God we have known. Denial of truth we have not known".

Mahatma Gandhi, the great apostle of peace in the twentieth century, considered non-violence a panacea for all our ills. He even identified it with truth. He believed that only a fearless devotes of non-violence could uphold the cause of truth and that those who separated truth and justice from non-violence did not understand the true nature of the creed of non-violence. According to him non-violence is a weapon of strong, and the brave and the fearless. Non-violence of his being free from hatred and bitterness. The philosophy of non-violence is hard to understand and difficult to act upon. The sprit of animosity which dominates man's thoughts, desires and aspirations creates in his mind a kind of live for violence. The sermons of saintly beings the Christ, the Buddha and Mahatama Gandhi have fallen on deaf cars. We are living in a world which is so completely dominated by the lure of power and material advantages that it cannot think and act in terms of non-violence. Non-violence is based on love for God's creatures and a desire to avoid doing any kind of harm to them.

According to Dr. S. Satyanaray, for Gandhi, non-violence is the best weapon to get what ever he wants. Through the method of his non-violence, Gandhi attracted the attention of leaders throughout the world. His method of non-violence is a continuous process of searching for truth that includes self-suffering. The process of non-violence resembles what is called passive resistance which civil disobedience, non-co-operation, demonstrations and fasting as tools for its successful conduct of a given conflict[13]. Dr. S. Radhakrishnan states that "Gandhi was the first in the human history to extent the principle of non-violence from the individual to the social and political place. On the other hand he entered politics for the purpose of experimenting with non-violence and establishing its validity"[14]. Gandhi, adopted the philosophy of non-violence to solve all problems, National and International. In his opinion "non-violence is meant not merely for Saints and Sages but for the common people also. Non-violence is the law of our species, as the violence is the law of brutes. Gandhi believed that "A non-violent revolution is not programme of "seizure of power", but it is transformation of relationships, canning in a peaceful transfer of power". Even in the struggle for India's Independence, he was persistent that we should adopt civilised methods of non-violence and sufferings.

Gandhi's stand for the freedom of India was not based on any hatred for British. He viewed that we must hate the sin and not the sinner. In his own words; "For me patriotism is the same as humanity. I am patriotic because I am human and humane. I will not win England or Germany to serve India". Such was his faith in non-violence. But unfortunately, the world's attitude is taking a more serious interest in violence and ignores or neglects other ways of freedom-fighting, which is basically wrong.

His Holiness, The Dalai lama, however, feels, genuine non-violence is something like an experiment on this planet. If they succeed, it gains new meaning. According to him, non-violence through human understanding and human love is something very new and very unique. If this experiment succeeds, it can be applied to other problems of the world[15]. His Holiness in one of his interviews was emphatic when he said; that he will never accept or condone violence.

---

13 Dr. S. Satyanarayana, "Peace and Non-Violence" published in Budhism and Peace (1991), P.101, edited by Prof.G. Sundra Ramaiah, Dr. K. Ravi and Dr. S.D.A. Joga Rao.

14 Krishna Kriplani, All Men are Brothers(1960) p.vii.

15 The Dalai Lama, Tibet, Tibet, China and the World. A Compilation of Interviews (1989), p.64.

Because as a Buddhist monk he thinks that violence is not good; he believes firmly and strongly in the Gandhian way of non-violence; violence is not their strength; their strength is truth, justice, reason and humane understanding. Tibetans have been trained centuries, in non-violence and ought to realise that in their hands non-violence should show all the brilliance that is inherent in non-violence.

One of the secrets to obtain mental peace is within ourselves. The compassionate attitude, loving kindness and forgiveness are ideal things and are the real source of inner satisfaction. Many people genuinely desire world peace and it appears some kind of a different human experiment is taking place.

According to Gandhi the principle of non-violence is the greatest force at the disposal of mankind. He believed that non-violence is mightier than the mightiest weapon of destruction devised by the ingenuity of man. In his opinion the so-called destruction is not the law of the humans. He proclaims that the first condition of non-violence is justice all round in every department of life. Gandhi further emphasised that just as one must learn the art of killing in training for violence, so one must learn the art of dying for non-violence[16]. Needless to say that a votary of non-violence has to cultivate the capacity for sacrifice of the highest type in order to be free from fear. he has also to cultivate endurance, besides love and compassion for all including their opponents. It is an old, established truth that violence can only be effectively met by non-violence.

Mahatama Gandhi traced the tendencies of non-violence even from the remote human history. In his opinion the attribute of non-violence is an inherent quality of man. To know the history of philosophy of non-violence, in his own words, "If we turn our eyes to the time of which history has any record down to our own time, we shall find that man has been steadily progressing towards non-violence". For example he says that our remote ancestors were cannibals. There came a time when they were fed up with cannibals and they began to live on chase. Next came a stage when man was ashamed of

---

16 Krishna Kriplani, All Men are Brothers (1960), P.110

leading the life of a wandering hunter. He therefore, took to agriculture and depended mainly on mother earth for his food. Thus from being a nomad he settled down to a civilised, stable life, founded villages and towns, and a nation. All these developments in man's life, are the stages of progressive non-violence and diminishing violence. Had it been otherwise, the human species should have been extant by now, even as many of the other species have disappeared. The progress of mankind must go on and the ultimate goal is world peace.

The true nature of non-violence should necessitate complete absentation from exploitation. The method of non-violence is, in fact, a power which can be used equally by all children, young men and women or grown up people provided they have a living faith in equal live for all mankind: When non-violence is accepted as the law of life, it must provide the whole being and not to be applied to isolated acts. However, the practise of non-violence would not mean a resignation from the challenge of wickedness. Complete and perfect non-violence may not be possible in a society but it may not be impossible also if may tries to be steadfast to the principle of non-violence.

The whole-hearted practise of non-violence will show the way for the individual as well as for national and international peace. To be practice and to put it in the words of Mahatma Gandhi; "My experience which is daily growing stronger and richer, tells me that, there is no peace for individuals or for nations without practising truth and non-violence to utmost extent possible for man. The police of retaliation has never succeeded. This is true of individuals and equally true of nations. Hans J. Morgentha in. "Politics Among the Nations", writes When a nation is engaged in war with another nation, it is very likely that the nation which anticipates victory will pursue a policy that seeks a permanent change of power relations with the defeated enemy. The nation will pursue this policy regardless of what the objectives were at the outbreak of the war. It is the objective of this policy of change to transform the relation between victor and vanquished which happens to exist at the end of the war into a new status quo of the peace settlement. Thus a war that was started by the victor as a defensive war for the maintenance of the pre-ware status-quo, transforms itself with the approaching victory into an imperialistic war, that is, for a permanent change in the status quo[17]. A nation that is at the peak of power is particularly exposed to the temptation to forget that all the power is relative. And it is likely to believe that the superiority it has achieved is an absolute.

Communism has been successful wherever its tenets of social, economic, and political equality appeal to the people for whom the removal of inequality has been the most urgent aspiration. The Soviet Union was indeed been the vehicle on which communism tried to conquer the world. But it could not achieve peace by force and violence. However, who can predict that in this regard China will not take tomorrow the place of the Former Soviet Union? The moral root of attempts to establish a stable and peaceful international order is to be found in the increase in the humanness and civilised character of human relations which the last centuries have witnessed in the Western World. The philosophy of the Enlightenment and the political and economic theory of liberalism postulates respect for human life and promotion of human welfare. According to Gandhi if the desired changes are brought about through non-violent means, with a view to achieve peace settlement, the world would not be deprived of the talents of the classes. He is prophetic when he says: In the non-violent order of the future, the land would belong to the State.

The Christian understanding of 'peace' is deeply rooted in the Biblical meaning of peace, 'Peace' is God's gift to those who subject themselves to his divine law. God is the ultimate source of well-being and fulfilment (peace) and anyone who comes into union with God enjoys peace. To attain 'peace' one should accept God as one's own total good and order one's conduct in conformity with God's law should respect and love one's fellowmen, created in the "Image and likeness of God"[18].

---

17 Hans J. Morgenthau, Policts Among the Nations (1969),pp 50-51.

18 Mireca Eliade (Ed), Encyclopaedia of Religion Vol. II, P. 221 (Macmillan Publishing Company, New York 1987). Also see Joseph Kuttianmickal, Concept of 'Peace' in the Bible (1991), P.203

To the ancient Hebrew mind, 'peace' (shalom) was not just the absence of war or conflict, but well-being and even prosperity. Prophets Isaiah and Micah bring out the positive content of peace in glowing terms in their prophecies. Proper Micah describes a state of peace, calm and security that will be established when people accept the reign of God and submit themselves to the law of God. In such a state of peace instruments of war have not place and as such they are converted into agricultural implements. To use the prophet's own expression. "... and they shall beat their swords into ploughshares, and their spears into pruning hooks; nation shall not lift up sword against nation, neither shall they harm any more ..." Violence has no place in the society and the people shall abide by non-violence and truth. Micah's description that every man would sit under his vine and fig tree, indicates peace and security. It also indicates that there is no place for injustice, exploitation and oppression where peace reigns supreme.

History tells us that every oppressed class gained true liberation from its masters through its own efforts. it is necessary that the people, more particularly the women learn the lesson, that she realises that her freedom will reach as far as her power to achieve her freedom reaches. Usha Bande, in an article, 'can violence be a way of life?", dwells on the thesis that oppressed will have to work for themselves for their emancipation and she writes :

"Camus, famous injunction "neither victims nor executioners be, recognises the existence of violence embedded in the historical process and the necessity to say a compelling "no" to the outside forces means a "yes" to self. This "yes" suggests an affirmation and an awareness: it becomes a voice of protest and reform and leads to progress; it is a become voice of protest and reform and leads to progress; it is a harbinger of change. When we talk of "violence in historical process", says :

We do not always mean violence which entails physical harm or assault. Even verbal insults or the tendency to deny someone his fundamental human right can be termed as violence.

Given this background of the traditions of non-violence in India and elsewhere, where have we arrived in India? All around us we see the cult and practice of violence to achieve ends that have little to do with social good of the common man. The question we have to ask ourselves is why ? Some of them are answered in the criminalisation of politics that has taken place over the past few decades, along with the greed to accumulate riches with the sole purpose of acquiring power that would lead to a further accumulation of wealth. It is a vicious circle that has trapped us from which there are few avenues of escape.

9

CRIME, CORRUPTION AND GOOD GOVERNANCE

Free India was born with massive problems and responsibilities of the new rulers were enormous. The country was to be kept secular, democratic, united, communal peace maintained, caste rivalries fought, poverty ended and jobs created. The nation had to be given a sense of direction of democratic institutions and instruments of governments of governance created to match its needs. Rightly, expectations of the people armed with adult franchise soared along with population, straining resources. The rulers should have kept up with the rising demands and used power as an instrument to meet them. With some expectations, they however, have not bothered to measure up to the challenge and instead have used power as instrument for personal and party ends. The result has been dangerous decline in quality and excellence of administration; a wide gulf between the rulers and the ruled and loss of moral and political authority of the ruler .

H.K. Dua[19] in an article, "Managing The nation", writes :

The authority of a government and the people who man it ultimately depends on the quality of governance, how sensitive it is to the social and economic needs of the people and how earnest it is in tackling their problems. The task of the rulers ultimately is to work for the betterment of the people. The people do not take long to notice a ruler's sincerity, which in turn increases his or her moral and political spectrum do not understand this simple and elementary truth about the governance.

---

[19] H.K. Dua, "Managing The Nation", The Times of India, October 9, 1997. P.12

Needless to say that a democratic political system enjoins on the political leaders the duty to provide the country better standards of governance than they have in the last several years.

Since Independence, politics gradually degenerated into a struggle for powers for its own sake. Power for personal ends became the supreme value. Politics became a lucrative profession and came to be regarded very much as the art and science of somehow getting to positions of powers and by all possible means staying there. In this scheme of things. Government was little more than the technique and the machinery of governing or ruling over the people, of keeping them under control, of the ruling classes of politicians dominating over the rest of populace, or the masters enjoying the exercise of power over the masses. Politics became the means to power and Government the manifestation of the quest for domination.

Those in Government are so pre-occupied with the struggle for survival in power that they have no time for addressing their attention to the problems of the people. Governance has become a casualty of Government. There has been a sharp erosion in the respect of the people for the politician. In large parts of the country. Government does not exist. Mafia gangs terrorise and rule, even the thin dividing line between the politicians and criminal has disappeared. Politics has been criminalised and crime politicised. Earlier the criminal sought the protection of the politician now it is the politician who needs the protection of the Mafia or the two have become one and the same person. Government have lost their credibility, legitimacy and even their representative credentials.

Article 37 speaks of certain "principles" being "fundamental" in the "governance of the country" but not "enforcement by any court". The following principles of governance to be followed :

a A social order, the promotion of the welfare of the people with social, economic and political justice for all [Article 38 (1)];

b Minimisation of inequalities in income and climnination of inequalities in status, facilities and opportunities among individuals and groups of people [Article 38 (2)];

c Right to adequate means of livelihood for all citizens - men and women equally [Article 38(a)];

d Opportunities and facilities for children to develop in a healthy manner and in conditions of freedom and dignity [Article 39(1)];

e Right to work, to education and to public assistance in cases of unemployment, old age, sickness, disablement etc. [Article 39 (1)];

f Just and human conditions of work and maternity relief [Article 42];

g A living wage for workers with conditions of work ensuring a decent standard of life and full enjoyment of leisure [Article 43]; Free and compulsory education for all children below 14 years [Article 45];

h Raising the level of nutrition and the standard of living and to improve public health [Article 47];

i Protection and improvement of environment and safeguarding of forests and wild life [Article 48A].

While it has become a fashion to blame the politicians for all that ails the nation, little is done to educate the citizens in the matter of their own citizenship obligations in a representative, participatory democratic polity. Freedom and democracy are tender plants and demand constant vigil from the citizens. Unless nursed by them with great care, these are bound to without away.

Indian Constitution is a beautifully drafted document. The sum and substance of Indian Constitution is the Preamble to the constitution;

the Fundamental Rights together with the Directive Principles of State Policy in Part IV plus Article 51A in part IV A, the Fundamental Duties. The Directive Principles are the mandate to the State as to what is expected of it in the governance of the State for the purpose of achieving the constitutional goals indicated in the Preamble. Only a few words of the Preamble are alone sufficient to keep us on the right track. The Preamble begins with the word, "We the People of India", which indicates the location of the political sovereignty. Justice of all kinds, Equality, Fraternity - Fraternity because there is a pluralistic society - and, of course, Liberty. In a pluralist society the concept of fraternity is very essential because unity in diversity is really the beauty of the Indian ethos. If what is said in Preamble, is kept in view along with the mandate to the State in the Directive Principles, the entire constitutional scheme becomes clear. The remaining provisions are merely to enable the achievement of these constitutional goals. Hon'ble Mr. Justice J.S. Verma[20], the Chief Justice of India, in his speech delivered at R.C. Ghiya Memorial Lecture, Jaipur, on June 28, 1997 said :

"The most valuable asset of any nation is its human resources. Now, to achieve perfect socio-economic justice, therefore, increase in the worth of this greatest national wealth is essential. Every thing which we can do in the sphere of governance as one of the three Wings of the state for development of human resources, for increasing he worth of human beings is going to contribute towards the growth and development of the nation interpretation Article 21 to mean life with dignity and not mere animal existence has the effect of increasing the worth of human beings". Mere guarantee of Fundamental rights in the constitution for benefit of the citizens of the country without ensuring that they become a reality is meaningless.

It there are three vices which are mainly responsible for cording the moral values in the country, one would have no hesitation in

---

20 J.S. Verma, "Constitutional Obligation of the Judiciary", AIR 1997, Journal section at P. 164.

pointing out one's finger towards lust for power, corruption and black money. They are close allies of each other, work in unison and have spread their tentacles to almost all walks of life;

I. Money was received by the politicians and other Government functionaries in cash without receipt and it was ensured that the same was not reflected in the account books. As the level of corruption rose higher so did the incidence of black-money. Things came to such a pass that according to financial experts the incidence of black-money in India was the highest in the world and it exceeded the white legal money in circulation.

II. As the heads of investigating agencies and vigilance officers owe their appointment and continuation in office to political bosses, the investigating agencies not only turn a blind eye to lapses but quite often instead of detecting the crime and bringing the culprit to book suppress the incriminating material and feel no hesitation in giving clean chits to the political bosses.

III. Springs of integrity and moral values have not altogether dried up in the country. We have still a number of persons in political life and administrative wing of the State who are possessed of impeccable integrity, honesty and moral values. But, their number seems to be dwindling like species of vanishing tribes.

Inevitably, by stages, economic reform on the one hand a bureaucratic-cum-business and banking class on the other produced the series of scams involving corruption at the highest levels, leading to a growing loss of faith in the system by all classes, and the growing scenario of chaos, confusion and what are called new "Experiments" in governance, presumably meant to provide social justice but in fact caught into their cobwebs of coalitions and endless 'parleys', 'adjustments', 'compromises' "carrying on somehow" but none of them able to deal with the basic malady of an increasing corrupt and criminalised as well as increasingly communal political culture. Political leadership is tottering and groping in the dark. People have thrown out the traditional hold of leaders. All existing political parties are rejected, be they rightist or leftist. They do not reflect he wishes of the people nor are they in a position to fulfil the aspirations of the people. People have lost faith in them.

On the whole, it can be stated that constitutional system is failing. It is system's failure. People are dismayed, not down and out. At this juncture, the leadership must emerge from amongst the people and it should be a people's democratic peaceful revolution.
We define good governance as "a system of governance that is able to unambiguously identify the basic values of the society where values of the society where values are economic, political and socio-cultural issues including human rights, and pursue these values through an accountable and honest administration".

Scams and scandals are the higher levels of corruption in which the elite and politically and economically powerful, manipulate the system in such a way that money is siphoned off from state projects to their pockets. They being in powerful positions and having inside information play a safe game. Networking ensures that they are not caught or if the scandals are exposed they neither loose money nor their positions.

The multi-national corporations have revolutionised the kickback market. Competing for the emerging markets in India they offer high kickbacks to bureaucrats and politicians in order to get a business deal through. A well known researcher on India wrote 25 years back "French, Americans and especially, West German companies are usually said to have the least inhibitions about bribing their way through. Japanese firms are said to be even more willing to pay up".

While India talks of discipline and accountability, in India it is a joke. While India talks about power to people, they only see more power going to the people in power. While India fiddles, India is burning with anger at the injustice of it all. The signs of modern Welfare State are just lacking.

In this dark period of history, we need leaders of stature of Rajagopalacharia who rightly philosophised in very lucid words :

"There is no country which can be governed more easily than India. You have only to appeal to tradition. All the great old kings of past - Janaka and Mr. Ram are still alive and governing our hearts. I am not the Governor General; Mr. Ram is. Treat my office always with respect". The administration in welfare state deserves to be inconsonant with the thought expressed by Rajagopalacharia. The ruler administrator should treat his office as trust; and himself as the trustee, in discharge of his functions. Rajagopalacharia is specific when he puts the words in the mouth of Bharat;

"This kingdom is RAM's. For the time being, he has asked me to be in charge. In my brother's place I have installed his sandals. Deriving authority from them. I shall do my work as king".

Thus Bharat performed the duties of the king as a delegate of Lord Ram, as a trustee. The modern State is a welfare State and the obligations of the welfare state are, to legislate for the purpose of ensuring social, economic and political justice; second, to provide essential services to the society through department for instrumentalities, by way of implementing the policies and programmes as directed by the Constitution and the Law; thirdly, to regulate and control the activities of individuals in every relevant sphere to sub-serve common good, and fourthly the ensuring of justice as between individual and individual and between individual and the State through the judicial wing of the State.

An analysis of the ancient Indian Polity would show that all the responsibilities, evolved and developed by the people, meant to secure the welfare and happiness of the people as a whole, as also the welfare and full blossoming of individual, had been conceived at the earliest period know to human history, and the instrumentality of the State was created and the King as its head was entrusted with duty and responsibility of its implementation[21]. The concept of a 'Welfare State' where in the Governmental tasks have increased by several folds, setting up various administrative agencies to carry out the objectives of a 'social' welfare state centres around the problems concerning 'social justice' and more particularly, the necessity balance between 'private' and 'social' interests.

The Welfare State is, in essence, a service state, which undertakes to redeem its subject from all miseries and risks of life. It is duty of State to safeguard human life from all possible perils. The social interest demands a prospers society with an evenly distributed economy where wants and sufferings have to be eliminated[22]. The Welfare State strives to gibe each individual his due, not only by protecting his life and liberty but also by providing him social and economic security.

Though the doctrine is traceable to Aristotle but the writings of Locke and Montesquieu[23] gave it a base on which modern attempts to distinguish between legislative, executive and judicial power is grounded. Locke distinguished between what he called : (I) discontinuous legislative power, (ii) continuous executive power; and (iii) federative power.

Good governance postulates: The rule of law prevails; economic and political power must be decentralised right down to the villages; people be given the rights over national resources such as air, water, land and forests. The Government must be transparent and clean. The people must have their right to full information about government policy and decisions. The State must be truly secular, i.e., guarantee rights to members of all religions and communities"[24]. Rule of Law

---

21 Justice Rama Jois: Seeds of Moern: Public Law in Ancient Indian Jurisprudence (1990) P.3

22 Dr. R.G. Chaturvedi: Justice Natural Social Economic and Political, (1990), P.779.

23 L'esprit Des Lois (1748) Ch.12, Also see: I.P. Massey: Administrative Law, Fourth Edition (1995) p.31

24 V.R. Krishna Yer, "NF-LF Must Shum Congress:, The Indian Express May 23, 1996, P.8.

is the pivot of good governance and evolves around it. All national wealth, must tackle down to the people and must not dwindle in between the resources of the State and the people.

People want quality governance and high standards of behaviour among politicians. With so many scams and scandals, the government's lack of dynamism and a sense of direction have been exposed The people feel that the last government's leaders were obsessed more with their own political survival than a desire to improve the country's political atmosphere and deliver goods. Mr. Rao's dismal governance and insensitivity to the problems of the people in general and the deprived segment of the population in particular wrought havoc for the party. The quality of its governance needed to be improved in as much as it was full of flaws, the laws and rules were slack and being exploited to weaken the entire system. In such a state of drift, shady characters with money and muscle rules the roost and only the dishonest, corrupt and hypocrite prosper. The polity needs a refreshingly different balanced approach, and responses to old and new issues and problems. Coalition politics require a new thinking process and an agreed agenda based on common programme as well as action plan Hari Jai Singh"[25] strongly feels; Gone are the days when the states were considered mere fields of the ruling party at the Centre. Regional satraps now mean business. They want a pride of place in the affairs of the nation. The strengthening of nation roots has to be seen as a two-way process. Once regional leaders develop a stake at the Centre, the national scene will, hopefully, change for the better.

The concept of good governance had linkage with the nationalistic vision of the architects of India's independence, and also a linkage with India's potential to emerge as a front-ranking nation in the world in the early decades of the 21st century. And when Sovernighty is further linked to the approaching major landmark in modern Indian History, the 50th anniversary of Swaraj it generated such a powerful

---

25 Hari Jai Singh, "exploring a New Agenda", The Tribune, May 19, 1996.

mass appeal that its practical manifestations are bound to be visible in the months and years to come.

The party of Hindutva has taken an awesome responsibility upon itself by seeking popular mandate on the promise of good governance. The people of India, stand for the sum of all ancestors down the ages past third have thought and done. Indians also, in part the product of influences and pressures exert from outside. Many are the strands out of which the fabric of Indian National life has been woven. Today a moral crisis is writ on every facet of life. Each one of us seeks consolation in accusing the others for all the maladies of Indian system. In the process, one or the other accusing finger is pointed towards every one of without an exception. They debates on morality, ethics, values, principles and virtues goes on unabated alongside a bashful demonstration of total absence of all these attributes in them. The truth is better revealed in the miscarries, hardships and numerous other problems starting at them directly on the face. Let us not forget that while several civilisations have perished through affluence, no civilisation has ever died of adversity. It is essential to replace the corrupt and the self-seekers by honest, consciential to replace the corrupt and the self-seekers by honest, conscientious and capable men. The major force is the public opinion, that will generate the wind in favour of simple living.

A government funded upon anything except liberty and justice cannot stand. All the wrecks on either side of the stream of time, all the wrecks of the great cities, and all the nations that have passed away al are a warning that nation founded upon injustice can stand.[26] Leadership seems to be laboring under misconception that governance is merely about keeping the ship of the state afloat, but surely it is also about giving a purposive direction to the state[27].

---

[26] American Lawyer Robert Innersole, also see: V.R. Krishna Iyer: Human Rights and Human Wrongs, (1990) P.17

[27] Bharat Bhushan, "Unable bad", The Indian Express, December 11, 1992, P.6.

Good governance seeks support from the rule of law which permeates the entire fabric of the constitution and indeed forms one of its basic features. The rule of the law excludes arbitrariness; its postulate is "intelligence without passion' and 'reason freed from desire'. Wherever we find arbitrariness or unreasonableness there is a denial of the rule of law. That is why Aristotle preferred a government of laws enacted by the legislative authority, howsoever, arbitrary or despotic it may be[28]

The rule of law has really three basic and fundamental assumptions; one is that law making must be essentially in the hands of a democratically elected legislature, subject of course to any power in the executive in an emergent situation to promulgate ordinances effective for a short duration while the legislature is not in session as also to enact delegated legislation in accordance with the guidelines laid down by the legislature; the other is that even in hands of a democratically elected legislature, there should not be unfettered legislative power, for, as Jefferson said: "Let no man be trusted with power but tie him down from making mischief chief by the chains of the Constitution" and lastly there must be an independent judiciary to protect the citizen against excess of executive and legislative power. It is worthwhile to recall what G.B. Shaw says: "Good people make good laws do not necessarily make people good". Governance at the hands of good, honest trustworthy people makes all the difference.

The concept of Rule of Law has developed many facts which are not only negative providing constraints on governmental action but affirmative also imposing in affirmative duty of fairness on the government. These various negative and affirmative facets have been summarized by Prof. Upendra Baxi thus: "One is that power should not be exercised arbitrarily. This has meant that it should be exercised for the purpose for which it has been conferred. It also means that power should be exercised within the statutory ambit; and purported exercise of it would not just be ultra virus, but in a

---

[28] Bachan Singh v. State of Pujab (1982): 3 SCC 24 at P. 50.

true sense of the term arbitrary. Simple negation of arbitrariness is, nowhere, not enough to preserve the Rule of Law values. Indian courts have gone further to insist on specific positive content of Rule of Law obligations. These include the rules of natural justice which have to be followed not just in quasi-judicial action but often also in purely administrative action. The scope and content of the requirements of natural justice have varied from time to time according to the judicial interpretation, but the broad insistence remains. In addition, access to information a to the grounds of decision has remained an important preoccupation of Indian judiciary, as any impediments to it have the tendency of obstructing judicial review of administrative action. This means that the courts have from time to time insisted that exercise of administrative power be accompanied by reasons, although the exact status of the obligation to give reasons is as yet indeterminate. The Rule of law notation has been in addition consistently extended to secure for the individual fair dealing by the State in its economic activities. For example, the government is held bound by its assurance to individuals in business transactions by way of estoppel"

The State has to follow some of the rules of natural justice before reaching decision that it would not trade with certain contractors or before blacklisting them. In matters involving governments contracts, the courts have been increasingly keen to insist that the ambit of fairplay is not lessened in view of the dominating capacity of the State over the individuals. In the area of losses and injury arising out of State economic entrepreneurial function courts have tend to restrict the scope of the defence of sovereign immunity in favour of the affected individuals.[29] It is heartening to see that the courts are making all concerted efforts to establish a rule of law society in India by insisting on "fairness" in every aspect of the exercise of power by the State.

Dicey's[30] formulation of the concept of 'Rule of Law", which

---

29 Upendra Baxi: Developents in Indian Asministrative Law Public Law in India, (1982), A.G. Noorani edn.) P.134-135.

30 I.P. Massey: Administrative Law, Fourth Edition (1995) P.25.

according to him forms the basis of the English Constitutional Law, contains three principles: (I) Absence of discretionary power in the hands of the government officials. By this Dicey implies that justice must be done through known principles. Discretion implies absence of rules, hence in every exercise of discretion there is room for arbitrariness; (ii) No person should be made to suffer in body or property except for a breach of law established in the ordinary legal manner before the ordinary courts of the land. In this sense, the Rule of Law implies: (a) absence of special privileges for a government official or any other person; (b) all the persons irrespective of status must be subjected to the ordinary courts of the land; (c) everyone should be governed by the law passed by the ordinary legislative organs of the State, (iii) The rights the people must flow from the customs and traditions of the people recognised by the courts in the administration of justice.

The modern concept of the Rule of Law is fairly wide and, therefore, sets an ideal for any government to achieve. This concept was developed by the International Commission of Jurists, known as Delhi Declaration, 1959 which was later on confirmed at Lagos in 1961. According to this formulation the Rule of Law implies that the function of the government in a free society should be so exercised as to create conditions in which the dignity of man as an individual is upheld. This dignity requires not only the recognition of certain civil or political rights but also creation of certain political, social, economical, educational and cultural conditions which are essential to the full development of his personality. During the last few years the Supreme Court in India has developed some fine principles of Third World jurisprudence, and developing the same new constitutionals further, the apex Court in Veena Seth v. State of Bihar extended the reach of the Rule of law to the poor and the down trodden, the ignorant and the illiterate, who constitute the large bulk of humanity in India when it ruled that the Rule of Law does not exist merely for those of the status quo which protects and preserves their dominance and permits them to exploit a large section of the community. What India needs today is the enforcement of the rule of law.

Rule of law is a patent instrument of social justice about equality in results. Social justice must flow from the legal system, as otherwise. 'Rule of law' will break down. 'Social Justice is a means as well as a device to ensure life to be meaningful, and liveable with human dignity, social justice and equality are complementary to each other, so that both should maintain vitality.

According to C.P. Bhambri,[31] "The crisis of governance in India is quite serious and all major political parties have made full contribution in the weakening of administrative institutions at every level in the country. While the Congress party is primarily responsible for politicisation of the administrative apparatus, the other parties have made their own contribution in the on going process of casteism and communisation of administrative functionaries. Indian administration has developed serious cracks in its structures and has lost its capacity to defend the 'rule of law' and because of this malady the whole culture of 'illegality' has taken birth in the country. A society where law is neither feared nor respected, any opportunistic political-coalition executive will further facilitate the ongoing process of deinstitutionlisation of India. Dr. Bhambri fells concerned when he writes: Indian bureaucracy is likely to be further politicised and fragmented because the experience of the past shows that a large majority of bureaucrats easily come to with the politics of flux for getting immediate personal and professional advantages from political leaders. Individual ministers belonging to various groups will operate as an empire within an empire and the bureaucrats of different departments will establish their quid pro quo with these individual group leaders. a weak government will further strengthen the existing culture of illegality and disrespect for the rule of law by politicians, bureaucrats, powerful social groups and lumpiness section of society. Arbitrariness of individual administrators increases if they have a protective political umbrella or a weak, vacillating, factionalism political coalition at the helm of affairs. The Central Government in India has to be in the driver's seal for making

31 C.P. Bhambri, "Coalition and Governance" The Hindustan Times, May 31, 1996 P.11.

collective decisions for an extremely diverse and complex country, and this 'collectively' cannot emerge on the basis of negative coalition partners. The basic goal of elections is to constitute a government and an opposition to ensure that democratic governance is conducted on the basis of accountability and transparency. The political situation in the Centre does not hold any hope for even minimum good and coherent governance because artificially created majorities cannot conceal the prevailing real vacuum in political power.

There must necessarily by close links of good governance with an environment of trust, integrity, and social consensus. There is too much of divisive tendencies already in the polity. These should not be augmented. There is far too much piling of litigation. It should not be increased further, if possible. The courts are generally barred from the election process and all efforts should be made to retain a political process as such. Individual action should not be separated from the context in which it has to operate.

The efficacy of the legal remedies needs first to be confirmed in the supporting arenas. Criminalisation is resulting in the politics of intimidation, coercion, climinimation of opponents and attraction that have made crime into an organised profession. The application and enforcement of law has been ineffectual so far against this trend and it can be mended. A mechanism of separating the political authority from controlling the processes of crime control in a partisan manner should be devised. Parliamentary accountability of the police need not be weakened but the means to end day-to-day executive dictation must be ended. The ending of the sovereign immunity of the police force will also breed responsibility. This package may be the minimum to change the current environment of lack of trust in the legal action where police power becomes the arbiter.[32]

Criminalisation and corruption go hand in hand. Corruption illegal under the law. Yet the increasing infrastructure of vigilance has led only to increase in the incidence of corruption. What is involved is

---

32 Kamala Prasad, "Interface of Politics and Crme:, Mainstream, September 13, 196, P.18.

protection to the corrupt, acceptance socially of the corrupt, respectability in the political association, and all this because of the power of patronage. The vigilance set up is hardly able to catch the really corrupt who carries on as a power-broker administratively and politically. It is the public-private sphere interface that determines the level of corruption and its social acceptance. We seem to have neglected to define the character of the civic society we are aiming to realise and organise and orient people towards that. Criminality deals with administrative corruption but social corruption is more endemic and influences both criminality and integrity. Politics has occupied a large space in the life of the country and must discharge its responsibility.

All this sums up the problems of governance. It is unfortunate that the government is accountable for everything. All institutions have been brought under direct political control. statutory delegations have been subverted under the misguided operation of political authority. Politics and centralised administration must be permitted to take over larger areas in the sphere of delivery of services including criminal domain and jails. They must assume the courage to resist authority where authority is misused. This is relevant to all institutions of the state and not just the executive domain. The coercive powers of the state should withdraw from the voluntary sector. Freedom must assume some new meaning rather than the swan song of lack of foreign domination. A good governance demands all this and is a precondition for freedom from criminalisation and corruption. In the current situation for freedom from criminalisation and corruption.

In the current situation, then, the cleaning of the election administration should be taken further by stages. The pressures for long-delayed reforms should not be slackened. The Lok Sabha resolution has already recognised this fact but is should be judged by urgency in moving ahead with actual legislation. Secondly, a minimal legislation on the issues brought in the Election Commission circular should be enacted. This is necessary to send a clear message to the country that Parliament has a consensus about dealing with criminalisation and electoral malpractice. Finally, a new style governance under the coalition implies a weak government rather than a government that safeguards the interest of the weak and the conglomerate of smaller interest groups must be removed. The voices of the weaker sections must not be submerged in the louder voices of the powerful as under majoritatarian rule by single parties. Regrettably, that is the impression. Actions speak louder than rhetoric and pronouncements. the parties t the present coalition should decide not to fail the trust their constituents have put in them.

A civil society built on the rule of law demands that once laws are framed they will be implemented faithfully and in an even-handed manner. In such a system there is no room for favouritism, special concessions, relaxation or discrimination depending upon who is closer to whom and who has paid the bigger bribe. The Council of Ministers in such a society would be competent to change the rules if this were in the public interest. It would not, however, be competent to do what many Chief Ministers now do, that is, minute on files that a certain thing should be don "in relaxation of rules and in anticipation of orders in Council". The rule of law demands that such relaxation of rules in the case of individuals which clearly benefits that individual in an abnormal manner should not be done by any person holding office, including the Chief Minister of Prime Minister.[33] All that the power permits is the act of governance, but within the framework of law. Those who forget this are the modern Pindaris because it is axiomatic that every arbitrary act is motivated by selfishness and indulged in only for a price. If arbitrariness is removed from Government, we may not need a special monitoring body to curb corruption. The rule of law will take care of this phenomenon.

The 1997 annual meetings of the International Monetary Fund and the World Bank in Hong Kong in September were held against the background of the currency turmoil in South-East Asia. The fund's ministerial-level Interim Committee noted hat the economic fundamentals of the South-East Asian countries remained solid an and their longer-term outlook was favourable. But these countries

---

[33] M.N. Buch, "The abuse of power", The Hindustan Times, September 30, 1997, P.13.

must strengthen financial systems, avoid excessive external deficits and reliance on short-term foreign borrowing Issues of "good governance" and combating corruption figured in the he deliberations and both IMF and the World Bank are now virtually authorised to take these issues explicitly into account in lending and other decision-making "when they significantly affect project or macro-economic performance". The general understanding is that the two institutions in conferring norms would operate within their respective mandate and not enlarge their operational freedom.

The cancerous spread of corruption has almost adversely affected every aspect of life and out political system is not untouched by it. The recipe for political success today is a mixture of MMI (money, muscle and influence). Politicians are regarded as inefficient crooks who sacrifice community interest for private purposes and hoodwink citizens. Criminalisation is proving to be the fallout of widespread political corruption. The Mafia works hands in glove with the demagogues and police seen to be in helpless situation incapable of catching influential criminals. the judiciary, too, let go the convicts due to lack of solid evidence.

We, the people of India, owe a safer, cleaner, richer and better future to generations where they can breathe in a free congenial, prosperous and healthy atmosphere, free from exploitation, injustice, partiality, divisions and reservations. The stagnant system needs to be given a new life and redesigned to secure renewed goals. Swami Vivekananda, who expounded the philosophy of Vedanta, once opined. "Let us perfect the means, the end will take car of itself.

10

MAFIASATION OF INDIAN POLITY

Mafia, violence, crime and guns have been an integral part of the struggle for the Rule of Law situation over years. A parallel government of militants - Mafia gangs has been the alternative code of conduct. And there is wide spread support for the Mafia-goons in action.

Mafia is the Sicilian word for a clandestine criminal organization so deeply rooted in Sicilian rural society as to amount to a counter-government administering its own law and justice. Established among the Italian immigrant community in the USA, the Mafia became the basis of various organized crime syndicates operating according to the same alternative code as in Sicily, the code of operetta, the Italian word for 'connivance'.

The Mafia hierarchy comprising broadly of antisocial gangsters, hooligans, musclemen and other lumped elements of the underworld, thriving on crime and vice, have been exerting a growing influence on industry, business, social organisation, educational institutions, politicians and political parties over decades. All political parties have links with the underworld which has not only played a very prominent role in all elections but it has spread its tentacles in other spheres too; and is found every where. In almost all cities and towns and even in the countryside the gangsters are active holding Indian society to ransom. They go about terrorising and kidnapping citizens, extorting money, molesting and abducting women and stabbing people, at will, in the streets. Even the country's capital is not free from the antisocial activities of the Mafia hierarchy.

The growth of Mafia hierarchy with political support has neutralized the police machinery. In some places like Bombay, Assam and

Bihar it is running parallel administration. Powerful gangsters have emerged who cannot be arrested even when they are involved in grave crimes, and no cases can be registered against them. These gangsters fight elections on behalf of politicians and even finance politicians for fighting elections from out of funds they are collecting through their illegal activities such as smuggling, gun running, drug trafficking with the blessings of the ruling party.

While a former Chief Minister of Goa had to spend a couple of months in jail under COFEPOSA for his reported links with smugglers, a minister had escaped unscathed despite his alleged association with the Menon Brothers, the prime suspects in the Bombay bomb blasts in March, 1993 and awaiting their trial under TADA. The Chief Minister, Dr. Wilfred de Souza was under tremendous pressure from his Partymen to drop the Industries Minister, Suresh Parulkar, whose link with the Menon Brotheers had been established based on evidence collected by the Intelligence agencies and Customs. This has led to insurgency in various parts of the country.

The insurgency in the North-East; accusations and counter-accusations on the funding of ULFA in Assam; the dinging battle involving terrorists, the proxy war in the Kashmir Valley; the lurking fear of revival of militancy in Punjab; the state of anarchy in Bihar; the ever-green political lawlessness in Uttar Pradesh; sheer helplessness of the two southern states to the dictates of Veerappar; the emergence of new Mafia groups to beat the prohibition regime in Haryana; Rampant corruption and bribery; the tightening grip of corrupt and unscrupulous persons on the polity.

Student, not politicians, have led all of Assam's agitations from 1960 to 1972, they fought for the acceptance of Assamese as the official language, followed by demands for "jobs only for the sons of the soil: from 1979 to 1985 they fought to expel 'foreigners' from the state.

And the seeds of militancy were sown. A section of agitators became restive over what Assam's leading intellectual Hiren Gohain calls Delhi's "insincerity and deception, opted for secession through violence and floated the United Liberation Front of Assam at Sibsagar on April 7, 1979. The present ULFA C-in-C Paresh Barua, who was then employed with the railways at Tinsukia, contacted ISSAC Murivah of the NSCN. The Naga outfit sent its men to Moran, Namrup and Sonari in upper Assam to "gauge the public mood".

Each time there is a kidnapping or abduction, a fresh bout of panic is unleashed. Many managers in high-risk areas like Darrang. Barpeta, Likhimpur and Tinsukia have sent their wives and children to safer regions. Ever since Assam became the largest of extremist attack a decade ago, the tranquillity of its tea estates has given way to turbulence. Nina Martyrs ventures into the beleagured outposts to investigate how the laid-back feudal lifestyle of the tea-sahib is now haunted by ambush and governed by the gun. "There was nothing to be afraid of', says a planter from Tezpur Club, Assam's oldest. "Today, the club-house is a skeleton of its former self. Now restrict Indian restrict themselves to tennis and polo and day-time functions. The weekly club nights and black-tie dinners are over. After 5.00 pm the social life is watching cable TV at home". And even to make it to the club in daylight, in Darrang district, all the sahibs from various gardens meet and leave together in a procession of Gypsys. Of the twelve Gypsys, six consist of security personnel, their guns pointed readiness for an ambush.

In fact, the state of Assam was beleaguered by two major insurgencies and has to bear the brunt of several other insurgencies in its neighbourhood. Several thousand people, including hundreds of Government officers and staff, security personnel and policemen have died while performing their duties.

In fact, several examples can be cited to underline the harsh fact of the emergence of parallel establishments that thrive on extortion, tortures, money power threats of violence and killings. What is more. Hari Jai Singh, in an article 'MAFIASATION Of Polity' writes:

"Like the parallel economy thriving on black money, it had become threateningly more forceful than the official establishment. Indeed, what we see today is a total breakdown of the established authority, at least in certain sensitive areas of national life. No wonder, the people's confidence in the system has got eroded. Nothing can be more ironic in this respect than the fact that out of sheer disgust even ordinary citizens have begun to look to the parallel set-up for protection.

The case of the Tata Tea estate in Assam is in itself a tell-tale commentary on how non-governance could create serious distortions in the thinking and working of the systems to the advantage of those out to challenge and destroy the existing order. Here I am not going into the merits and demerits of the explanation trotted out by the Tata Tea authorities. What is relevant in the present discussion on the MAFIASATION of the polity is the gravity of the overall situation prevailing in different parts of the country.

Problems do vary. So do responses. But in all these aberrations of the system and its working, it is same old story of non-governance and the absence of political will to tackle the pressing problems existing at different levels. The question here is not of apportioning blame. We jolly well know what is what and who is to blame for the drift. A major share of the blame, of course, must lie with the political parties and their leaders who have ruled this country over a long period and have made a mess of everything in order to play their petty power games and mint money in the spoils system. In this gloomy scenario the "new rajas" and "leaders" have come to bank upon trigger-happy Mafia groups.

Take, for example, the Mafia raj in Mumbai. Facts are very simple. The dreaded underworld there makes its own laws and executes them to carve out as well as enlarge it sphere of influence. Ironically, underworld operators happen to be well entrenched in some of the powerful sections of Mumbai society, Most Mafia leaders are in league with the police. They act as collaborators of small time politicians of different shades who, in due course emerge as big names.

The underworld of smuggling, liquor trafficking, drug peddling. Call girl rackets, gambling and gun running is thriving in collusion with criminal politicians and police, and big money is involved. With the mushrooming of criminal gangs, the support they receive from politicians, and the easy availability of firearms. India has entered an extremely dangerous phase since late 1960s.

Nations emerging from foreign rule have all been marked by the rise of gangsters; even in established democratic governments, underworld activities manifest themselves in several ways and in varying degrees but they are checked and effectively controlled by the government. Para doxically, the developing nations are weakest in their law and order resource and little is done to curb the antisocial activities of the gangsters that threaten to make a clean administration impossible.

During the early years of Independence gangsters were kept subdued because those were the days when a galaxy of national leaders, both at centre and in States as well as in the opposition, steeped in normal values and personal integrity governed country. Those were the days when a person with a criminal background never dared to seek elections on any party tickets. All was well.

We have slide downwards from the "Age of Heroes" to the "Age of Pygmites. the downhill drift of politics and politicians was swift with disastrous consequences. Today, politicians accused each other of hiring gangsters to kill their rivals, attack polling booths and loot polling boxes during elections. Gangsters have emerged extremely powerful. They are fighting elections. providing finance to political parties, becoming MPs, MLAs and ministers. They wield more power than the Government itself.

Gone are the days when the gangsters were a pawn in the hands of politicians. The position is practically reversed today. It is the gangsters who are using politicians and political parties as instruments for their personal advancement. It is no longer the dog that wags the tail but the tail that is wagging the dog.

The stranglehold of the Mafia hierarchy over the politicians has been so menacing that despite a democracy formally in existence, for more than four decades the rulers have surrendered their powers to gangsters, who have formed a ring around them for the success and stability of their rule. Any country where elections are fought with the support of gangsters and guns, instead of the ballot, can hardly describe itself as a functioning democracy.

What is more worrying is the fact that the growing nexus between politicians, the underworld and the police has made nonsense of the machinery to keep the peace. As it is, part of the police force seems to have become an extension of the underworld. Informers find that information given to the police get back to the criminal within minutes. Complaints against gangsters are not registered by the police and complaints, who ventured to report, are threatened by the police and asked to seek redress elsewhere. The law makers and law breakers are perceived to be inextricably linked up with the underworld, impairing the safety and security of law abiding citizens. the classic example is the massacre of thousands of innocent law abiding Sikh men, women and children during the anti-Sikh riots in the country's capital on 31 October and 1st and 2nd November 1984 following Prime Minister, Indira Gandhi's assassination. Politics is now brutalised in the Hindi speaking and Eastern States where gangsters have emerged every powerful as the result of political struggles. over the years. Here, criminal activities do not affect the respectability and social standing of politicians. Every political party in the region maintains a cadre of antisocial and gangsters. A few cases of nexus between politicians and gangsters, including notorious absconding dacoits are given here. there cases can be multiplied.

A minister from Bhagalpur, Bihar, harboured notorious dacoit Sudama Mandal, wanted in a number of cases of dacoity, some of them with murder, and on whose arrest a reward had been declared. The Indian Nation. a Patna based English newspaper dated 9 December 1980 demanded the arrest of the minister.

Notorious dacoit Kamdeo Singh was killed in a police-encounter in early 1980 in Bihar. Ministers of Bihar not only went to the gangsters house to offer their condolence to the bereaved family but transferred all police officials involved in the gangster's killing.

A Bihar Congress (I) MP was arrested from brothel in Calcutta a few years ago, but nobody took any notice of the incident. His standing did not suffer when he was accused of leading a criminal gang to attack the striking teachers of the Ram Lakhan Singh Yadav College near Patna. Another Congress (I) Rajya Sabha MP patronised the Jehanabad (Bihar) criminal gang. Both of them had been revered figures in Bihar's corridors of power and wielded enormous influence in the State Government.

A few years ago, two MLAs from Jehanabad district, Bihar, namely Ram Jatan Singh and Sardar Krishna were involved in a court case in Patna. The order passed by the Patna High Court is a revealing reflection on the State of affairs in Bihar. the Judge said: "The case presents a true picture of politicians today - a picture of post-election gang warfare. On group was led by the petitioner Ram Jatan and the other led by Sardar Krishna. both members of Bihar Legislative Assembly. The two group fired at each other. The Central Reserve Police Force (CRPF) intervened and the result was that one CRPF soldiers and four other were killed. Indian democratic pattern of society stands in great danger from persons like the petitioner...." But scathing observations have had little impact on the political system.

A case that created a sensation in the Bihar Assembly in 1988 was a letter allegedly written by Mritunjoy Prasad. deputy superintendent of police. Naogachia sub-division in Bhagalpur district to Dineshwari Gohri, a notorious dacoit asking the latter to send Rs. 7,000 with the bearer of the letter. In the same letter, the deputy superintendent of police advised Gohri to lie low for some time as his exploits turned out to be a cause for much embarrassment to the police as well as to (minister). The deputy superintendent of police was suspended by the Chief Minister, Bhagwat Jha Azad, but it proved beyond doubt the politician - criminal and police nexus.

Various distortions that have been taken place in the working of the polity over the past two decades have however, added an altogether new dimension to the whole problem, and created a situation which now threatens the very existence of the Indian Union and its democrat polity. Over the past two decades. a close nexus has developed between contractors. leaders of Mafiosi and criminal gangs and many persons with criminal antecedents. including prominent politicians, and a stage has now been reached when the leaders of Mafiosi and criminal gangs are entering the ponals of State legislatures, and even the National Parliament as members. The close link up between prominent politicians has made it virtually impossible in many states to maintain satisfactory law and order, as there is often interference by influential politicians, some of them holding cabinet ranks, with the normal functioning of the law and order machinery. As might be expected, there has also been growth of rampant political and administrative corruption. Visibly, there is no short cut to the task of weeding out corruption from the public life. In the permissive atmosphere power is chased to promote and protect personal and family interests. The general tendency everywhere is to get rich overnight by hook or crook.[34] Thus, corruption is no longer the preserve of public servants, contractors, politicians but it has permeated every section of the society. Indian bare existence as a respectable free nation is in jeopardy. the remedy is not easy to find.

Every political party which ruled Bihar ever since late 1960's maintained close rapport with Suraj Deo Singh the Dhanbad coal field gangster. Ministers of Bihar a called on him and accepted his invitation at his house breakfast. He was arrested along with five others in 1988 as part of clean up operation, since more than a dozen of criminal cases including murder. rioting. extortion and attempted murder were pending against him. He obtained his release, on bail from Court. The Deputy Commissioner (District Magistrate) and superintendent of police were transferred since the was instrumental for his arrest.

His influence was so great that though he was owner of several trucks/lorries, he paid no road tax; nor did he pay entertainment tax for the cinema houses run by him. There was no limit to the firearms, both licensed and unlicensed that and his gang possessed. He dictated transfers and postings of law enforcement officials in Dhanbad. The station House officers and the police station staff paid obeisance to him every day.

The lynching of Gopalganj district magistrate G.Krishnaiah by a

---

34 Panchod Prasad, in "Politics of Corruption: The Goddness that Failed', (1995) P.184, by Shashi B. Sahai.

mob led by Bihar People's party chief Anand Mohan and his wife Lively Anand symbolises the rot. Laloo Prasad Yadav. Chief Minister. Bihar encouraged criminals like Dular Chand Yadav to fight what he called the Brahmin dominated social order and was not ashamed to get himself photographed with Dularchand. Bihar had sent to Parliament a number of M.P.'s including Mohammed Taslimuddin, who adorned the Gowda's United Front Govt. as a minister so state in the home minister. He was involved in several cases of rape and kidnapping.

In Uttar Pradesh politicians have worked as informers to dacoit gangs of Chambal ravines and supplied arms to them in return for their help during elections. M.L.A.'s in Uttar Pradesh harboured dacoits wanted In police cases in the Darulshafa legislators multi-storied buildings in Lucknow. A senior police officer equipped: "If the police were allowed to raid legislators, rooms at Darulshafa it would definitely ferret out a couple of dacoits wanted by the police. Duralsafha has been a dacoit-den".

Chief Minister Ram Naresh Yadav, it was alleged, go thumping majority from a Nidhanli Kalan because dacoit Alwar's influence in the area. A fortnight later Alwar who too was a Yadav, was short dead by the police in an encounter. During the Janata rule, the industries ministers of the Lok Dal was charged with sharing his dies at a public meeting with a notorious dacoit, Vikram Mallah. A former Zamindar of Agra district and a minister during the Janata rule close to the ruling party was reported to be friendly with the dreaded dacoit Malkhan.

In the eleventh Lok Sabha elections Bandit queen Phoolan Devi, who had killed 22 persons, was elected as MP on Samajwadi Party ticket. At present Kanpur Court is trying 10 cases against her including one in which she is accused of shooting 17 Thakurs and three others. It has been issuing summons to her and asking the Uttar Pradesh and Madhya Pradesh Governments why she has not been produced in Court as yet. If she becomes an honourable minister, investigating agencies will have to take permission from the government before proceeding against her.

Phoolan Devi has others for Company. They include Ramakant Yadav of Azamgarh, M. Hussain of Kairana, Ram Singh Sakya of Etawah and Pratap Singh of Amroha of the Samajwadi Parti. Cases have been instituted against all of them. The Robin Hood of Western U.P.., D.P. Yadav is Bahujan Samaj Party MP from Sambhal, the constituency he preferred to his home town, Bulandshahr. Involved in several cases of kidnapping, loot and murder, he was minister in the U.P. government. He is entering Parliament for the first time. Yadav is the most well known former outlaw after Phoolan Devi.

Ganga Charan Rajput "God of Bundelkhand's oppressed" leads the BJP's collection of former outlaws in Parliament. The BJP had sent 13 MPs with criminal backgrounds. Rajput was elected from Hamirpur constituency. He was involved in sheltering a notorious dacoit, Dadhna. He also formed an organisation called Ekalavya Sena to protect the weaker sections. That Phoolan Devi was made its president proves that party affiliations have not come in the way of brotherhood among ex-outlaws. U.P. sent 28 MPs from different parties, with criminal records to Parliament in 1996. Major criminal cases are pending against 52 MLAs, some of whom are ministers.

In Madhya Pradesh, police officials still recall that home minister Narsingrao Dixit used to entertain dacoit gang leaders in his house while the other senior officers of the government waited outside to meet the Minister. It was reported that when the minister was camping in Gwalior circuit house, the dreaded dacoit Mohar Singh had free access to his bedroom.

Prim Minister Indira Gandhi's 20-Point Programme Implementation Committee at the state district and block levels formed for overseeing the official execution and charting out new plans, had been packed with murderers, rapists, smugglers and underworld dons. Office bearers of the Committee at the State level had been given the status of a minister and impressive perks and privileges that go with it including police guards for their security. Every Chief Minister after assumption of office blamed his predecessor for packing the Committees with gangsters and criminals. It is interesting to note that a feudal overlord, aged 39 years of Chhatarpur district and dubbed as the terror of Bundelkhand, who happened to be member of the State Committee was reported to have used pythons to terrorise women to submit to his will. There are other stories about him. As many 32 criminal cases were pending against him.

Chief Minister Vora, announced on 11 March 1987: "Police screening is a must for committee membership. We shall not allow criminal elements to become members". The same story was repeated by Arjun Singh when he succeeded Vora. Vora had dropped 1300 members after screening. When Arjun Singh returned to power he brought in 1,200 new members increasing the committee's strength to 3000. Again when Vora succeeded Arjun Singh he dropped the pro-Arjun Singh elements. These members misused their powers by allotment of plots of land meant for landless poor, to their family members as well as to the family members of MPs and MLAs. For the 20,000 ruling party members, accommodated at the State, district and block levels, the help has been in the shape of sharing the spoils of power.

In Porbandar, Gujarat, the birth place of mahatma Gandhi, ten hard-core criminals had been released to enable them to contest the municipal elections there the 108 candidates in the fray were known to have criminal antecedents. The police records disclosed that some of the councillors had been charged for murder.

Over 42 criminals convicted and sentenced for long terms in cases of murder, dacoity and looting had jumped parole in Gujarat. The lot included dreaded criminals such as Babu Satyam Bhaiya (35). a gangster who had been convicted in a triple murder case along with his accomplices Dilip Shankar Rao Maratha (32) and Mahendra Singh Rathod (27).

A known extortionist and smuggler who also ran gambling houses. Bhaiya, was accused in a murder case but was acquitted in late 1970s. Bhaiya's political influence grew when he gunned down three of his rivals in broad day light in Ahmedabad in 1982. He and six of his associates were sentenced to life imprisonment by the Gujarat High Court.

While in Vadodara jail, Bhaiya moved a parole application in July 1988 on the ground of his wife's illness. His case was recommended by Surendra Rajput, MLA and the Government cleared a five - day parole. Thereafter, he got his parole extended for times and upto one hundred days at a stretch. His case for parole was recommended twice by the MLA Rajput and once each by the State Minister for Roads and Buildings and two other MLAs.

In 1990 Congress (I) leader Chimanbhai Patel patronised criminals in order to remain in power Ashik Bhogilal Patel, former Congress (I) treasurer was gunned down a day before he planned to topple Chimanbhi Patel ministry.

In Tamil Nadu, political parties which harbour criminals in the name of cadre building often used them to settle scores. Vicious attacks on the critics of the ruling AIADMK including lawyer K.M. Vijayan and former IAS Mrs. V. Chandralekha are cases where gangsters had been used by the ruling party.

During the height of the naxalite movement in West Bengal the Congress(I) ministry and the left dominated ruling political party had been charged by the APRD, a human right group, with committing hundreds, if not thousands of political murders. The Bowbazar blasts in March 1993 exposed the links between Satta don Rashid Khan and the ruling Left Front government. It must be said to the credit of Chief Minister Jyoti Basu, who had been ruling. West Bengal for over 18 years. That he has kept the administration free from criminal-political links.

The Emergency marked a watershed in Delhi politics and that was when Sanjay Gandhi initiated the patronage of the Mafia hierarchy to punish Indira Gandhi's adversaries. The system flourished after Sanjay Gandhi's death. The anti-Sikh riots in the country's capital in October and November 1984 in the wake of Indira Gandhi's assassination established clearly the close rapport between the underworld and ruling Congress (I) party.

The nexus between the underworld the ruling political parties in Bombay India's most flourishing commercial and industrial capital, has a long history Indian economic system prohibited import of goods the people craved for and this led to large scale smuggling of gold, silver, liquor, electronics and other consumer goods in demand, ever since late 1960s. The number of smugglers increased but no organised criminal gangs existed in Bombay as we find today. With the rapid growth of smuggling, corruption increased in leaps and bounds and encompassed not only politicians but also touched the police, customs and even the judiciary at the lower level.

In the sixties, the gang leaders were kept under control by politicians such as Bombay's erstwhile strongman S.K. Patil. They guided the activities of small groups paying small donations to police. But they were kept within the rules of decency and decorum and there was no serious confrontation with the public or the police.

A perceptible change came about late 1960s. Politicians had now learnt that to attain power they required money and muscle. They also learnt that they could use the licensing system to acquire money and they could take the help of bureaucrats, many of whom were willing to co-operate. They also found that they could get money and muscle from the underworld. Here they required to rope in the police. Since the police were answerable to politicians and bureaucrats, they could be easily subverted. There was no dearth of policemen at the highest levels who were willing to join hands with the corrupt politicians for a life of ease. The latitude given to the underworld by the nexus that had evolved between politicians, criminal and police helped them to expand their empires. It spread corruption in the bureaucracy and the police and polluted the entire body politic. The police shut their eyes by receiving greater weekly donations which were collected at lower levels with a distributing system functioning within the police hierarchy.

In course of years, with the blessings of politicians criminal gangs led by Mafia leaders such as Haji Mastan, Yusuf Patel, Varadarajan Mudaliar, Karim Lala, Alamzeb, Arun Gawali, Babu Reham, Dawood

Ibrahim, Shabir Ibrahim, to name a few, came into prominence. Their activities were concentrated in thickly populated localities. They resorted to looting of matka and liquor dens and resorted to stabbing and killings in the streets. The control of the streets passed on from the police to the gangsters of the underworld and they ruled the streets with impunity. Quarrels broke out between different competing gangs over the area of operations and, as a result, gang wars became a common feature. Powerful gangs could enlist the support from the politicians and police by paying protection money. Gradually, the gangs extended their activities to other areas such as business transactions as the usual civil Court proceedings were lengthy and time consuming.

Hari Jai Singh[35] speaking in an article, "MAFIASATION of Polity: Some disquieting signals", writes: Haji Mastan, who was a known smuggler having links in Dubai and other places. Of course, he used to donate a certain percentage of his income to a religious cause. However, with his money power, he got into the film industry, spread his tentacles in the media and political circles and, as a final act, he launched his own party. Haji Mastan is no more. I am giving this only as an example to show that how the Haji Mastans and mini Mumbais continue to multiply and thrive in our system of sleaze and spoils, bereft of values and ides, thanks to the patronage extended to them by the so-called respectable and honourable members of society.

Unfortunately, even in the state of Haryana, we find disturbing signs of his MAFIASATION. We know it for certain that there is liquor-smuggling on a large scale in the state But under whose patronage ? Liquor smuggling cannot be organised by the new class of "lumped" elements without the connivance of police and petty political bosses. In fact, small time operators, village-level small and inconsequential politicians have all joined hands under some politico-police patronage to make money. The have acquired systems the latest communication and weapons to keep themselves in the business of liquor smuggling.

---

35 Hari Jai Singh, "Mafiasation of Polity: Some disquieting signals", The Tribune, September 27, 1997.

What is disturbing in the process is hat the basic fabric of Haryana society is getting destroyed. It is creating new imbalances in money and power sharing right at the village levels, which is bound to lead to serious consequences for Haryana tomorrow. Still, there is no realisation of this new form of mafiaisation taking place right at the grassroots level in the State.

I am not saying this with a view to decrying prohibition as a state policy. My concern is about the shocking fallout of the whole exercise as a weapon of arrogance or of power. It has to be seen objectively and in practical terms> And I have reasons to feel concerned about a new form of mafiaisation taking place in Haryana. People know about it. So do those who are supposed to enforce the law. Still, we continue to turn a blind eye to the realities because vested interest have stakes in enlarging their sphere of influence by amassing wealth!

Who gains in such a state of affairs ? A handful of small time operators, petty politicians, policemen and corrupt bureaucrats. The sufferers are the people who want to see the process of development and progress so that they have more comfort in their life Perhaps, we think that the people have a short memory the can be fooled for sometime but not all the time Democracy, of course, does not provide short-term answers to serious aberrations around us.

Meanwhile, MAFIASATION sets in tits own momentum. And we see drift practically in every part of the country. The system is destroyed as the MAFIASATION process gains strength. The values get eroded. Society is debased. Are we to accept a situation like this? Are we to allow frauds to be perpetrated on the people in every nook and corner of the country so that crooks, criminals and their collaborators thrive and flourish in the name of democracy.

India is not for crooks and criminals. As citizens commented to the well-being of the nation. We ought to challenge this Mafia raj. Mere bloated rhetoric and self servers can lead us nowhere. We must be able to resist the raw vitality and blandishments of the old and new gondas hovering around the corridors of power.

The gangsters feared law till Justice Krishna Iyer's historic judgement laid down the judicial principle of "Bail and not Jail". The judgement set a new trend in judicial dispensation. Not only were those accused of crimes like murders, robberies, rapes and dacoities granted bail but even some convicts who had appealed against their sentences were set free. This emboldened them to commit more crimes since all the sentences would be served simultaneously.

A thief commits crime for his survival. If he is apprehended he is beaten up by the people of neighborhood and even by the police to extort confession. But a member of an organized gang can strut through the streets of his locality, inspiring awe, and even respect. The gangster is protected by an invisible skein of patronage that includes politicians, police and sometimes even by Courts.

Gang activities and gang wars will continue to plague the city of Bombay till the nexus between politicians, gangsters and police is broken. And that can only be done after (I) electoral reforms are introduced to obviate the need of money and muscle to win elections and (ii) the police are made accountable only to the law and not to the politicians.

In Andhra Pradesh, the link-up between home minister K. Prabhakar Reddy (Congress government) and the gangster Kotha Das reportedly led to a conflict between the home minister and the Hyderabad City Police Commissioner P.V. Pavithran. Kotha Das's gang was arrested by the police in April 30, 1981 and immediately after the arrest of the gang the Police Commissioner was asked to proceed on leave. In the statement duly signed by him and counter-signed by five police officers Kotha Das said: "My gang politically supports Prabhakar Reddy, the present home minister, irrespective of his political affiliation....."

Today, in several States political rivals are falsely implicated as dacoits and shot in police encounters along with genuine dacoits. In such cases it become extremely difficult to pinpoint the limits where political rivalry or caste conflict ends and plain dacoity begins. The police are in a complete mess due to politicisation. The situation is already pretty drippy and one does not have to very sensitive to feel the sensation of damp seeping through as one looks at what is happening to our political system. When the day of reckoning comes, illusions, old or new, will offer no protection.

A political offered an explanation for the phenomenal rise of Mafia in politics. He said that he criminals first hired by political leaders to capture booths. Gradually, these men grew in importance and began to feel that they could achieve greater power and position themselves. Thus many of them fought and got elected either on the ticket of a political party or as an independent candidate. In the latter case they joined whichever party was in power. Such incidents were unheard of till the end of 1960s because the leadership of the country was based on ethical norms and elimination of persons of doubtful integrity from political parties.

In a monumental work on criminsalisation of politics with reference to Bihar the most criminalised state in the country, Vikas Kumar Jha[36], a daring journalist, writes: "Viewed as a whole, Indian politics went on being criminalized by the continuous decline of democratic-constitutional, values in India. The abominable prescriptions of power-greedy, power drunk politicians resting upon casteism, communalism and regionalism for keeping power, destabilised the society. In this way, socio-political instability finally enhanced the status of criminal elements from society to power....Today every one is worried over the question how to push out criminal elements from politics. Who will have to take the initiative for this? The common people or top politicians? But it is the view of competent political thinkers that unless we eliminate criminal elements from politics no improvement could be made. People's power is the ultimate arbiter. If the society and common people of society decide from then history sheeters to be and criminal dons will naturally remain confined between jail and court dock: they will not adorn the Parliament and Vidhan Sabha."

---

36 Vikas Kumar Jha, "Rajmit Ka Apradhikaran (Criminalisation of Politics) 1992.

Reflecting over unprecedented violence during State Assembly elections in Bihar early in 1990, Indrajeet Singh[37], a senior reporter of 'Nav Bharat Times', Patna edition, wrote: "A candidate went to a village to ask for votes. One villager said: what for should I give my vote to you? During the last election it was pointed out that there was no proper arrangement for cremation in the village. You promised to get a cremation place made on winning election. Five years have passed since that promise and no cremation place has been made in the village. Hearing this, the candidate said, "Please give me one more chance. This time I will get a cremation place made in every house". The reporter goes on to add: "The famous Jain saint, Acharya Tulsi had made a mention about this event in one of his sermons. He has to say, such persons are at least getting cremation grounds prepared for democracy. If democracy is to be saved, it has to be prevented from passing into the hands of such persons".

Infiltration of persons with criminal records into politics had a modest beginning. As politics increasingly became agenda less, winning elections itself became the sole agenda. Politicians started soliciting the help of known outlaws with muscle and arms. In the process, a person with criminal antecedents and potentialities came to be regarded as a valuable resource by election managers and criminality an important input for electoral success. As the story goes, when a politician (who rose to be a Minister) was being garlanded by his supporters on being elected to the State Assembly in 1980, he asked them to garland a notorious outlaw instead, to whom he owned his election.

For the criminal elements, it was but a short step to win elections themselves. And they seized the opportunity with both hands. With the cult of booth capturing growing fast, they could win elections on their own with muscle power. And political parties were not wanting either in obliging them with party nominations. In the Bihar Assembly election of 1977, the Mafia King of Bihar coal fields, involved in

---

37 Indrajeet Singh, "Chunavi Hinsa Se Milne Wale Sabak" (Lessons from electroal violence) Nav Bharat Times, 4 March, 1990.

around a dozen and a half serious crimes including murder, attempt to murder, rioting etc., was nominated by the Janta Party

Rulers have not allowed the police to discharge their law enforcement duty within the rule of law. Politicians have jam-packed the police force by infiltration of party cadres, violating all rules of recruitment and turning it into a completely unless instrument for impartial enforcement of law. Today, two-third of station house officers in charge of police stations are political appointees. Anti-social have made inroads into the police forces and their loyalty is more towards the political party who helped in their recruitment rather than to the police hierarchy.

Discipline is the key to police efficiency. Exemplary discipline, strict regimentation and implicit obedience and loyalty are indispensable in a police force. Forerunners of indiscipline are insubordination, disloyalty and involvement in politics. When discipline goes out of a police force, it is not the first to go, nor the second or third to go, it waits for all the rest to go; it is the last.

Many policemen, even in the higher ranks are known to have close association with terrorist groups. Escapes of terrorist prisoners from police custody are frequently reported. Most of the terrorist prone States have to depend more and more on security forces.

Mafia gangs entered trade unionism in the late 1960s when they were used to break up strikes in Bombay. With the growth in trade union rivalry in the industrial areas, the number of gangsters required for such operations increased. Gangsters are used to collect subscription from workers, and union leaders, mostly involved in money lending business at high rates of interest, retain gangsters to threaten and beat up workers who defaulted in the repayment of loan or in the payment of interest. For example, in the Bihar's coal belt, Dhnabad, the unions with help of gangsters control lives, property and women of the workers, turning them virtually bonded labour.

Managements are not sitting idle. They have also hired musclemen to ideal with militant unions. Allegations and counter-allegations about use of gangsters by unions. Allegations and counter-allegations about use of gangsters by unions and managements have surfaced in recent years. Tea garden managers have been killed. Jute mill owners stabbed. Police resorted to firing at several places to prevent violent activities of striking workers.

Business rivalry has often led to the hiring of gangsters for the extermination of rivals. This phenomenon is mostly prevalent in Bombay. The fee could be as high as Rs.One Lakh to Rs. Fifty lakhs. There are two alleys - Pakmodia street and Tumkar street opposite the J.J. Hospital junction in Bombay's Street where one could hire killers and establish contact with the underworld.

During the last few years quite a few criminals belonging to rival gangs, police informers, and important witnesses, both in criminal and civil cases, have been killed by professional hit-men inside court premises. Only a few years ago the dead body of a customs officer was found in central Bombay with marks of injury. It was suspected that head been killed by gangsters employed by smugglers involved in the shipping of brown sugar to Mauritius.

Real estate is an area where the use of criminal gangs is widely prevalent in some of our metropolis; it is a flourishing business in Bombay, Calcutta, Ahemdabad and Delhi. Landlords employ gangsters to evict tenants because of the failure of our legal system. For example, if the owner of a flat wanted to evict his tenant and the latter refused to move, all one can do is to file a case against the tenant. But the law is so heavily titled in favour of the tenant that the landlord is likely to lose the case. And even if the landlord is fortunate enough to win by appealing to higher court against the decision of the lower court, the tenant can tie the case up in the courts for years. If, however, the landlord instead of taking the matter to the court, approaches a gangster he would be able to recover the flat by paying the latter heavy compensation.

Sometimes gangsters would offer to buy flats at half or even a third of its market value. As this low price still represented a net gain from an otherwise dead asset it is an attractive offer. Once the gangster owns the flat he would use strong arm tactics to evict the tenant and sell the flat at its true market value.

Or, take the case of a person wanting to acquire a property from a builder. As is usual in such cases, the builder will take 40 percent or even more of the price in black. Then, he might as well refuse to transfer the property to the purchaser. If one goes to the court, it could take nearly a decade for the case to be decided in his favour. And, even then the builder would return the "white" component of the purchase price. No documents would exist to prove that the purchaser even paid him the black component in cash. The alternative is to go to the underworld route. The gangster, on the other hand would approach the builder, threaten him and get the money back. For this service, he would take 10 to 20 percent of the money recovered. In the circumstances, more and more citizens are depending on the underworld, rather than courts.

The changing pattern of society is changing the nature of underworld activity. As the demand for real estate grew the activities of the underworld extended to this area. Builders of multi-storeyed flats often took the help of the underworld to get the slum area, on which multi-storeyed fats are to be constructed, vacated. For builders interaction with the underworld became a necessity to prevent obstruction and stoppage of work by local people.

The number of transactions with a high black money content is increasing. When one party on such a transaction refuses to keep his commitment, then obviously, the aggrieved party can hardly go to the police or court. Leading gangsters of Bombay's underworld such as Hazi Mastan Mirza, Karim Lala Pathan. Yusuf Patel, Vardarajan, to name a few had done remarkably well in land and house property deals. Their interventions in property matters are legendary.

Rare though, is the man who complains to the police. Most know that to go to court in Bombay, could mean instant death. And indeed, the end result of all this "parallel justice" has been the frequent use of the underworld in property disputes. Many leading lawyers of Bombay are reported to have referred their clients to the gangsters.

Gangsters are involved in the collection of (Protection money) from shopkeepers, bootleggers, jewellers and diamond merchants, businessmen, cinema houses, hotels, restaurant, taxi drivers, persons dealing with back money. The minimum protection money could be Rs.2000 to Rs.3000 per month. Non-payment could result in assault, kidnapping and even murder. In tea gardens in Assam, collection of hafts is widely prevalent. Owners and managers of tea gardens are kidnapped and murdered if they failed to pay protection money. In some placed the collection is shared by the police.

The hawala business of informal money lending, mainly for stock market operations is so large that many consider its operations comparable to that of the Reserve Bank of India. In this parallel banking system interest rats charged are as high as 30 to 35 percent per annum and the business is conducted on faith. Since there is never a shred of evidence to prove that the hawala money has changed hands debtors often deny having taken it. In Bombay, specialised gangs deal with elusive debtors and the demand for such services is so high that a creditor often has to wait for months before a going could be available to take up the job.

There is a parallel flourishing banking system of notes and promissory notes that conduct its business entirely in black. The problem with all black money transactions is that by definition they have to be conducted in secrecy. For example, a businessman carrying lakhs of rupees to a place cannot complain to the police if he is waylaid and his cash snatched. All these people end up turning to the underworld. And so, a gangster escorts a businessman. And the one who has the hope of even seeing his money again will turn over his notes or promissory notes to a gangster for 25 to 50 percent of its face value and leave it to the gangster to retrieve the money with interest from the borrowers.

Trading in sex and girl running is very profitable business in which the gangsters play an important part. Flesh trade has been flourishing in India in various places and in different forms - whatever it is in the red-light areas of our metropolis; in the fringes of our industrial belt; in the dark alleys of cities: in the growing multi-storeyed apartments; in the government offices; in the industrial houses: in the hotels and bars: in the garb of sales girls, call girls, dancing and singing girls and prostitutes in temples: in the film world; and in the university campuses.

Flesh trade and girl running require active participation of gangsters and Mafia network is discernible in all such activities. Ordinarily, kidnappers of women and girls are females. These female kidnappers are often escorted by respectable looking gangsters so that they cannot be checked or interrogated by police en route.

Flourishing Mafia network operates at checkpoints in the international border through which trafficking of women and girls takes place, day and night, every day, all the year round in league with the police and security forces.

All brothels function under the protection of gangsters in exchange with free sex. Prostitutes are protected from molestation by customers. Women and girls who operate as call girls in hotels and multi-storeyed apartments have underworld connections. They seldom operate openly and always without the knowledge of their parents or husbands, they are easily lured into the call girl racket by the gangsters.

A survey conducted by a team of social scientists and reported in Sunday dated 19-29 July, 1987 that about 200 housewives and college girls were involved in call girl racket in Goa. These women and girls were from respectable families, some residing in the heart of Panjim, Goa's capital, were on the list of those who frequented a posh hotel on the outskirts of Panjim. Further investigation disclosed their connections with underworld.

In another case, a massive police contingent headed by an Assistant Commissioner of Police and assisted by the Anti-Corruption Bureau raided the eight storeyed King's hotel in Bombay city on 4 July 1980 midnight and pulled 34 call girls out of the rooms. 15 call girls were arrested and the remaining. 19 minors were sent to a rescue home at Chembur. It was alleged that a former minister in the erstwhile PDF Government was active trying to protect the hotel proprietors and gangsters involved from the police drag-net. During the search of a hotel an album containing photographs of girls were found. The call girls operated under fake names to conceal their identity[12].

All sea ports in India and the residential areas where dock workers, labourers, etc., live are virtually under the control of criminal gangs who operated and thrive on smuggling, pilferage, gambling, money lending brothel keeping and prostitution. The gang leaders who are in control of the area are split into different zones of operation with itself-appointed godfathers. There is intense gang and political rivalry because gangs are divided on political lines. Old gangs are busted by the police and new gangs are formed.

For example, the entire 130 km waterfront of the Calcutta port, stretching from the Howrah bridge in the north to the sandheads in the south is a paradise for smuggling and well organised Mafia gangs over the decades. Smuggling is rampant, both inside and outside the vast estate of the Calcutta Port Trust. The smugglers indulge in illegal stocks and gambling in the brothels and gambling dens run by the criminal gangs extort money from customers.

Garden Reach, surrounded by Garden Reach Road, Paharpur Road and Taratolla Road, the colony of dock workers, labourers, machine workers with squalor, crimes, smugglers, poverty and prostitution, clashes among rival criminal gangs is always trouble prone. The sound of gunfire breaks the silence of the night. Next morning it would bc a common sight to see some persons lying either dead or grievously injured. The police only arrive to remove the dead body to the morgue or get the injured admitted in a hospital.

The area is prone to Hindu-Muslim communal riots due to the infiltration of Muslim nationals from Bangladesh. Thousands of them infiltrate into India through West Bengal check-post gates and many find shelter in the Garden Reach area for employment.
A former president of a unit of the Forward Block in Garden Reach,

was reportedly one of the biggest smugglers and happened to be a close associate of the former deputy speaker of West Bengal Legislative Assembly. It had been allege that a few years ago he had masterminded the murder of Vinod Mehta, Deputy Commissioner of Police (Port) whose untiring crusade against the criminal activities of criminal gangs, smugglers and corrupt local police and customs officials created many enemies. Smugglers and criminal gangs attempted to gain over Mehta to a blind lane in the Garden Reach area ad chopped him to death. Mehta was deserted by the local police at the time of his death.

With scores of ships and travellers coming to see ports, every day, laden with gold biscuits, narcotics, electronic goods, etc. there is an ever increasing demand for people who are ready to act as a carrier of the smuggled goods. The business community dealing with smuggled goods depend entirely on the underworld. Highest profits are in smuggled goods which required criminal connections.

Haji Mastan Mirza with his associates Karim Lala Pathan and Yusuf Patel ruled Bombay's underworld for óver two decades. Mastan started from rags and worked his way to power and riches. He concentrated most of his activities to gold smuggling from Dubai. Karim Lala Pathan, Mastan's close associate ran a drug running operation and latter established himself as a leader if a powerful gang.

Ulhasnagar, a growing township on the outskirts of Bombay, occupies a unique place where the laws of the land do not apply. The township is virtually under the control of gangsters who provide protection to gold and narcotics smugglers, illicit liquor business, land grabbing and video piracy. The township shot into national prominence when on 30th March, 1990 a 16 year old girl student, Pinku Patil, was burnt alive in the examination hall of a local school by her alleged lover with the active assistance of a local gang. In 1989 as many as 32 persons had been killed in this growing township, mostly with firearms. V. Narayanan, a local journalist work for the newspaper the Blitz, who had exposed the activities of the Mafia gang was gunned down.

Kasargod, on the north-easter most tip of Kerala, about 50 km south of Mangalore has always been a smuggler's paradise. Being a part of Malabar coast. Kasargod has trade links with Gulf countries. Earlier, the Arab dhows used to come to India for spices, but, they mostly carry gold from Dubai. Gold running was a big business in Kasargod. Kerala's best known smugglers are Abdul Rehman, K.S. Abdullah, Kallatra Abdul Haji, Soopy and many others.

The calm sea which flows parallel to the national highway in most places makes Kasargod coast ideal for smugglers Abdul Rehman, the Kingpin of smugglers gang is based in Dubai from where he operates through his relative K.M. Abdullah, based in Bombay. Rehman is said to possess a dozen of passports and visits India frequently.

In 1987 Rehman's gang was caught with gold worth Rs. 2 crore in Delhi and at Cangoli, near Mangalore in Karnataka, the police seized Rs. 10.5 crore in year 1988. Yet again in December Rs. 6 crore worth of silver was recovered from his gang members at Chidambaram in Tamil Nadu. Because of his political influence his name does not feature in police records.

Illicit liquor and narcotics is a very lucrative business and needs underworld support. The total turnover of bootleggers every year in Gujarat is reported to be over Rs. 1000 crore. 25 % or Rs. 250 crore goes to the politicians and police and excise officials. The illicit liquor and narcotics trade has been going on for decades. The underworld has such a command over the politicians of all varieties that they were instrumental in bringing about the downfall of Gahanshyam Oza ministry in early 1970s.

The "spirit scandal" in Tamil Nadu and Kerala led to the appointment of two commissions of inquiry, one by the Central Government and another by the Tamil Nadu Government. Rectified spirit is unauthorisedly transported from Tamil Nadu to Kerala to make country liquor and exorbitant rates, depriving government of lakhs of rupees. Examination of documents revealed that thousands of gallons of spirit had flowed into Kerala in the past on fictitious permits making some politicians rich overnight. In 1989 T.K. Ramakrishnan, Kerala's Excise minister was accused of stage managing a government liquor auctioning favour of a powerful gangster. The trade thrives on adulteration of liquor because the supply seldom meets the demand and the market is controlled by criminal gangs. Hundreds of persons are killed every year in various parts of the country after drinking adulterated liquor.

Varadarajan was controlling a sprawling liquor network, a fresh trade run by an eunuch and a chain of video parlours showing blue films in his area. He operated a large number of vehicles which transported liquor from the locations of illicit manufacturing centres to different parts in Bombay and acquired a number of assets which included a restaurant in Koliawada; a rubber plantation at Kalladikode in Palghat. His empire prospered with impunity as a result of support he received from politicians and law enforcement officials.

On 27th March, 1983 the Directorate of Revenue (DRI) raided different places where Vardarajan and his gang operated seized property involving rupees several crores and arrested him and members of his gang Varadarajan was exerted from Bombay and subsequently died in Madras in a cardiac attack. When his dead body was brought to Bombay in a chartered aircraft, mourners included some politicians and filmstars who had been financed by Varadarajan.

A survey of past communal riots and reports of commission inquiry revealed that it was the gangsters who spread rumour of various types, deliberately concocted to stir up trouble and fanned the flames of riots. They are the main shock troops of the riotous mobs and mainstay of riots, Through them, weapons of offence and defence are distributed, before, during and even after a riot to prepare them for the next riot.

The aftermath of the Hindu-Muslim riots raises several questions. Political leaders are accused of inciting the riots and pressurising the police for not arresting the gangsters involved. Even some who are arrested are released. Those few convicted are granted pardon and reprieve. Political interests are sought to be consolidated with the help of gangsters.

Indian universities, mushrooming after Independence, have been under the grip of the underworld. Gang warfare has assumed :apocalyptic proportions: in many of the universities. In many universities, hostels shelter criminal gangs all the year round and turned them into liquor and narcotics dens and arsenals. In almost every campus in Bihar and Uttar Pradesh molestation of women teachers and students in different forms is rampant. S.D. Singh Commission of Inquiry appointed in 1977 to investigate and report on sex abuses and activities of antisocials on Lucknow University campus, had warned of the existence of a Mafia gang who terrorised girls and enticed the latter into flesh trade.

Securing admission in universities at gun point has been a regular feature in some of the universities in Bihar and Uttar Pradesh Leaders of rival unions are murdered with firearms. Gangsters with political support are operating in the campus. Examiners and invigilators at examination centres are threatened, beaten up and even murdered.

A vice-chancellor in the Hindi speaking State maintained gangsters, with the knowledge of the government, to enforce discipline on the campus. Cases of assaults on Vice-chancellors and teacher within the campus are reported.

In August 1980, pitched battles were fought by political parties with the help of criminal gangs during the annual elections to the 50,000 member strong Delhi University Student Union (DUSU). Rival groups were attacked with lethal weapons, bombs, soda water bottles and bombs and known criminals of the city provided the necessary security to candidates supported by different political parties. Justice G.D. Khosla Inquiry Committee Report on the violent incidents during the student union elections during August-September 1980 disclosed the involvement of criminal gangs.

Criminal gangs operate at places of entertainment, such as, cinema houses, social functions, sports and athletic meets, fairs and festivals, places of public workshop and centres of tourist attraction.

Involvement of criminal gangs in the black marketing of tickets at places of entertainment is well known. They resort to molestation of women, snatching, pick pocketing, robbery and even kidnapping of abduction of women and children.

A peaceful crowd witnessing soccer and cricket matches often turned violent at the investigation of criminal gangs whose activities spread from the stadium to the streets. The presence of a well organised gang, on all such occasions, has been a serious development. What is becoming increasingly evident is that hooligans in soccer and cricket matches has precious little or nothing to do with the game. The ugly scenes of wanton violence and destruction of property are the work of antisocial who gather in large numbers and make the life of soccer or cricket fans a misery. Race courses have often been the scene of Mafia activities. It is well known that large scale betting takes place on all such occasions and Mafia gangs are very active.

On January 1, 1967 on the occasion of the second test match between West Indies and India at Eden Gardens, Calcutta, widespread violence took place and a number of antisocial had been arrested. The West Bengal Government set up a Commission of Inquiry headed by a Judge of High Court. It was found that the Mafia gang had been responsible for the violence and destruction of public property inside the stadium and private property in the street on their way back from the stadium.

A few years ago Aslem Kader, Bangalore-based jockey was found guilty of "stopping" a winning horse and banned from the race track for three years. On questioning he said that he had acted under pressure from a gangster who had threatened to fill him if his horse won.

A simple fact of everyday life in India today is that organized crime has become a regular feature in almost every walk of life. Whether it is sports like races or football and cricket, politics or any other form of social activity like music festivals or worships organized gangs are required to enforce some semblance of control and discipline. To take a simple example like travel. Large railways stations and inter city bus stands are favourite hunting grounds of organized gangs of touts who would take care of all your needs for a fee like booking tickets, reservations and even supplying you with liquid refreshments for the journey. Bona fide passengers have been known to have been active in court premises, near women's colleges, hospitals and their public places. Shoot-outs have taken place inside courts and inter-gang warfare has often come out in the streets. Such cases are too numerous to be cited but every major city would have a story or two recount in the last two years.

The big question is: where do the arms come from? Manufacture of illicit firearms is a cottage industry in Bihar, Uttar Pradesh, Punjab, Haryana and West Bengal. The gun manufacturing units are run by the gangsters under the patronage of powerful politicians to 1985 just before elections, the police in Bihar sealed a number of factories making guns and other firearms cladenstinely. But the police beat hasty retreat after they found that these units had the blessings of some MPs, MLAs and even ministers, some of them, allegedly, financed these units.

In Uttar Pradesh, the police seized over 10,000 illegal firearms and over 20,000 cartridges from raids on the hideouts of criminal gangs in 1985. In addition, 281 illegal gun manufacturing units were detected the same year. Gangsters are deeply involved in the gun running from across international borders are prized postings and are auctioned.

Anti-terrorist measures require a highly motivated, impartial, honest and loyal police force operating under an efficient leadership with complete unity of purpose from the highest level down to constables, who are the final agencies for implementation. The force down the line to the constables must be fully trained, adequately equipped with weapons superior to the militants with up-to-date communication facilities. There must not be any economy in manpower. In anticipated dangers of terrorism intelligence has to be ruthlessly objective in its analysis. Simultaneous tasks are evaluation of intelligence reports and executive action.

Most of the above mentioned factors are wanting. Our intelligence machinery is in a bad shape when we consider the assassinations of Indira Gandhi and Rajiv Gandhi. Look at the high efficiency of the French Secret Service which saved President De Gaulle from more than 18 assassination attempts between 1960 and 1965.

A machinery which has been rendered useless, except for carrying out illegal verbal orders, even for fighting routine crime could hardly meet a more serious threat posed by terrorists. An efficient and corruption free law enforcement has paled into insignificance and the law and order machinery has broken down so badly that terrorism could flourish at ease. Many politicians, bureaucrats and policemen have close links with the militants. Even senior civil servants, who supervise the working of the police under the Police Act are open to purchase. A classic example is Tamil Nadu where a Home Secretary was arrested for having links with underground LTTE. How could Ibrahim Dawood and Menon Brothers with their associated stockpile powerful explosives for months which killed hundreds of innocent persons in bomb blasts in Bombay have succeeded?

MAFIASATION is a world wide phenomenon and has manifested itself most prominently in the former Soviet Union. Whatever Russia's success may be in curbing violent crime, in our context it has fatal consequences for every segment of society. The Vora Committee report has confirmed the fact of criminalisation of both the political and administrative apparatus. Linkages between the underworld, politicians and the police are clearly evident in the Bombay blast cases of 1993. The Committee has gone to the extent to say that an almost parallel government has pushed the State apparatus into irrelevance.

Both it is not merely the political-criminal nexus that has deeply undermined the Indian state. Interest groups and lobbies have proliferated which in turn have their own connections with the underworld. It could be safely asserted that many crucial decisions that have been taken by bureaucrats and politicians are on a quid pro quo basis and not on merit.

EXTRA MATERIAL TO BE CONSIDERED FOR CORRUPTION BOOK

Optimists predict that the intensity of cross-border for insurgencies in India will decline, now that the Pakistan economy is sputtering. They forget that is only a fraction of this support comes from the regular budget. The bulk of the funding comes from the profits of the drug trade, which is a pan-Assam context is conservatively estimated at $ 75 billion, of which around $ 20 billion goes to Pakistan-based syndicates and around $ 40 billion annually to South East Asia-based syndicates with linkages to China. Around $ 5 billion is generated by India-based groups, many linked to the Chinese and Pakistan syndicates. Thanks to the drugs trade, many officers in the Pakistan army - as well as structures in China - have accumulated fortunes.

Their common interest in this profitable business is an important reason for the close fraternal ties that bind Beijing to Islamabad, apart from the common need to contain India. Think tanks in the West seems to surrender Kashmir to Pakistan, tensions between the two powers would subside. In fact, Kashmir is just an excuse for the Pakistan army and the ISI to keep alive the terrorism that acts as the internal rationale for the drugs trade. There is no way the ISI and the Army would easily surrender the milt cow that is the drugs trade.

Despite its ponderous intelligence networks, Washington seems to be blissfully unaware of the reach of the Chinese triads and their fundamentalist allies in Afghanistan and Pakistan. During the late 1930s and well into World War II, there was a similar 'ignorance' over the fate of people professing the Jewish faith in Nazi-controlled Europe. Hopefully, unlike in the case of the Jews when it woke up only after millions belonging to that faith had perished, the US will improve its intelligence-gathering in Shanghan, Hong Kong, Canton. Peshwar and Lahore and join with India in leading an anti-drugs was in Asia with the same vigour with which it is being waged in South America.

Indeed, the Asian variety has even worse implications for international security than the South American one, linked as it is to fundamentalist terrorism. New Delhi has been even more oblivious than Washington of about the effects of the drugs trade on regional security. Indeed, one of the more successful Indian multi-national corporations, the 'D' Company headed by that benefactor of the film industry Dawood Bhai Ibrahim, has become a media celebrity.

Laws against drug trafficking in India are much weaker than those in countries such as Singapore and Malaysia, and are hardly enforced. Unless the becoming industry is checked, terrorism will continue its rampage over most parts of the sub-continent.

Tackling Myammar and ignoring China while confronting the drugs trade, or lecturing Iran and ignoring Pakistan and Saudi Arabia while discussing the funding of terrorist discussing the funding of terrorist networks, is a little like swabbing the throat in a case of tuberculous. In the case of South Asia, the US has been part of the problem in the region, thanks to the unreal expectations generated within Pakistan of the American capacity to pressurise India. If not for this illusion, Islamabad may perhaps have accepted the current reality in Kashmir rather than huffing and puffing away in an attempt to blow, away the Indian security structures there. The terrorism spawned by the drugs business may cost its existence in a few years time. (Article from The Times of India dated October 7, 1997 by M.D. Nalapat)

CATCH THE CORRUPT!

There is a well-known story of a Maharaja who got fed up with the corrupt practices of his minister. As a punishment, he shifted him to the coastal town of his kingdom and directed him to count the waves. Undeterred, he started stopping shops and boats passing by on the plea that their movements were interfering with the job assigned to him by the king. Knowing his reputation, the boatmen got the hint and started greasing his palm. Very soon, he amassed a fortune from the job the Maharaja thought to be corruption-free. But hold and behold, he proved the king wrong! The moral of the story is simple: the corrupt finds his devious ways and means for his black deeds. The Himachal Government's latest "catch the corrupt: scheme, however, does not suggest any punishment posting of counting waves or trees for shady civil servants. Instead, it has evolved a novel way of identifying the corrupt. There is, of course, a James Bond touch about the Himachal Pradesh Cabinet's proposal. It promises a reward of Rs. 1 lakh to the person who provides "information" about unaccounted wealth possessed by government servants and corruption in offices. The Income-tax Department has a similar scheme in operation, which is apparently based on the theory of "you spy on the neighbour". One wonders whether operation "catch the corrupt" will work at the government level. We all know that the system in this country indulges in shadow-boxing rather than work on a concrete action plan. Perhaps, Chief Minister Virbhadra Singh would soon discover to his horror that tackling corruption is not a child's play. Nor can this task be entrusted to the neighbor's prying eye. It is a serious business which has to be handled carefully and in a transparently determined manner. We know that corruption, like water, flows from top to bottom. So the starting point of handling corruption has to be the government itself, beginning with ministers. Otherwise, it will be yet another "drama" of a wild goose chase which is bound to have an element of witch-hunting. This is simply because corruption in the Indian stings is seen through political angles. Every political party sees corruption at the other wide of the fence without caring to see things under its very nose. Well, this is how the politics of corruption goes on in his country. (Article from The Tribune, October 8, 1997, page 10)

The extent to which corruption may flourish in a particular country, depends largely on the attitude of the public, which in the case of India is one of apathy. In fact public apathy is the unconscious sanction to Governmental corruption. This is, to some extent, due to ignorance, but the prime reason is historical. Since times immemorial, the people of India have been crushed by invaders and in between invasions, they have fared no better under the local rulers and Maharajas. Rulers, whether foreign or indigenous, have, with some exceptions, been unconcerned with the behaviour of their officials towards the general public as long as the demands of the State Exchequer were met.

Corruption in public administration is something not peculiar to India. It exists in all the countries, and India is by no means the worst in this respect. Corruption needs only two prerequisites - first, there must be a predisposition on the part of an individual to accept gratification, and second, he must have some discretionary power to affect some sections of the public. When both these factors combine, corruption most prevail. No wonder that the Independent India is a fertile ground for corruption.

The old British system was primarily designed for the maintenance of law and order and the collection of revenue. Now in the Independent India, in addition to its above function, it is oriented to the needs of a developing economy. As a result, the senior officers are heavily burdened with additional work and, therefore, the degree of supervision over their subordinates has decreased. On the other hand, with the expansion of Government functions, the opportunities for corruption have increased. In the districts the basic structure of administration - the revenue administration - has remained unchanged in almost all the States. The Patwari, who is entrusted with the land records of his circle and can play havoc with the titles and possession of land of the agriculturists, who form nine-tenths of the rural population, wield sufficient power to extract gratitifications from his clients. Over the years, the Patwari's power has increased because of the relaxation of the direct supervision. Even if discrepancies are detected in his records, he generally gets off lightly because of the protection afforded by the service rules.

In the good old days, corruption was confined only to officialdom. But since the dawn of Independence, the non-officials, who have been associated with the administration, have also joined the trade in a big way. The reason for this is not far to seek. In the more advanced democratic counties, most of the non-officials, who join the administration, for their elective terms, are men of integrity, who already have some standing in business or one of the professions.

In India, the public men are the people, who are politicians by profession. There are some notable exemptions, no doubt, but the rank and file of politicians consist of gentlemen who have no other ostensible means of livelihood. In India, the only criterion for an average politician is that he should have a loud voice and should be able to speak a lot of nonsense on any subject for any length of time. As this "profession" has vast potentialities in a newly independent country, it has attracted a horde of self-seekers.

The introduction of Panchayati Raj has increased the opportunities for amassing of wealth in a short space of time. The programme, though well intended has not worked the way in which its sponsors had contemplated. Complaints are rife that subsidies and loans are given by the Panchayaati Raj Institutions to people as political favours rather than on the basis of actual needs. Very often, no security for the loans is insisted upon, with the result that recovery becomes impossible. The cost of local projects is over-estimated in order to secure a large Government contribution which is normally 50% of the estimated cost. In most cases, the Anti-corruption Departments in the States are the hot beds of corruption. Wherever, the Departments are free from corruption, they are not free from political interference which means an indirect encouragement and protection to the corrupt. These departments specialize in catching the small fish to keep up the facade of departmental efficiency, but conveniently drop the big catches which prove too hot to handle, or are just allowed to slip through the net. The political executive keeps the reports of the Anti-corruption Department officials in cold storage till the time to blackmail them carrying out its whims under threat of exposure.

The Vigilance Commissions, which are in a better position to function freely, merely pass on their findings to the State Governments for suitable action which they seldom take. The result is that majority of cases come to a dead end. Since Independence, the political executive has systematically taken over the power of the officials and reduced them to mere scape-goats for their own acts of omission and commission. Many cases have come to light, where officials had to take the rap, though it is common knowledge that they had acted under instructions.

The main reasons for the steady growth of corruption in India is the advent to get rich quick professional politicians on the scene. They make hay while the sun shines as also encourage corruption among the officials to suit their own ends. The only remedy, therefore, lies in separating the function of the politicians and the officials. The work of the politicians should be confined to laying down policies and they should not have anything to do with routine day-to-day administration, except to see that the policies laid down are effective. It is also important that eminent men of standing with a spirit of dedications should come forward to replace the professional politicians so as to make for a cleaner administration. There is also need for the government to give up its penchant for controls In certain circumstances, controls on the distribution of foodgrains and other essential commodities in short supply are essential but their essential commodities in short supply are essential but their continuance long after they have outlived their usefulness simply perpetuates corruption. It results in harassment to the public which is the breeding ground for corruption.

NO HONEST EFFORT TO PREVENT CORRUPTION

The Santhanan committee appointed in 1962 by Lal Bahadur Shastri, the then Home Minister, to study the problem of corruption and suggest remedial measures had stated in its report of 1964 that "There is a widespread impression ... that some ministers who have held office during the last 16 years have enriched themselves illegitimately, obtained good jobs for their sons and relations through nepotism, and have reaped other advantages inconsistent with any notion of purity in public life".

To curb corruption among ministers, the committee had recommended that specific allegations against any of them should be investigated by "an agency whose findings could command respect". For this purpose the committee suggested the constitution of a "national panel" of eminent persons by the President Allegations of wrong-doing and corruption against any minister could then be referred to an ad hoc committee of three persons out of the larger national panel. This ad- hoc committee should inquire if there was any prima facie truth in the allegations to justify the initiation of further legal action under the Prevention of Corruption Act, 1947.

The suspect minister as a matter of convention was also expected to resign if a prima facie case was made out against him. To deal with the problem of corruption the committee felt that "absolute integrity on the part of ministers at the Centre and the States is an indispensable condition for establishment of a tradition of purity in public services. No action was taken, however, on these recommendations. The recommendations of the Administrative Reforms Commission of 1966 to set up the institution of Lokpal to investigate cases of political corruption against ministers at the Centre was also not implemented. Five times in the past (i.e. in 1968, 1971, 1977, 1989 and 1985) some kind of Lokpal Bills were introduced in Parliament but all of them were allowed to lapse. The sixth and the latest Lok Pal Bill of 1996 is still pending before Parliament. This new Bill, however, provides for a rather weak Lokpal. Even if installed, he will be a toothless and in all probability a corruption friendly Lok Pal. He has been forbidden to act on his own but only when a complaint is lodged.

To deal with corruption among public officials, the Santhanam committee had recommended the setting up of an independent Central Vigilance Commission keeping ministers out of its purview but bringing all public servants of the Central Government and the PSUs within its jurisdiction. This Commission was to be headed by a Central Vigilance Commissioner (CVC) with the same measure of autonomy and status as of the Comptroller and Auditor-General of India and the Election Commissioner. The Commission was to be given a statutory basis by a parliamentary law.

Unfortunately, the Vigilance Commission scheme approved and notified in 1964 fell far short of these recommendations. The basic weakness of this scheme which is till in force is that the Commission has no statutory basis. It continues to be the creature of the 1964 resolution which is liable to frequent changes. This has in fact been happening, affecting adversely both the nominal independence of the Commission as also its jurisdiction. For example the tenure of the Vigilance Commissioner initially was for a period of six years like that of the CAG, the Election Commissioner and the UPSC Chairman. In 1977 the tenure of the CVC was reduced to three years, extendible by another two years by the Government: This virtually demolished whatever independence the Commission was intended to have. The tenure was again raised to five years in 1990. Such changes make the CVC vulnerable to the Government's pulls and pressures.

Further by a mere circular of the Bureau of Public Enterprises in October, 1996 the jurisdiction of the Central Vigilance Commission over the officers of the PSUs save the Board level appointees, was withdrawn. The Commission has also not been given the recommended power to decide on its own the initiation of disciplinary action or prosecute of any public servant. This power continues to rest as before the Government but is exercised after obtaining the Commission's advice". Cases of disagreement with the Commission in its "advisory" role can be included by it in the Commission's annual report to Parliament. Such reports are, however, not to be sent directly to Parliament by the Commission but through the Ministry of Personnel and Training, the designated administrative ministry.

The Prevention of Corruption Act was first passed as early as 1947 and later replaced by a slightly improved version in 1988. But without effective enforcement agencies such laws cannot prevent corruption, particularly at higher levels. A special anti-corruption police force was created in 1941 to deal with wartime corruption generally confined to lower levels of administration. This force, known as the Delhi Special Police Establishment Act 1946. Later, it became a division of the CBI on its creation in April 1963. But the CBI has no other legal basis yet except the Delhi Special Police Establishment Act, 1946 with limited jurisdiction. As a result the CBI has no power to investigate cases in any power to investigate cases in any State without their prior consent. (Article published in The Hindustan Times dated October 10, 1997 page 13 by U.C. Agarwal).

CAN CORRUPTION BE CURBED ?

Corruption in Government is an age-old problem, but a new subject of study for economists concerned with economic growth. Within the past year, organizations such as the World Bank and the IMF have begun to argue that corruption can deter investment and retard growth. In the beginning of August 1997, the Fund suspended a $ 220 million loan programme for Kenya, to punish the Government for its failure to root out graft. In future, according to a newly adopted IMF policy, its aid may be suspended or delayed on account of poor governance, if there is reason to believe it could have significant macro-economic implication.

How, though, are governments to curb poor governance? One common recommendation for poor countries is to increase the pay of civil servants. Clerks and police officers earning $ 50 a month, the reasoning goes, have no choice but to take bribes in order to feed their families. If governments paid their public officials better, such people would have less need to supplement their incomes illicitly, and more to lose by getting caught.

The fly in this ointment is the assumption that officials are driven to corruption by necessity. They may simply be driven by greed. And the balance between these motives will affect the amount by which their pay needs to be raised in order to make them less corruptible. In a recent paper two IMF economists try to work through these complexities. One surprising implication of their findings is that while higher pay for public servants may indeed reduce corruption, the benefits may be smaller than the added costs.

Measuring malfeasance' Quantifying costs and benefits in this murky domain is difficult, so the researchers have drawn on a multinational corruption index devised by a company called Political Risk Services. The index is based on surveys of business opinion, and tries to assess the relative likelihood in different countries of high government officials demanding back-handers in return for favours, as well as the extortion of smaller bribes by petty officials. Regrettably, the authors refuse to disclose how individual countries rank on the corruption index, lest the IMF be accused of labelling some of its members corrupt.

The economists then rank bureaucrats pay in 25 developing countries by the ratio of government wages to manufacturing wages. This provides a rough estimate of the difference in regards available to workers in the private and public sectors. And they adjust for national differences in the chances of a corrupt official being caught and punished by using an index of the effectiveness of national legal systems developed by the same risk-assessment firm. In addition, they factor in Political Risk Services attempt to measure the relative quality of public administration in the different developing countries.

The results of all this are not entirely reassuring. One encouraging finding is that there does indeed appear to be less corruption in countries where public servants are paid relatively well compared with other workers. The relationship is strong enough to suggest that raising average civil-service pay from 100% to 200% of the manufacturing wage reduces corruption by about one unit in the corruption index. This would be a substantial improvement, equivalent broadly to reducing the amount of corruption in China to that of Hong Kong, or from that in Argentina to the amount in Spain.

And yet this numerical correlation does not prove that governments can merely increase pay to eliminate corruption. For one thing, the inverse relationship between wages and corruption does not always hold; El Salvador, for example, pays its bureaucrats far more than the average factory worker but still ranks towards the bottom of the corruption index.

Moreover, paying civil servants enough to persuade them to reject bribes and kickbacks is itself costly. The paper estimates that government wages need to be between 2.8 and 7.4 times the wages paid in manufacturing, depending on the other factors in each country, before corruption would become negligible. Singapore has the best ranking in the corruption index, but its bureaucrats more than twice than average manufacturing wage.

Establishing a statistical link between low wages and corruption does not show which way causation flows. Extensive corruption might reduce a government's tax take, limiting the amount it can pay to employees. Or perhaps some governments deliberately keep wages low because they take it for granted that customs inspectors and driving-licence clerks will supplement their official pay.

Although it is plausible to suspect that low pay encourages government officials to seek extra income, a strong correlation is hard to draw. A telling finding from the research is that when its authors looked at trends in individual countries over a 12-year period, changes in public-sector wages had no significant effect on the reported extent of corruption.

This may be, the authors say, because relative pay levels are unlikely to have changed enough ever over a dozen years to show up on an index of corruption that is broad and subjective to begin with. The study argues that a doubling of the relative wages of civil servants is needed to reduce a country score on the corruption index by a single unit.

Still, there is another reason to question the efficacy of paying officials more. Arguably, the type of corruption that most damages economic growth is not petty bribery but rather the massive theft of state funds by venal politicians and their senior henchmen. It is hard to believe that corruption at this level is much influenced by official pay scales. And the pettier forms of corruption are anyway much harder to control when office juniors see their masters filching vast quantities of other peoples money. (Courtesy Article of The Economist Newspaper, October 1997 - News Panorama of India and World - Topic of the day pages 30-31).

11

POLITICAL CORRUPTION

Corruption has bothered many great Indians in the past. Gandhi had warned of its dangerous effects at the beginning of independence. In 1963, the then President of the Indian National Congress, D. Sanjivaiyya Reddy had observed that Congressmen who were paupers in 1947 had become millionaires without having any ostensible source of income. The Swedish economist, Gunnar Myrdal called India a "soft State" where nothing moved unless a bribe was paid. Since Myrdal days the level of corruption has risen from leaps and bound. It was become so widespread that the credibility of the entire political system is at stake. Let us not forget that at the final stage of transfer of power to India, the then British Prime Minister Winston Churchill said, "They (Indians) are all corrupt and they will not be able to run their administration". We scoffed off at Churchill's observations. His prediction has come true.

In the list drawn up by the German non-governmental organisation known as : Transparency International, India has been placed as the "most corrupt nation". This body had drawn up an index of corruption on the basis of a study in 45 countries in 1994. The survey shows the United States (USA) as being a more "Corrupt nation" than the United Kingdom (UK) and Germany. Scandinavian countries are relatively free of corruption. The survey, however, does not find a single nation to be entirely corruption free.

Corruption was rampant in the UK at both the national and local levels. In France, at least three ministers had been embroiled in financial scandals. There were kickback scandals over arms sale in Belgium which implicated the secretary general of the North Atlantic Treaty Organisation (NATO). In West Asia, a political corruption scandal in Histadrut, Israel's largest labour union discredited the Israeli government. The Saudi Arabian monarchy is getting shaken as wasteful public spending and kickbacks come to light. Financial scandals have been reported routinely in countries with divergent political systems-Italy, Japan, Korea, China, the USA, the UK and former USSR. The Frunze trial reported in Izvestia (July 22, 1962) and Sovetskaya (January 9, 1962) was one of the most important events in the history of the former USSR. The number of accused was as high as fifty four. They included ministers and officials, who were sentenced to various terms of imprisonment with confiscation of property. Leaders of the plundering band were sentenced to death.

On March 17, 1981 the special branch of the Italian police in charge of financial probes raided the residence of Licio Gelli. The documents they seized sparked one of the worst scandals in Italy's recent history. The list of 962 members included cabinet ministers, Generals and journalists. Gelli's secret organisation had penetrated the nerve centre of Italy's political and financial institutions. The government tried to stall a probe. But with magistrates forced publication of the list Gelli fled to South America. None of those whose names appeared in the list was spared.

The Lockheed Aircraft had paid bribes to Japan and other countries to boost the sales of its planes. This information exploded all on a sudden in February 1976 during hearings of the Sub-Committee on Multinational Corporation of the U.S. Senate Committee on Foreign Relations. In July 1976 the former prime minister of Japan Kakui Tanaka was arrested in Tokyo. Many a head rolled thereafter.

In the USA and Japan heads of government have been removed for corrupt practices. The French minister of industry had been jailed for corruption under public pressure. A president and prime minister had been imprisoned in Bangladesh on Corruption charges. In Italy, a prime minister found guilty of corruption was imprisoned. Colombian president is awaiting his impeachment by Parliament for receiving massive contributions from drug-traffickers.

In all democracies, the most effective watchdog is free press which is free to comment and criticise as they feel inclined and the vocal public opinion against declining norms of conduct in public life. Most of the countries have enacted harsh laws to ensure purity in the corridors of power. For example, the United States Ethics in Government Act 1978 enacted by the US Congress at President Jimmy craters instance in the wake of the Watergate scandals and the United States Independent Council Reauthorisation Act 1994 apply to the President, vice-presidents, members of cabinet, judges of the Supreme and Federal Courts, senators Congressmen and officials serving them. We shall revert to the details these laws later. In the UK, the Court has the power to ask a political functionary to appear before tribunals in order to testify about government's functioning.

Political corruption in post-independence India has undergone a sea-change from the Nehru-Shastri era (1951-66) to Narasimha Rao's rule (1991-96) and the worst period has been after Narasimha Rao assumed office of prime minister. His personal integrity has been questioned like no other prime minister before him. Taking a cue from his approach to corruption, the ministers and bureaucrats amassed huge fortune as if they are accountable to none. It left an impact on State ministers who started filling their coffers by illegal means.

Narasimha Rao's rule is a story of how the rule of law was systematically subverted and greed, swindling, forgery, fraud became governing virtues. Not merely Rao himself but most of his cabinet colleagues are allegedly involved.

About eight years ago, we had Bofors scandal involving Rs. 640 million. Then, five years later, there was the securities scandal, the scale of which was in thousands of million. Now we have Jain hawala, where the sum is not all that big, but is considered as the 'mother of all scandals' for the sheer number, range and stature of political personalities involved. Each successive scandal has been of greater magnitude than the preceding one and is a proof of our rotten political system where political thieves, with double standards, cannot be brought to book. Over the years ministers, bureaucracy and civil servants who lined their pockets would have retired peacefully had it not been for the series of happenings that emerged from the recovery of Jain diaries. The nation is entitled to know, no less from everyone of those, without a single exception, who figure in Jain diaries. It is shocked by the sheer range of the personalities cited, the vast scams involved, the security aspect and gross betrayal of the public trust. Bare denials by the political thieves carry little weight. A full disclosure is called for.

But for the press which broke the story, alert citizens who filed petitions to which the Supreme Court responded promptly, the hawala scam would have been buried. The most elementary qualification demanded of a minister is honesty and incorruptibility. It is, however, necessary that not only he should possess these qualifications but also that he should spear to posses them expressed Chief Justice Hidayatullah when K.B. Sahay, Chief Minister and other ministers of Bihar challenged the appointment of a Commission of Inquiry.

While the law weaved its web around Narasimha Rao in JMM bribery case, forgery in the St. Kitts case, in hawala case and nepotism in the urea deal involving his son, Rao continued in office as prime minister; and, worst still the C.B.I. over which he exercised control was investigating into his conduct. He should have given up his office to facilitate the C.B.I. to carry out their lengthy questioning without fear and in a free atmosphere. Would Nehru or Shastri have continued as prime minister even for a day if a single incident had involved them personally?

Let us examine the political corruption from Nehru-Shastri era (1951-1966) to Narasimha Rao regime (1991-1996). It has undergone a sea-change.

Nehru-Shastri era (1951-1966)

Whenever there was a scandal over money, both Nehru and Shastri got agitated. Nehru-Shastri era ensured that their cabinet colleagues were men of high stature. But when corruption of any of them surfaced there was no hesitation to take firm action against him.

For example, T.T. Krishnamachari, Union finance minister was forced to resign as a result of Mundhra scandal, after the publication of Justice Chagla Commission of Inquiry holding Krishnamachari guilty; K.D. Malviya, minister of mines and fuel had to resign for having accepted money from mining contractor Seerajuddin and Co. Justice S.R. Das Commission of Inquiry held Pratap Singh Kairon, Chief Minister, Punjab guilty of corruption and he was forced to resign. There were Commissions of Inquiry against Chief Minister K.B. Sahay, Bihar and against H.K. Mahtab, Chief Minister, Orissa and they were all removed from office.

It was during Nehru's rule that Santhanam Committee, on prevention of corruption, was set up in 1962 to deal with growing corruption among bureaucracy after the commencement of the second Five-Year Plan, with its emphasis on industrialisation and closer rapport between industrialists and politicians.

The Delhi Special Police Act, 1946 (SPE) established after the war to tackle high incidence of corruption among bureaucracy was strengthened by the establishment of the Central Bureau of Investigation (CBI) in 1963 and appointment of a Central Vigilance Commission to advice the C.B.I. Both the director of the C.B.I. and the Central Vigilance Commission were headed by persons of high integrity. On the recommendations of the Santhanam Committee, every State government set up a separate vigilance and anti-corruption organisation to fight corruption at every level of administration. Since the political corruption was left out from the purview of the Santhanam Committee, Commission of Inquiry was the only instrument left to deal with corruption charges against ministers.

Indira Gandhi (First) rule (1966-77)

The period can be divided into two phases. During the first phase political corruption was limited to collection of funds from large industrial houses for the purpose of elections. It was very much limited. It expanded after Sanjay Gandhi came into the picture and

Indira Gandhi depended on him to boost up the Congress election funds. Sanjay established direct relationship with industrialists. A new breed of wheeler-dealers appeared who would offer the party, cuts on everything imported from outside towards the growth of industrialisation in the country. However, neither Indira Gandhi nor his son Sanjay was ever accused of corruption at personal level.

Janata Rule (1977-79)

Since the Janata government, comprised of a Medway of several political parties, and the new governments attention was mostly directed against Indira Gandhi and her government during the Emergency it did not give much attention towards development projects. Raising money through industrialists or through licence-quota-permit system received a set back; the industrialists did not know whom to pay. Moreover, prime minister Morarji Desai, a politician with high integrity and honesty ensured the country a clean administration after all that had happened during the Emergency. These factors helped to put a check on political corruption.

Indira Gandhi (Second) Rule (1980-84)

Licence-quota-permit raj achieved remarkable growth during this period with Sanjay Gandhi's support. Large industrial houses vied with each other to secure Sanjay's favour. Industrialists were willing to donate money to the Congress(I) funds, controlled by Sanjay. The Kuo oil deal provided the best evidence of how the sums had grown larger and how hard currency kickbacks were appreciated.

Indira Gandhi's decision to host the Asian Games in 1982 provided opportunities to an entirely new class. The brokers who subsisted in making deals and getting huge commissions were the most sought-after propel. At this time Surender Jain (S.K. Jain) came to the limelight and was helped by then law minister P. Shiv Shankar and Indira Gandhi's most powerful yogi Dhirendra Brahmachari. The shifting of P. Shiv Shankar to the Petroleum ministry came as a windfall for Surendra Jain. In the Oil and Natural Gas Commission, a public sector undertaking, contracts ran into several hundred crores. Surender was able to secure most of the contracts due to his close proximity to Shiv Shankar.

Rajiv Gandhi Rule (1985-89)

Assassination of Indira Gandhi in 1984 and Rajiv Gandhi's ascent to prime ministership saw a boom time for brokers. This was also the period when Rajiv and his advisers took a decision to change the track of election funding and lean more and more on the kickbacks that would come by way of the foreign deals. The thinking was that the Congress would not have to approach Birla, Tata, Ambanis, etc. for funds. The Congress had to depend on the services of the people such as Surender Jain to ensure that the Congress party coffers were full. Lalit Suri, a hotelier of Delhi was very close to Rajiv Gandhi and was a major fund-raiser for the Congress. Suri could secure contracts for exporting Basmati rice to the Soviet Union.

This was the period when kickbacks and illegal commissions, from foreign companies, to politicians started flowing. Allegations had been made that Arun Gandhi, Union Minister of State for Internal Security in the ministry of home affairs, in Rajiv Gandhi cabinet struck a Rs. 22 crore deal with a Czech firm Merkurias for the purchase of 55,000 pistols. Within months of the receipt of the first consignment of the pistols, on examination, they were found to be of sub-standard quality. The deal was finally scrapped. This triggered off trouble. It had been alleged that Arun Nehru and an additional secretary in the ministry of home affairs received huge kickbacks from the Czech firm. To pacify Parliament, the C.B.I. registered a FIR against Arun Nehru and additional secretary D.P. Singhal in this connection. During the investigation of the case, Arun Nehru told the C.B.I. that the deal had been arranged through the help of Italian businessman Ottavio Quattrochi, who happened to be a close friend of Rajiv Gandhi's family. Arun Nehru's disclosures greatly embarrassed Rajiv Gandhi and the C.B.I. case was dropped.

The Bofors pay-off case was the greatest scandal during this period. It was alleged that in the purchase of Bofors guns amounting to over Rs. 600 million from AB Bofors of Sweden, the prime ministers name surfaced for having accepted kickbacks from the deal. After 11/2 year long preliminary inquiry, the C.B.I. registered a case on 22 January 1990 against several persons including Martin Ardbo, former president of Bofors, Win Chadda and G.P. Hinduja who were all reportedly linked to the deal.

Director C.B.I. Katre, who was in charge of the Bofor's probe from the beginning, it was alleged, had delayed it purposely and thus made himself indispensable to Rajiv Gandhi. He secured two extensions and finally left the C.B.I. with the end of Rajiv Gandhi's regime. The C.B.I. chose not to raid the house of Win Chadda, the main accused in the case till he had fled the country while Katre and his team travelled around the world in search for the kickback recipients.

Janata Interlude (1989-91)

No centralised corruption but by then earning kickbacks through deal making had become a way of life. Money was made on every item from telephone equipment to State Trading Corporation (STC) purchases. Chandra Sekhar's ministers were more corrupt than V.P. Singh's, but actually there was little to choose between them.

Important cases registered by the C.B.I. during this period were: HDW Submarine deal registered on March 5, 1990 in which several bureaucrats were named in the FIR; Air bus A-320 case registered on 29 March 1990 in which several I.A.S. officers were among the accused in the Rs. 2,500 crore deal; and St. Kitts forgery case in the which godman Chandraswami, a very close friend of prime minister Chandra Sekhar and Union Minister external affairs P.V. Narasimha Rao was involved. FIR registered against godman Chandraswami and his associate K.N. Aggarwal alias mamaji, K.L. Varma, A.P. Nandy, Larry Kolb and G.D. McLean for falsely implicating Ajeya Singh son of prime minister V.P. Singh in a bank fraud case. When N.K. Singh, Jt. Director C.B.I. wanted to interrogate godman Chandrawamy, in the St. Kitts case not only prime minister Chandra Sekhar did not give him permission to do so but transferred Singh out of the C.B.I. (see N.K. Singh's book: Plain Truth) much before the High Court's order was received directing godman Chandraswamy to appear before Singh for interrogation. P.V. Narasimha Rao, as Union minister of external affairs was suspected to have been the brain behind the case to embarrass V.P. Singh and discredit him politically.

P.V. Narasimha Rao's Rule (1991-96)

No government was ever involved in as many scams as the Rao government; no prime minister's name was ever dragged into as many scandals as P.V. Narasimha Rao. Nothing has so far been proved against him, yet few are ready to give him even the benefit of doubt. Loss of power after his fall has not freed him from the stigma of scams; rather, even before the cobwebs of the past had been cleared fresh ones entangled him. His conscience keeper had been godman Chandraswamy, a crook and shady character who is involved in power struggles, pay off scandals, scams, forgery, shady international arms deals, frauds and FERA violations in a large number of cases. He remained immune to arrest and prosecution under Narasimha Rao's umbrella; although Rao denies his acquaintance with Chandraswamy.

St. Kitts Forgery Case

In March 1989 when V.P. Singh, as head of the Janata Dal was fast emerging as the prime political challenger to Rajiv Gandhi in the Bofors scandal, an elaborate plan was conceived and carried out to implicate Ajeya Singh, V.P. Singh's son in a foreign bank scam. It was made out that Ajeya had defrauded the First Trust Corporation Bank Ltd, a bank in the Carribbean island of St. Kitts of huge sums of money. But, suddenly the whole thing exploded and allegations were made that the incriminating documents against Ajeya Singh were, in fact forgeries. And the brain behind the forgeries was none other than external affairs minister, P.V. Narasimha Rao. At the instance of prime minister V.P. Singh the C.B.I. instituted an FIR charging Chandraswamy, several Indian officials and foreign nationals with criminal conspiracy and forgery. A separate cell was set up under Jt. Director N.K. Singh to investigate into the case. With the fall of V.P. Singh government when a breakthrough in the case seemed imminent after the confession of A.P. Nandy, deputy director, directorate of enforcement, who figured as one of the accused in the case, the investigation of the case had to be slowed down due to the interference of Chandra Sekhar government. N.K. Singh was transferred out of the C.B.I. Details are highlighted by N.K. Singh in his book: Plain Truth.

Goldstar

A spin-off of the securities scam, the Goldstar scandal did not implicate Narasimha Rao directly but centred on his son, Prabhakar Rao. This Andhra Pradesh based Company - Goldstar Steel Alloys Ltd. was co-promoted by Prabhakar Rao, who entered into a Rs. 2 crore deal with one of the accused stock brokers of the securities scam, Hiten Dalal. The way the money was routed through the Andhra Bank Financial Services Ltd. raised many eyebrows and many questions were raised in Parliament. A belated FIR was registered by the C.B.I.

Joint Parliamentary Committee (JPC)

On the securities scam, involving crores of rupees, a high powered JPC was set up under the chairmanship of Ram Niwas Mirdha on 6 August 1992 with 30 members 15 from the ruling Congress and remaining from different opposition parties. It submitted the report on 21 December 1993. Apart from none brokers, 14 banks, high officials from the Reserve Bank of India, the report recorded severe criticism against government functionaries including ministers for being participants in the securities scandal. S. Venkitaraman, former governor, Amitava Ghosh, former deputy governor and R. Janakiraman, former deputy governor of Reserve Bank of India were criticised for their omissions and commissions; B. Shankaranand, former minister, Petroleum and Natural Gas Ministry, Rameshwar Thakur, former minister of State, ministry of finance, were lambasted for investing funds to help Harshad Mehta.

While recommending the removal of Shankaranand from the Union cabinet, the JPC observed that this was the minimum concession the government should make to parliamentary sentiment.

Prime minister took no action to implement the recommendations not even on the report of the C.B.I. on 5 September 1994 recommending the prosecution of Shankaranand for cheating under Section 420 IPC. Shankaranand resigned on 22 December 1994 along with two other ministers Rameshwar Thakur and Kalpnath Rai.

Since the JPC report was unanimous and the majority of members belonged to the ruling Congress party it was thought many heads would roll. Moreover, the prime minister Rao was also bound by a previous promise that he would not spare the guilty. When he took no action on the findings of the JPC, people were convinced that the prime minister's power rested on giving total freedom to his coterie of corrupt ministers.

When the summary of the JPC report appeared in the press, the intelligentsia was happy with its observations, conclusions and recommendations on banks, and the indictment of the Reserve Bank of India chief and his deputies. The public welcomed the suggested action against eight public sector undertakings and critical comments on Manmohan Singh, Rameshwar Thakur, B. Shankaranand and Madhav Rao Scindia.

But the public was disappointed when the prime minister and his finance minister took no effective action. If they had, more scandals could have perhaps been prevented. The JPC is potentially a vital corrective and it is the denial of constitutional remedies that compels people to approach the courts.

Sugar Scam

The genesis of sugar scandal can be traced to the end of September 1993 when sugar stocks were several lakh tonnes lower than they had been in the same month the previous year. The sugar position at September end has traditionally been the amberlight which alerts government to the need to decide whether imports will or will not be required. The Cabinet Committee on prices met within a fortnight of the end of September, eleven days to be precise, on 11 October 1993 and decided that Kalpnath Rai, the Union food minister should examine whether "marginal imports"might not be required.

On 9 March 1994 the Cabinet Committee on Prices decided to put sugar imports on Open General licence so that private traders could import the 'marginal quantities' require to offset the marginal increase in open market prices than anticipated. Two months later, the open market price of sugar shot up from Rs. 15 to Rs. 17 per kilo. There were two proximate causes for this; for one Kalpnath was not responsible. It was the failure of the State Trading Corporation (STC) to effect imports in time. The other cause for which Kalpnath must bear the sole responsibility is that he cut down the sugar release into the freesale market in May 1994 by 2.25 lakh tonnes. This represented about 0.25 per cent of India's annual consumption of sugar.

Gyan Prakash Committee was set up by the prime minister to investigate the sugar scandal on 17 July 1994. The Gyan Prakash report held Kalpnath entirely responsible as he curtailed sugar in the free market so that the shortage become more acute. Worse, says the report, the poor who relied on public distribution system

(PDS) through ration shops was also affected because traders raised the price of sugar in open market and the Food Ministry reduced the supplies of sugar to the PDS as well as the open market. Thus, the report says had the effect of favouring sugar mills. The policy of granting licences to set up new sugar mills to augment production was followed in such a skewed way that it helped only a few. The report raps the cabinet secretary and A.K. Antony, a person of high integrity, Union Minister Civil Supplies for lack of co-ordination. Antony resigned in protest against Gyan Prakash report which commented against him. Kalpnath did not resign and continued in office till the C.B.I. arrested him under TADA for his links with terrorist Dawood Ibrahim and his group. There were wild rumours that Kalpnath shared the profits of sugar scandal running into lakhs with the prime minister but it will never be known.

Harshad Mehta and Suit Case Story

A stock broker by profession, Harshad Mehta's rise has been spectacular. In the course of interrogation into securities -banking - political scam, Harshad Mehta alleged that he had handed over two suitcases stuffed with Rs. 1 crore to one of prime minister Rao's most trusted factotums, R.K. Khandekar when Mehta visited Rao's resident at 7 Race Course Road to meet him as per prior appointment. Rao denied the receipt of money and the pro-Rao circle in its cover up action produced evidence that Rao had spent the day in question, November 4, 1991, cooped up in his office. As he was not in residence there was no question of Mehta paying money to Rao.

Although Rao denied Mehta's allegation it was a powerful indictment of the nexus among brokers, bankers and politicians. The C.B.I. came in for severe criticism for lapses such as not seizing the relevant records at the prime minister's residence, in particular, the visitor's register and the telephone register; failure to interrogate business associate Mohan Khandelwal who had accompanied Mehta and prime minister's private secretary R.K. Khandekar; and security personnel on duty on 4 November; failure to follow up Mehta's interrogation and withholding from the JPC some of the evidence it had collected; failure to verify the stories of denial put out on behalf of key witnesses Sunil Mittal and Manmohan Sharma; and its failure to register a FIR on the information of Mehta.

Defrauding Lakhubhai Pathak

A UK-based pickle dealer Lakhubhai Pathak alleged that he had paid $ 100,000 to godman Chandraswamy on New Years Day 1993 in a New York hotel for securing two government contracts for the supply of newsprint and paper pulp in return for the dollars. At the time of payment of the amount to Chandraswamy and K.N. Aggarwal alias Mamaji were present. The C.B.I. registered a FIR under Section 420 and 120-B, IPC for cheating against Chandraswamy and Mamaji. During investigation Pathak said that prime minister Rao not only witnessed the deal but also added his assurances about Chandraswamy's clout and ability to carry the deal through. The C.B.I. arrested Chandraswamy and Mamaji but released them on bail the same day. The C.B.I. did not investigate into Rao's angle.

Urea Scam

This is the latest of Narasimha Rao's scams. It is a deal in which the corruption is of a magnitude that is unprecedented in the history of independent India. Most deals involved kickbacks. But the urea scandal is different not because of the size of the kickback nearly US four million dollars are alleged to have been paid to Narasimha rao's son, Prabhakar Rao and others but because the transaction was essentially, fraudulent. Over Rs. 133 crore of taxpayers money was transferred abroad to a shady Turkish firm nobody had heard of before or after, and all the routine safeguards were dispensed with and then finally, even the urea never arrived. This was one deal where the connections went right to the top. One view is that if

Rao's government had not fallen this urea scam would never have come to light.

The history of the urea scandal can be traced to 31 October 1995 when National Fertilizer Ltd. (NFL) a public sector undertaking operating under the fertilizer ministry, negotiated to purchase 200,000 metric tonnes of urea raw material used for the manufacture of fertilizer, from a Turkish Company called M/s Karsan Danishmanlik Turizm Sanyai Ticaret. Nobody in the fertilizer business had ever heard of Karsan before the September of that year.

All such transactions are ordinarily conducted with bank guarantees, letters of credit and insurance to protect the buyer. But in this case, no bank guarantee was secured from Karsan and no letter of credit was opened. There was only limited insurance cover in case of damage during shipping. If Karsan defaulted on the delivery, as it turned out subsequently, there was no way in which the Government of India through National Fertilizer Ltd (NFL) could recover the money. It was unprecedented for a public sector undertaking to enter into a transaction with an unknown non-existent Company and agree to purchase 200,000 tonnes of urea for Rs. 133 crore and to pay the entire amount in advance.

When a company makes an advance remittance, the entire Reserve Bank of India (RBI) procedure involving a Bill of Entry comes into play. The State Bank of India (SBI) Delhi South Extension branch, used by NFL, flouted wilfully the bank regulations and remitted promptly the amount. All these irregularities could happen because of the involvement of prime minister's son, Prabhakar Rao in the transaction.

The RBI says it was misled by the SBI Delhi South Extension Branch, NFL's banker. It claims that the SBI asked for permission after it had remitted Rs. 1.33 crore or one per cent of the amount. It wrote to the RBI on 10 November stating that the money had been sent on 2 November and asked for permission to remit the remaining 99 per cent. The RBI replied on 12 November asking for more details and documents. But it says, the SBI promptly remitted the other 99 per cent without furnishing these details. Later the RBI denied permission for the remittance. But the money had already gone. Several officials of the SBI were suspended over this issue and the investigation of the case is still pending.

It was alleged that even though there were enough irregularities committed by the NFL in the urea deal, neither the fertilizer minister, Ram Lakhan Singh Yadav nor prime minister Rao were interested in following up the allegations because their sons Prakash Chandra Yadav and Prabhakar Rao and prime minister's another relation Sanjiva Rao were deeply involved in the urea scandal. For example, on December 20 Janata Dal leader Sharad Jadav allegedly met prime minister Rao in connection with the telecom scandal. He told the prime minister that the urea deal stank. The following day, Jadav claimed, he had sent a letter to the prime minister asking for a C.B.I. inquiry as he suspected grave irregularities perpetrated in importing urea. Prime minister did not order any inquiry but passed on the letter to fertilizer minister Ram Lakhan Singh Jadav asking him to check on it. From 20 December 1995 till 19 May 1996 the inquiry was confined to NFL and on 19 May a complaint was forwarded by Fertilizer secretary Indrajit Chowdhury to the C.B.I. On 28 May, the C.B.I. registered a FIR against Ramakrishnan, Managing Director NFL; D.S. Kanwar, executive director (marketing), Sambhasiv Rao and several others. Ramakrishnan, Kanwar and Sambhasiv Rao were arrested by the C.B.I. on 1 June 1996. During interrogation Sambhashiv Rao told the C.B.I. that the deal involved Prabhakar Rao, Sanjiva Rao and Prakash Chandra Yadav. The C.B.I. kept this to itself but by the weekend (7-8 June) the details had leaked out to all the newspapers.

According to Sambhasiv Rao US four million dollars were deposited at an account in the name of Edible Foodstuffs at the Dubai branch of the Standard Chartered Bank. This was a post-box account in the name of a shell company because the money was quickly moved out and the account closed. Sambhashiv Rao said that the four million dollars were then converted into rupees through hawala and sent to Prabahakar Rao and Sanjiva Rao. All Sambhashiv Rao got, he claimed, was Rs. 37 lakh from this sum. But he was made to buy land at Nampalli in Hyderabad for Prabhakar Rao and Sanjiva Rao.

The C.B.I. discovered through interrogation of Ramakrishnan and Kanwar that another US 200,000 dollars were sent to an account in the USA in the name of Rea Brothers, a front company for Prakash Chandra Yadav.

Prakash Chandra Jadav and Prabhakar Rao were interrogated by the C.B.I. Both pleaded innocence and denied all knowledge of the scam. Narasimha Rao's critics say that Ram Rao, director C.B.I. will give protection to prime minister Narasimha Rao's son Prabhakar Rao just as he did during the Goldstar investigation. It remains to be seen how sincere would be the United Front prime minister Deve Gowda with his new C.B.I. director Joginder Singh to deal with the case impartially, without fear or favour.

Prabhakar Rao's interest in the NFL represents fraction of his entire holdings. He is a director in the Goldstar group of companies which has an estimated turn over of Rs. 250 crore. He owns Rs. 2.75 crores of the Rs. 71 crore equity of Goldstar Steel and Alloys Ltd. Goldstar is a group of six companies against which several questions had been raised. Among them are Goldstar holdings and Goldstar Cements. The Companies are owned by Krishna Mohan, a family friend of Narasimha Rao. The Janakiraman Committee report mentions a Rs. 2 crore loan that scam-tainted Andhra Bank Financial Services Ltd. (ABFSL), the merchant banking branch of Andhra Bank arranged for Prabhakar Rao from Hiten Dalal, who was accused in the securities scam. When the C.B.I. investigated the Goldstar case it found nothing. The case was dropped. There could be no investigation against a son of the prime minister.

Prabhakar Rao had interests in Sinclair Holdings and Investments Ltd, formed in July 1984 with a capital of Rs. one lakh and now stands at Rs. 3 crore; Sphinx Investments and Finances Ltd. started with an authorised capital of Rs. 10 lakh in 1986. Its net assets came down to Rs. 4000 in March 1990. In 1993 the Company had equity capital of about Rs. 4 crore; Navnirman Investments had an equity capital of Rs. 1 lakh when it was formed in July 1989. In 1993 it was worth Rs. 2 crore.

Government Housing Scam

The Central Government housing scam was a massive racket involving 8,768 allottees and crores of rupees. The asking rate for an out-of-turn allotment in the capital varied from Rs. 10,000 to Rs. 50,000. Senior bureaucrats admitted that they had been asked to pay to be allotted a house. On 14 February 1995 the Supreme Court, on receipt of a public interest litigation petition, directed the C.B.I. to probe the scam.

The racket dates back to 1991 when Sheila Kaul, belonging to prime minister Rao's inner circle was union minister urban development ministry and M. Arunachalam and P.K. Thungon were ministers of State. The malpractice in the allotment of houses and shops were uncovered by public interest litigation following press reports about irregular allotment. It had exposed many VIPs who had been either unauthorisedly occupied houses or had houses larger than their entitlement. It was found that even secretaries and joint secretaries had to pay bribes for routinely deserved accommodation.

Thungon had power to allot type I-IV houses out of turn while type V-VIII allotments could be made only by Sheila Kaul. The charge was that all senior bureaucrats posted outside Delhi retained allotments in the capital. A senior bureaucrat was reportedly told to pay for entitlement to a D-I flat though he was allotted it in Sheila Kaul's presence. When he went to claim the key, he was sternly told no D-I flat was vacant. That night, he began getting anonymous calls demanding money for a D-I allotment.

The scam involved allotments to artists, scientists, social workers, freedom fighters, sportsmen, journalists and all categories of government servants. Middle level bureaucrats complained that hundreds of them had to wait patiently for 15 to 20 years for an allotment while juniors managed out-of-turn allotments from ministers' discretionary quota through bribes.

Many VVIPs who do not occupy the houses allotted to them sub-let them to industrialists, stockbrokers, businessmen and even to smugglers, and when they visit Delhi they are put up as free guests. This has been going on for years and it would be foolish to think that the prime minister would be unaware of these developments.

The C.B.I. implicated Sheila Kaul, former Union Minister for Urban Development in the housing scam, accusing her before the Supreme Court of allotting 43 commercial shops and stall in prime localities in New Delhi to close relatives and friends in "utter violation" of norms without issuing any public notice inviting applications from eligible persons.

Till June 1994 there were 30 bungalows and flats occupied illegally by ex-ministers, ex-MPs, ex-governors and other VIPs. Amounts that are due from these illegal occupants for electricity, water charges and other expenses run into lakhs of rupees. Some of them such as former Congress MP Darbara Singh's family (Darbara Singh died of a heart attack two years back) continued to occupy the bungalow on Krishna Menon Marg, owes the government Rs. 15,59,823; speaker of the Lok Saba G.S. Dhillon had moved over to his home State, Punjab several years ago but he still retains his official accommodation in New Delhi; Vasant Sathe, former information and broadcasting minister had been staying in his 2 Krishna Menon Marg bungalow for over ten years now; Subramanian Swamy's Rajya Sabha term came to an end in April 1994 but he still retained his bungalow at 5 Safdarjung Road to name a few.

What makes the problem of illegal occupancy of bungalows in prime areas of Delhi more serious is the fact that according to the prevailing market rate the government had been losing lakhs of rupees every month. A type 6 independent bungalow which is allotted to ministers fetch a rent of Rs. 25,000 per month; a type 7 more than Rs. one lakh per month; and a type 8 bungalow, four of which are occupied by the prime minister Narasimha Rao and by ministers like Arjun Singh would get a rent of over Rs. 3 lakhs every month says a property agent.

Refusal of Sheila Kaul to appear before the C.B.I. for interrogation on the ground that as long as she held office of governor (in Himachal

Pradesh) she acquired immunity from her appearance before the C.B.I. An upright and honest prime minister like Lal Bahadur Shastri would have himself resigned or directed Sheila Kaul to tender her resignation to the President when such frauds are perpetrated. 'When such frauds are perpetrated on the Constitution by persons holding the reigns, and crime is committed, surely there has to be a way out to bring such persons around even if such persons enjoyed immunity' the Supreme Court observed: 'the rope was being tightened around the necks of small fry like personal assistants and private secretaries of ministers in the housing scam, and the big people were going scot-free' adding 'either we must have a Lal Bahadur Shastri, who even at a little finger being pointed at him was ready to quit office, or else the law should step in and find a way out'. The judges pointed out that Article 361 of the Constitution only granted a governor or the President immunity for something done while holding that office, and not for something which had been committed earlier.

The minister had allotted two of the shops to her own grandsons, one to the maidservant of her son Vikram Kaul, who was living in Dubai, and another to the manager of a handloom shop who was related to her close friend. The minister had allotted one shop to the nephew of former minister of State for Urban development P.K. Thungon. While making the allotments of these stalls, the minister had favoured her relatives, friends, personal staff and some officials of the directorate of estates. There were also similar allegations against other 'high ups' involved in the housing scam against whom the C.B.I. was still carrying on investigations. In several cases government's decision to waive dues amounting to Rs. 15 million from the 127 VIPs for accommodation was under scrutiny and a committee had been appointed to examine the reasons.

Besides the public interest petition on which the Supreme Court is acting, it had received over 200 anonymous complaints that urban development ministry officials were making allotments of houses on the payment of bribes. By pursuing the issue with firmness, the Supreme Court has conveyed the reassuring message that no one is above the law. Its activist role might, in the long run, actually prove a deterrent to the abuse of power.

The C.B.I. believed that P.K. Thungon, former minister of State, urban development used a part of the money illegally obtained through the housing scam to contest the 11th Lok Sabha elections. The C.B.I. detected an account in the name of Thungon's wife at the State Bank of India, Bomdilla branch which had Rs. 50 lakh in a short-term deposit. This account was frozen by the C.B.I. (India Today, 15 August, 1995-Scandal in Allotments). The apex Court fined Sheila Kaul Rs. 60 crore for abuse of power.

Railway Scam : Corruption Runs Deep

Railway ministry which employs over 16 lakh workers, pays more than Rs. 7,000 crore in wages annually and spends approximately Rs. 16,000 crore on operations has been charged with high level corruption, involving foreign deals,.running into crores of rupees. What is perhaps more relevant is how recommendations made by M.V. Srinivasan, member traffic - the key adviser on matters relating to the use and requirements of rolling stock (coaches, wagons and locomotives) to constitute a full board committee, consisting of representatives from the traffic, finance, electrical, mechanical and planning departments to assess the need for these locomotives and coaches, the routes on which they would be used and to evaluate foreign exchange requirements not only for the purchase of locomotives and coaches but also for the purchase of spares was not implemented.

Controversial deals were import of 20 high-power diesel locomotives from General Motors of the US at a total cost of Rs. 132 crore; 21 high-speed coaches from Linke-Hoffmann Busch, Germany at a total cost of Rs. 136.6 crore and 19 million dollars electric locomotives from Asea Brown Boveri (ABB), Sweden by the Union railway ministry under C.K. Jaffer Sheriff. Negotiations for the import of railway rolling stock was floated on November 1, 1986.

Names of Madhavrao Scindia and C.K. Jaffer Sheriff figured in the S.K. Jain's diaries. The former was alleged to have been paid Rs. 75 lakh and Jaffer Sheriff was alleged to have been paid Rs. 10 lakh for awarding contracts to Jains for various railway projects imported from abroad and Jains were middlemen to some of the foreign firms which executed the orders. Both Scindia and Jaffer Sheriff, however, deny of having received any money from Jains. Some MLAs in Karnataka brought allegations against Jaffer Sheriff, who hailed from Karnataka, for amassing assets through land deals violating the provisions of Section 79B of the Karnataka Land Reforms Act and bought a palatial bungalow in Indira Nagar, one of the Bangalore's posh residential areas, for Rs. 59 lakh on 16 January 1992 when he was railway minister, in the name of his wife. (Sunday 7-13 November 1993).

Earlier when Jaffer Sheriff was a minister in Veerappa Moily's cabinet, M. Rajasekharamurthy, MP demanded an inquiry into the alleged land encroachment and also allegations of falsifying documents and violation of Karnataka's land reforms Act. Moily had referred it to a Cabinet sub-committee which never took up the matter and things did not change even after the new Janata Dal under Deve Gowda assumed office. (Sunday 19-25 February 1995). Against previous background the induction of Jaffer Sheriff in Rao's Cabinet, as a railway ministry, surprised everyone.

The CBI conducted raids on the properties of the former railway minister Jaffar Sheriff on 18-1-97 and allegedly seized documents to show that Sheriff had amassed Rs. 2 crore in excess of his known sources of income. The CBI probe revealed that Sheriff owns two palatial bungalows, a housing complex comprising 16 flats, a shopping complex and three farm houses. The CBI teams which went to search five other premises allegedly belonging to Sheriff and his sons found locked. Sheriff had declared income of Rs. 94.85 lakh during 1977-95. Documents value his properties at over Rs. 2 crore. (The Telegraph dated 19-1-97)

J.M.M. Bribery Case

When prime minister Narasimha Rao faced a no confidence motion against his government in July 1993, the situation was not in his favour. The Congress party needed 265 votes to win and it was running 15 short. Congress party managers had, by then, broken the Telegu Desam Party, the Shiv Sena and the Janata Dal but just before the 28th July motion of confidence, they were still running short. In August 1992 the Janata Dal of Ajit Singh refused to go along and Ram Lakhan Singh Jadav and six others split. Along with them, four Jharkhand Mukti Morcha (JMM) MPs Suraj Mandal, Simon Marandi, Shailendra Mahato and Shibu Soren also voted with the Congress. At that time, it was generally believed that huge sums of money had been paid to effect the defections. Newspapers identified such Congress MPs as V.C. Shukla, R.K. Dhawan and Haryana Chief Minister Bhajan Lal among them. There was a huge uproar then. Narasimha Rao won the confidence motion and by the end of next year, had secured a comfortable majority in Parliament.

On 1996 New year the bombshell struck. Ravindra Kumar of the Rashtriya Mukti Morcha (RMM) sought to get the C.B.I. to register a FIR against Narasimha Rao, Shukla, Dhawan, Ajit Singh, Captain Satish Sharma, Bhajan Lal, hotelier Lalit Suri and Suraj Mandal and three other JMM, MPs for entering into a conspiracy to effect the defection. There was no response.

A month later, another reminder was sent to the C.B.I. but no reply was received. Rs. 30 lakh in cash had been deposited in a savings bank account of Suraj Mandal in the Punjab National Bank, Naroji Nagar Branch on August 1, 1993 after the confidence motion. He had no way to earn such amount. On February 22, P.N. Lakhi, counsel for the RMM in the JMM case filed a petition in the Delhi High Court and the next day, Justice Y.K. Sabharwal and Justice D.K. Jain asked the C.B.I. to explain. On 27 March the C.B.I. registered four separate FIRs against Suraj Mandal, Shibu Soren, Simon Marandi and Sailendra Mahato, none of which made any mention of either Narasimha Rao, Shukla, Dhawan, Satish Sharma,

Ajit Singh, Bhajan Lal or Lalit Suri. Four different FIRs were deliberately registered so as to avoid the conspiracy angle. If a conspiracy could not be established, Narasimha Rao was safe.

The draft FIRs registered offences under section 13(1)(D) of the Prevention of Corruption Act. This refers to a public servant receiving an illegal gratification for himself or anyone else. In the actual FIRs, this was diluted. This was pointed out in a RMM petition to a Division Bench of Delhi High Court. J.J. Sabharwal and Jain accepted this and in a ruling on 17 May they observed that the C.B.I. director Vijaya Ram Rao had himself deliberately filed weak FIRs. When the additional solicitor general and the C.B.I. Counsel, A.N. Jayaram sought to defend the C.B.I., the judges passed strictures against the C.B.I. The C.B.I. moved a special leave petition before the Supreme Court requesting that the strictures against the C.B.I. be expunged since the High Court's observations amounted to interference in the C.B.I. investigation and be stayed.

Satish Sharma's farm and his houses were raided in Delhi on 12 October, 1996. Over 150 documents were reportedly seized from his house. At last, the C.B.I. identified the source from where the money came in the JMM bribery case. While the case against Satish Sharma in the JMM case was pending in the court, he had already been fined a sum of Rs. 50 crore by the Apex Court in connection with the misuse of power in the distribution of dealership in petroleum products.

Jain Hawala Scam

The term 'Hawala' (reference in Hindi) denotes a wide range of secret and sophisticated techniques for laundering dirty money. For anyone seeking to avoid official banking and tax channels, underground operators provide attractive exchange rates for foreign currency, facilitate duty exemption on bogus exports and help transfer slush funds to outlets abroad.

Black money funnelled through the hawala network comes back to India through the banking system in a recycled form as foreign currency. Hawala has evolved into a vibrant international racket with credibility among the salaried expatriates in the Gulf and the middle class at home. Businessmen and traders book losses or expenses for official consumption, moving their hard cash to destinations where no questions are asked. Through the hawala network, black money is converted to dollars and deposited abroad in secret bank accounts. Rich residents of India take on the liabilities of non-resident Indians who flush funds into numbered accounts elsewhere, for favours done or assets in India are swapped for assets abroad.

For about five years, the Jain hawala scandal was, in the public notice, synonymous with political and bureaucratic corruption at the top. It came to light in March 1991 with the arrest of Kashmiri militant Ashfaq Hussain Lone of the Hizbul Mujahideen was a devastating exposure of the ubiquity of corruption in the political system.

The C.B.I. launched a massive probe in the spring of 1991 into the dealings of hawala operators, who among other things, were accused of funnelling the funds that financed terrorist and secessionist activities in Kashmir. When the case was first detected the most serious concern was about payments to Kashmiri militants. It was reported that Ashfaq Hussain Lone and Shahabuddin Gauri were paid Rs. 16 lakh for stepping up terrorist activities in Kashmir, laying down extensive wireless network for subversive purpose, procurement of sophisticated weapons, recruitment of volunteers for subversion, etc.

The money was allegedly sent from the United Kingdom and Dubai. Two names were identified in London one Mohini Jain and another Dr. Mahammed Ayub Thakur, who is also a patron of Islami-Jamaat-e-Tulba. A third person identified in Dubai was Tariq Ali and supposed to be connected with Dawood Ibrahim. Another Kingpin of hawala operator was a man commonly known as Amir Bhai. It was reported that he was the brain behind the illegal transfer of nearly Rs. 48 crore to S.K. Jain (Surinder Jain) in his multi-crore pay offs to politicians and bureaucrats.

The C.B.I. tried to interrogate Mohini Jain and Dr. Mahammed Ayub Thakur in London but failed. Tariq Ali could not be interrogated in Dubai as he was absconding. Moolchand Shah, a Mumbai based hawala operator, known as having close links with the Menons and suspected in the Mumbai bomb blasts in 1993 was arrested by the Mumbai police.

The investigation of the Jain hawala case, by the C.B.I., was marked by very slow progress after the recovery of diaries. It pulled in different directions due to the involvement of top politicians. The amounts paid to them were mentioned against their coded names which were not difficult to decipher. S.K. Jain reported to have paid Rs. 65 crore between 1988 and 1991.

When the entries in the diaries became known journalists Vineet Narain and Rajinder Puri and advocates Kamini Jaiswal and Prashant Bhusan moved the Supreme Court through public interest litigation petitions charging the C.B.I. with delaying the probe intentionally. The C.B.I. confessed about the recovery of diaries and seizure of lakhs of rupees in foreign exchange in June 1991 which the Jains could not account for. Suddenly, the case took a serious turn when, shortly after the raids on Jains, the C.B.I. caught one of its own senior officials, O.P. Sharma, a deputy inspector general trying extract the last instalment of the bribe money. Sharma was in charge of the investigation of the hawala case against the Jains.

A number of others denied receipt of payments and they are bureaucrats. K. Padmanabhiah, then attached to the energy and power ministry (presently home secretary) denied any payment. Vijay Karan, former director, C.B.I. denied any payment and said that the code words V.K. used in the diary was not him and meant someone else. Vijay Karan's defence was found to be true.

It has been established beyond doubt by both the C.B.I. and DOE that S.K. Jain had been a part of an international chain involving illegal transfer of money. During investigation Jain made a clean breast of the network through which he operated. Entries in diaries and his telephone bills provided adequate materials of the nexus between Jain, top politicians and bureaucrats. Although both S.K. Jain and J.K. Jain (diaries were recovered from his residence) were arrested and examined they avoided to answer several questions put by the C.B.I. involving them taking cover under Article 20(3) of the Constitution which permits an accused not to disclose facts that will incriminate him before the Court. This has made the position of the Directorate of Enforcement embarrassing; the C.B.I. seems to be faring no better. By issuing the charge sheets, the C.B.I. has confirmed the entries in diaries and Jain's confessional statement. The same evidence will apply against ministers (who are all public servants) and top bureaucrats to prosecute them under Section 13 of the Prevention of Corruption Act which deals with abuse of official authority for granting favours and taking pecuniary advantage in return.

The importance of Jain's statement is that he decoded the names and said how and why he handed over the money. The diary entries are meaningless without the confession. But strictly under the law neither the diaries nor the confession mean very much on their own. The cases will depend on the evidence of quid pro quo and the end-use of the money by the recipients.

S.K. Jain, the main accused in the case, had stated that prime minister Narasimha Rao also was a recipient of his largesse to the tune of Rs. 3 crore although his name does not appear in the diaries. Jain had disclosed during his interrogation by the C.B.I. that he had routed the payments through godman Chandraswamy and minister Satish Sharma; he had paid Rs. 2.5 crore to Chandraswamy and Rs. 50 lakh to Satish Sharma in March 17, 1995 under instructions from prime minister Rao. The C.B.I. did not pay much attention to Jain's statement and concentrated on the cases of those mentioned in the diaries.

Jain's statement was full of contradictions so far as prime minister Rao's involvement is concerned. 'We interrogated S.K. Jain several times over last two years. He did not say anything about payment to prime minister rao's involvement till his last interrogation in March 1995". Even if the money was paid through Chandraswamy and

Satish Sharma invoking the name of the prime minister Rao it could not be taken for granted that the money was received by prime minister Rao. However, a preliminary inquiry was conducted by Amod Kanth, DIG, C.B.I., who was in charge of the investigation of the hawala case after suspension O.P. Sharma, DIG, C.B.I. who was in Jain's pay and reportedly came to the finding that prime minister Rao did receive money from Jain. With this revelation, Amod Kanth could not be retained in the C.B.I.; he was transferred out of the C.B.I. by the Prime Minister's Office (PMO) and also his immediate superior B.B. Lal.

Jain's powerful friends were not confined to the ministers and politicians of the ruling party. They belong to BJP and Janata Dal. Only left parties were free from Jain's influence. Jain himself was not a hawala dealer. His role primarily was a intermediary to work out the level of commissions to be paid for the deals and then distribute the money amongst those who mattered. The kickbacks and commissions were deposited in a foreign account of some hawala dealer and an equivalent amount handed over to Jain. The funds were spread thin over the entire political system. It was, perhaps, due to this that neither the hawala scandal nor its dangerous import on the security of the country was ever raised in Parliament. Jain's relationship with top politicians was mostly to secure contracts. His business started from Bhilai Steel Plant and spread to other parts of the country.

The nexus between contractors, corrupt bureaucrats and politicians has resulted in the subversion of public sector undertakings. The politicians have no compunction to amass illegal money to fight elections. Several of them acquired vast property out of the crores of rupees received by them from Jains. Needless to say the subversion of democracy through black money power has been a redeeming feature in Indian democracy. All these years politicians have handled crores of rupees as election funds and not included in their income tax returns as if they are accountable to none. The recent message of the Supreme Court that politics is a matter of accountability to courts have sent shockwaves among politicians.

Besides kickbacks and commissions, some politicians and bureaucrats had been drawn towards Jain whose high life-style was an added attraction. The farmhouse that Jain purchased in Mehrauli named 'Panchavati' has temperature controlled swimming pool, a basement discotheque and a landscaped area dotted with bars and statutes made of Italian marble, where Jain threw lavish parties with choicest food and foreign liquors flowed like water. There was no dearth of society women in colourful dresses in attendance. MPs, ministers and top bureaucrats made a beeline to parties which continued throughout the night. During Diwali, New Year's day and birth day Jain hosted card games for his guests. Different card tables had different stakes starting from Rs. 1000 to Rs. 2 lakh. Jain's farmhouse 'Panchavati' was a convenient place to cultivate powerful politicians and top bureaucrats in the nation's capital.

Lucrative contracts from all sectors of the government such as NTPC, SAILs, TELECOM etc. were available to Jain's companies for the mere asking. In 1975 Vishwanath Menon, a member of Rajya Sabha, in a letter reportedly addressed to the energy minister K.C. Pant had detailed the modus operandi of Jain's lobby which was using corruption as an instrument to destroy public sector undertakings. He alleged that some of the Jain's companies secured contracts in public sector undertakings, fraudulently, at exorbitant rates. After they had collected bills, they deliberately delayed infrastructure projects by either demanding higher payments or doing only those jobs which were profitable. They also used trade union leaders to queer the pitch of the management. Since Jain had established close rapport with Sanjay Gandhi, Menon's letter to K.C. Pant did not cut any ice. Jain continued to prosper. It was only Mohan Kumaramangalam, steel minister an honest and upright person who put his foot down and refused to be influenced by Jain. Contracts for steel plants went to contractors, other than Jain's companies. This period was short lived as Kumaramangalam died in a plane crash.

True to his father, P. Rangarajan Kumaramangalam tendered his resignation as General Secretary All India Indira Congress and former Central minister began his fight by exposing prominent

Congressmen and their relatives who had links with the underworld don Dawood Ibrahim. He released a copy of his notes dated 8 February 1996 highlighting that the prime minister's brother P.V. Manohar Rao had accepted free tickets and hotel accommodation from East-West Airlines and last year (1995) Ghulam Nabi Azad gave East-West the contract for chartering flights for Haj pilgrims. The notes mentioned that these flights came back loaded with gold and other smuggled goods. Although the government denied these charges, the enthusiastic crusader was unfazed. Ranga, who had helped the Vohra Committee said that these materials are in the files of Vohra Committee. On being questioned whether he had asked prime minister Rao to resign, he replied, 'I have asked the President to ask prime minister to resign. There is a lot of difference. If you have an investigation pending against you, you cannot head the agency that is investigating you (Sunday 18-24, 1996).

So formidable was Jains' money power that even the C.B.I. was afraid to touch him as if he was the government. The C.B.I. booked two Kashmiri militants connected with the hawala scam under TADA. The hawala dealer Shambhu Dayal Sharma and his mentor Mool Chand Shah were also booked under TADA. But when it came to S.K. Jain, his patrons were powerful enough to grant him immunity from TADA. His case was neither reported to the income tax nor enforcement authorities for evasion of tax and FERA laws; he was also liable for action under the Prevention of Corruption Act. Jain's companies had allegedly secured more than 200 government contracts in the coal, power, and steel sectors.

He flaunted his closeness to prime minister Rao and boasted that he could make anyone minister or remove him from the ministry. Nemesis caught up with him when the Supreme Court came into the picture after receipt of public interest litigation petitions. The Supreme Court asked the C.B.I. on December 5, 1994 for a report, observing that If we are meant only for punishing people for petty offences and letting people who spend lakhs on birthday parties go scot free, we had better close down the Courts. It appears that Jains are too hot to handle and the only way to keep them quiet is to let them do what they want. It is difficult to believe that a thing so simple which can even a Policeman from a police station could solve is beyond C.B.I.'s calibre. The Judges Verma, Bharucha and Sen, consisting of the division bench of the Supreme Court, who heard the case, made it clear that they would not sit idle and allow the government to carry on its business of 'cover up'.

The Supreme Court was very critical about the failure of the C.B.I. to trace and interrogate Ameer Bhai alias Ameer Dean Habib who had allegedly supplied more than Rs. 50 crore to S.K. Jain to pay off politicians and bureaucrats through the hawala channel. Ameer Bhai had fled India. Arrest warrants were issued and order to attach his property, one of the devices to break the back of economic offenders, was resorted to but nothing tangible has come out of these measures so far.

Reacting to the C.B.I.'s delay in charge sheeting three cabinet ministers for want to sanction from the PMO, the Court remarked, 'if there is any delay from any quarter in procuring permission, we shall intervene'. Again on 16 January 1996 Justice Verma told the C.B.I. 'If 10 people are named and you charge sheet nine, leaving out even one, we will not be happy about it'.

The hawala bomb had surfaced since 1991 and it took five years to explode. The seeds of the scam had been largely sown during the rule of Indira Gandhi and watered during the regimes of Rajiv Gandhi, V.P. Singh and Chandra Sekhar. And, now the harvest was ripe for picking up and Rao was doing it at his own choosing. The explosion discredited all major political parties - Congress, BJP and Janata Dal. Since largest number of politicians belonging to the Congress was the beneficiaries of Jain's largesse, the reputations of the Congress, painstakingly built up over the years, fell by the wayside. Except for the Left, no party escaped unscathed.

The ideological and moral vacuity of the ruling Congress can be traced from the demise of Lal Bhadur Shastri and rise of Indira Gandhi to power. Obsessed with power and the advancement of her own family, she treated the country like a feudal estate. She sacrificed everything including democracy at the alter of her overriding ambition. She nationalised banks with the object of helping the rural poor but utilised them for her and party interests. Bank boards and officials at the highest level were packed with her as well as the ruling partymen and their relations. Money, running into crores were siphoned from banks without any accountability and ushered in 'loot mela' in the name of 'loan mela'.

She, in the name of 'Garibi Hatao', introduced Programmes for the benefit of the poor but they were subsequently pitchfork into a complete eyewash because the ministers and bureaucrats, who were supposed to implement the programmes, were themselves highly corrupt and no wonder the programmes fell by the wayside.

S.K. Jain Opens a Pandora's Box

Extracts from the statement made by S.K. Jain to the C.B.I. under Section 161 Criminal Procedure Code between 5 and 11 March 1995 is given here. Legally a statement made to a police officer is not admissible in evidence. They are not intended to prejudice, in any way, the rights of the accused or interfere with the administration of justice or fair trial but simply to report on facts:

"I came in contact with Quattrocchi, an Italian, who was a representative of Snam Progetti in India sometime towards the end of the year 1982 or in the beginning of the year 1983. He was introduced to me Mr. Gerni, who was a manager of Onsaldo, a government undertaking of Italy. I met Gerni for the first time in Delhi in connection with discussions of a tender which he had quoted for erection and supply of steel structure and boiler, etc. for Rourkela Steel Plant. He had come to know that my company BEC had a good name in this field.

Quattrocchi was interested in taking up the contract of supply, fabrication and erection of a boiler in the captive power plant, Vishakapatnam. It was a 60 x 3 MW project. It was an understanding between me and Quattrocchi that if they got the contract, they would give me a sub-contract for erection and fabrication of the boiler etc. Quattrocchi had submitted a tender for the project in the name of Snam Progetti. The prices quoted by Snam Progetti were very high and that is why we did not pursue this contract. This was ultimately allotted to BHEL. Quattrocchi was involved in many businesses like fertilizers, ONGC, pipeline, etc.

"In and around 1987, the contract of the hydro project of NHPC at Dulhasti in Jammu and Kashmir came up. It was awarded to M/s Ceglec Company of France. I and Quattrocchi had assisted Ceglec to get this contract from NHPC.

"During those days, another hydro project of Uri also came to be tendered. M/s Scanska of Sweden, which was a consortium of several companies had also tendered for the same: ABB also one of the companies in the consortium.

Mr. Benbourn, the executive vice-president of ABB in India was known to me. He had been introduced to me by Arun Nehru at the residence of Shri Shivshankar, minister, who was a close friend of mine.

"I took Benbourn and introduced him to Quattrocchi. There after, Quattrocchi put Benbourn in touch with Rajiv Gandhi for discussing and finalising the said contract at Uri. Quattrocchi worked as the middleman for getting Scanska the Uri contract and Ceglec the Dulhasti contract, both through Rajiv Gandhi, the then PM. The Dulhasti contract was for about Rs. 800 crore and the Uri contract for Rs. 1,200 crore - Rs. 1,300 crore, as I roughly remember. As per my undertaking with Benbourn and Quattrocchi, I was to get the work of erection and fabrication in the Uri project for about Rs. 300 crore - Rs. 400 crore. In the meantime, some terrorist activities started in Uri and I lost interest in the said jobs. These works were then done by ABB themselves through some other contractor.

For the help which I and Quattrocchi rendered ABB in getting the Uri contract. I was to get my commission of 3 per cent and Quattrocchi, 7 per cent. For the Dulhasti project too, I was to get a

3 per cent commission. With regard to the commission pertaining to the Uri project, I had insisted to Quattrocchi that he give me the payment in Indian rupees and in India. Therefore, he brought a certain Amir Bhai to my office and introduced him to me saying that he would make the payment to me in Indian rupees. He had told me that Amri Bhai was residing in Bombay. J.K. Jain had also met him in my office at that time. Amir Bhai was about 45 years old, 5 ft 6 inch height, medium-built and with a medium complexion. He used to speak both English and Hindi and was a very close confidence of Quattrocchi's. Amir Bhai met me at the Oberoi Hotel in Bombay where J.K. Jain also met him on two-three occasions. I do not know his telephone number or his address, since J.K. Jain kept in touch with him for collection of money. As far as I know, Amir Bhai has left India about three years back and his location is not known.

"After the work of the Uri project was allotted to Scanska, my share of the commission was decided at about $ 18 million $ 19 million as I can now recall and Quattrocchi had transferred the said $ 18 million - $ 19 million into Amir Bhai's account who was living in Bombay, to be delivered in Indian rupees as and when I asked for the same. Quattrocchi had a bank account in ABN Bank at Antwerp (Belgium) or Geneva/Zurich in Switzerland and possibly Amir Bhai had also got Bank accounts in the said banks. Amir Bhai had been passing on the money to me through J.K. Jain as and when I asked for it. Whenever Amir Bhai used to pay the money to J.K. Jain, he used to account for the receipts against secret heads 'A', 'AB' and 'K' in the diary. I had been thus getting my share of commission in Indian rupees through Amir Bhai in the manner stated above.

"I had a desire to become the biggest industrialist of India and to grow on the lines of Dhirubhai Ambani of Reliance. I had known that Ambani had risen with the help of his close contacts with politicians. I also wanted to come into close contact with politicians and highly placed public servants by paying them money by way of commissions. I started giving money to various politicians and highly placed public servants from the year 1987 which continued till 1991.

"During 1989, the work of Kawas project as Gujarat was being retendered and was pending clearance in the Ministry of Power and Energy. Arif Mohammad Khan was then minister for power and energy. GEC Alsthom were the lowest bidders in this contract. Revviellon was then the vice-president of Alsthom and was looking after the export works of Alsthom in India. Revviellon met me and requested me to get a clearance for the contract file, which ultimately had to go to GEC Alsthom. After the allotment, a sub-contract for about Rs. 20 crore-Rs. 22 crore, pertaining to erection and fabrication works was to be given to me the GEC Alsthom, but ultimately, when the contract was awarded, they gave me a sub-contract of about Rs. 4 crore - 4.5 crore only.

"For expediting the Kawas contract with Arif and as compensation for the loss of work, I told Revviellon to give me Rs. 10 crore, which he transferred to the accounts of Amir Bhai (with ABN Bank). I had introduced Revviellon to Amir Bhai for this purpose. Amir Bhai had taken this amount also in the common pool of my earlier credits which he was holding on the transfer of commission for Uri and Dulhasti. Out of these Rs. 10 core, I paid Rs. 6.5 crore to Arif Mohammad Khan in three instalments during May to August, 1990, which he used for setting up the charitable hospital in Bahraich.

"Also in 1989, the work of the cantering plant of Durgapur Steel Plant was awarded to M/s Tyago Permo Export, a government of Russia undertaking. I have been in contact with the said companies because of my old contacts with Bhilai Steel Plant with which they had old associations. Mr. Egnevf of Russia was the president of the company. At the time of the awarding of the contract of Durgapur Steel Plant to M/s Tyago Permo, there was a demand of Rs. 10.5 crore towards political expenses at Delhi. Since Tyago Permo was a government undertaking, they could not make any direct payments to anybody and therefore, they suggested they could make the payments to our company, BEC.

"The understanding between us and Tyago Permo was that they would compensate us in the export orders at the inflated price we would be quoting to them. With this background, Tyago Permo gave an advance of Rs. 15 crore by cheque to my company, which I deposited in my company's account. Against the said payment of Rs. 15 crore, I paid Rs. 10.5 crore in instalments to Satish Sharma in Lalit Suri's presence in Holiday Inn, New Delhi, which was later sent to Rajiv Gandhi's house. I had met Satish Sharma in Rajiv Gandhi's house and had known him quite well since 1985.

"I had paid Rs. 4 crore to Rajiv Gandhi during March and May 1991 because he had demanded the said amount for making payments to Jayalalitha in Madras. The sum of Rs. 2 crore was collected by Mr. George, private secretary to Rajiv Gandhi, from my residence in the month of March 1991. I had kept the said amount with me after collecting the same from J.K. Jain. J.K. Jain, however, knew that this amount was given to Rajiv Gandhi and therefore, he had entered the said disbursement in the diary under the code RG during March 1991. The other sum of Rs. 2 crore was given by me and J.K. Jain to Sitaram Kesri, treasurer of Congress Party at his residence in Delhi in two instalments. One instalment of Rs. 1 crore was given to him on May 2, 1991 and the other Rs. 1 crore was given after about 10-15 days after that. Since the diaries had already been seized by the CBI by that time, there is no entry in respect of the payments to Sitaram Kesri.

"After the assassination of Rajiv Gandhi, Narasimha Rao, the present PM, became president of the Congress Party. Shri R.K. Dhawan, MP, who is known to me from the time of Rajiv gandhi's government, took me to Shri Rao at his residence at Motilal Nehru Marg, New Delhi. R.K. Dhawan told me in the presence of Shri Rao to give Rs. 50 lakh to the party fund, saying that I would be compensated for the same. I had agreed to the same. Shri R.K. Dhawan, meanwhile, further told Shri Rao that I would be giving Rs. 5 lakh for his (Narasimha Rao's) expenses also on the elections, etc. I agreed to make the said payments also.

"Since I already had the flowing money from the channels of Amir Bhai, I had no difficulty in making these payments. After about 2-3 days, I paid Rs. 5 lakh to Rao at his residence at Motila Nehru Marg. On or around 27th May`1991, I also paid Rs. 50 lakh to R.K.

Dhawan for party expenses when Rao was to leave for UP for electioneering. After about a month or so when Rao became PM, Satish Sharma called me to his own farmhouse where Chandraswami was already present. I left my car at the farmhouse of Satish Sharma and went along with Chandraswamy in his car to the PM's house at Race Course Road. Shri Rao talked to me separately and told me to pay Rs. 50 lakh to Satish Sharma, who at that time was not in the cabinet. Rs. 50 lakh to Shri Rao himself and Rs. 2 crore to Chandraswami I had agreed for the payments. At that time, some large-scale modernisation work was likely to be started at Rourkela Steel Plant. I expected some work in the plant to be given to me also and in that expectation I agreed to pay Rs. 3 crore as mentioned above. I met Rao on nine occasions during those days. Chandraswami is not checked and his car has free access to the PM's residence. I was also, therefore, not checked any my name was not recorded at the reception whenever I accompanied Chandraswamy in his car. When I went separately on 2-3 occasions my name was recorded at the reception and I was also checked by the security staff.

"In one of these meetings, Shri Rao told me that I may give his money of Rs. 50 lakh also to Chandraswamy. I thus paid Rs. 50 lakh to Satish Sharma and Rs. 2.5 crore to Chandraswamy at their respective residences in instalments. These payments were required for the purpose of effecting defections of some MPs in support of Congress Party which was being planned during those days by Satish Sharma and Chandraswamy. These amounts were also from the same channel of Amir Bhai which I have been receiving through J.K. Jain as mentioned above. Since the diaries had been seized by the CBI by then, none of these payments are entered in the said diaries. I went to the residence of Rao in the evening prior to Holi of 1992. He again asked me to pay Rs. 3 crore Rs. 4 crore more for party work which I could not pay.

"The other receipts of money through hawala channels is Rs. 1.9 lakh which I had received in US dollars at Dubai during January 1989, when I had visited Dubai for 3-4 days with my wife Poonam and daughter Geetika during the New Years' celebration of 1989. I had received this amount through the above mentioned channels at Dubai and that is why it is accounted for in the diary against the account only under code'A'. The first two pages of the diary contain the receipt of Indian rupees from AB against the conversion of US dollars at Hawala rates prevalent during the relevant period. This gives the account of about 22.65 m US dollars which were received by us from AB which I had distributed to different persons and business organisations as mentioned in detail in the two diaries and two files in coded words and figures.

"The other receipts shown in the names of my family members and other contractors, etc., are the receipts of black money from my business earnings or the intra-family transactions which also included refund of some amounts received by them from the amounts received by J.K. Jain from the channel of AB, etc. My brothers N.K. Jain and B.R. Jain knew about such receipts from the channel of AB mentioned above and they also knew the sources of the said funds. The amount of Rs. 13 lakh shown as received from one ABBI is the receipt of black money through one contractor P.N. Abbi for sale of steel scraps, etc. at Bhilai. I do not know the exact whereabouts of P.N. Abbi now.'

The two diaries, two files and two note books seized the C.B.I. were in the handwritings of J.K. Jain. He maintained them under the instructions of his boss, S.K. Jain. They were written month wise and needed verification as the entries could not be accepted as genuine books of account. They would all have been consigned to the oblivion were it not for the petition filed in the Supreme Court by Vineet Narain, editor Kalchakra in which three others had joined.

But for the Supreme Court's intervention the hawala scam would have been buried. Despite its intervention, politicians who figure in the diaries cutting across political lines have failed signally in their duty to account to the public or even to realise the gravity in the matter. The diaries seized sparked one of the worst scandals in independent India's recent history. Like murder, scams will be out, each in its own manner. With allegation against prime minister Rao that he was paid Rs. 3 crore the nation is bewildered and does not know whom to trust. A poor country like ours cannot afford to have such pervasive corruption among the rulers, who have become easily purchasable commodities. When people read loans of Rs. 250 billion are to be raised by March, 1997 they might ask how much there is in it for the ministers and politicians of the ruling party.

The upshot of the hawala scandal which is rocking the nation is that it has highlighted the case with which the nations complex foreign exchange control and regulation laws can be and have been contravened. Ways and means must be found to strengthen our foreign exchange laws to prevent foreign exchange holdings of Indian citizens in illegal bank accounts abroad; today Indian citizens illegal bank accounts abroad are estimated by the Reserve Bank of India at $ 180 million (Rs. 550,000 crore).

Bank Scams

Massive loss reported by the Madras based Indian Bank for the last financial year, 1994-95 is a scandal that goes beyond the figures in red. As Rs. 1336.40 crore, the quantum of the loss reported is the highest ever recorded by an Indian bank to date. The bank, which the previous year reported a capital adequacy of 8.5 per cent is now in the ignominious position of having its entire net worth capital base of Rs. 654 and reserved Rs. 412 crore fully wiped out. What is worse, however, is the irrefutable evidence that the bank has been guilty of fudging its accounts for the past few years. In this, it seems to have been aided by the negligence as well as incompetence of both the regulatory authority and the bank's statutory auditors. After all, such fudging of accounts would not have been possible had the auditors and the Reserve Bank of India (RBI) inspectors done their job properly. Additional provision of Rs. 980.02 crore for bad loans and Rs. 190 crore for reversal of interest is reportedly responsible for the huge loss. The net profit of Rs. 14 crore reported by the bank for 1993-94 is also suspect. The RBI as the regulator, can hardly absolve itself of the blame (The Economic Times, 16 August 1996-editorial). Chairman and managing director, M.

Gopalakrishnan was given extension thrice for allegedly obliging Tamil Nadu Congress president G.K. Moopanar in sanctioning loans to hundreds of persons recommended by him. The scandal assumed political overtones as some politicians belonging to the Tamil Mannila Congress were linked to it.

The C.B.I. filed cases against six bank officials, namely M. Gopalakrishnan, former CMD; B.B. Shetty, former executive director; T.P. Karunanandan, former GM (Credit); A.V. Shantamugasundram, former AGM; V.R. Chidambaram, former Zonal Manager, and P. Srinivasan, AGM - all working at the Madras branch of the Indian Bank during the period. The FIR stated that they had released the loan to the borrower D. Natarajan without observing the norms and procedure of the banking administration.

The disease of corruption has spread enormously among bank employees and officials posing a serious threat to the functioning of the banking industry. The Public Estimates Committee had submitted a detailed reports regarding rampant corruption in the banking industry. It is not always the small fry in the banking sector who are involved. It is the big shots who seldom get caught and who are responsible for massive frauds. Chairman and Branch Managers are not always above board in this wave of corruption sweeping the banking industry.

Gurudas Das Gupta CPI, MP in his letter to the prime minister had said that 70 per cent of profits earned by nationalised banks are lost in meeting bad debts and the amount of bad debts has been rising steadily every year. A Chairman of a nationalised bank with its headquarters in Madras wrote off Rs. 10 lakh as bad debt a day before his retirement. A leading hotel in Madras which had got over Rs. 1 crore as loan from the bank, was the beneficiary. The amount written off was the interest that the hotel was to pay to the bank (The Statesman, 15 December 1988).

In 1985 the officers' Association of Allahabad bank levelled serious charges against the then Chairman of the bank. It was alleged that the bank management had sold securities worth Rs. 500 crore to

Citibank of America for only Rs. 300 crore. According to the Association, the Chairman had accumulated extensive properties in Bangalore, Madras, Delhi and Bombay. The C.B.I. had unearthed crores of rupees after conducting raids in the premises of the chairman of different banks in the past and also recently. The Public Estimates Committee concluded in its report that banks have left other government departments far behind in respect of corruption.

In one of the biggest case reported from the State Bank of India's Shivaji Nagar branch in Bangalore was defrauded to the tune of Rs. 12 crore. Investigations disclosed that the concerned officer had a house in a posh colony in Bangalore and quite a few foreign cars. He was fond of changing foreign cars frequently but strangely enough the management was unaware of his activities. In Lucknow and Jamshedpur branches of SBI cases had been unearthed by the C.B.I. where peons defrauded these branches. A peon in Lucknow branch, it was later found, never travelled except by air.

There are innumerable cases in which bank officers granted loans to fictitious and even dead persons taking the money themselves and investing it in business, carried on by their wives or relations. The system of taking commissions for sanctioning loans has become widespread in Indian banks today. Under the various integrated rural development programme (IRDP), bank officials take commission for financing rural schemes.

Almost all co-operative banks are in red. Losses run into crores of rupees every year. Poor agriculturists do not get the benefit of these banks and the beneficiaries are the rich landlords who control the banks. The biggest scandal in the history of banking was the acceptance of even Gandhi maiden, Patna and Platform No. 2 of Patna junction railway station as security against a payment of advance of several lakhs of rupees by the Patna Urban bank to one of the close relations of chief minister, Bihar.

On an average, 70/80 raids are conducted by the C.B.I. almost every year, in the country, on the residence of bank officials to unearth cases of assets disproportionate to the their legal sources of income. Many cases do not come to notice due to collusion between the management and union leaders, who prevent investigations, threatening strikes. The Vigilance departments of banks do not function at all in the banks.

Over the years, the public sector banks have become the veritable pork-barrel of political patronage ever since Indira gandhi's rule. Not only have the chief executives been chosen on political considerations, but an overwhelming majority of non-official directors of the nationalised banks had been drawn from the ranks of ruling party. Though the Banking Registration Act stipulates the appointment of the nominees of depositors, artisans, industry and farmers on the boards, these interests had all too often been represented by the ruling party workers, pro-party journalists, ministers relatives, defeated ruling party MPs and MLAs (India Today, 15 March 1982).

For example, in the case of Punjab and Sind Bank, one director, Jamuna Solanky was a former Congress(I) MLA from Madhya Pradesh. Another, Surinder Singh Virdi was the son-in-law of President Zail Singh. A third, Keshav H. Kulkarni was a leader of the Congress-affiliated Indian National Trade Union Congress (INTUC) and a fourth, Jaswant Singh Kochar was a Congress(I) leader. In the case of Andhra Bank, Sunil Jakhar, son of Lok Sabha Speaker Balaram Jakhar was a director. In the Central Bank of India Ravi Krishna Datta, prominent Congress(I) worker of the Ghazipur district, Uttar Pradesh was director.

K. Sambhasiva Rao Congress(I) MP, a director of the Andhra Bank managed to secure loans worth Rs. 3.92 crore from the bank for the Progressive Constructions Private Ltd. of which Sambhasiva Rao was a major shareholder, for assets he mortgaged at half the value. What was worse, the company also received advances from various departments from Andhra Pradesh and Uttar Pradesh governments to the tune of Rs. 5 crore by offering, as security, the same assets (Indian Express, 6 September 1984).

In 1981, Parliament was rocked by the then Finance Minister R. Venkataraman's admission that his officials were looking into allegations that the directors of various banks were obliging each other with loans totalling over Rs. 20 crore. The RBI too was flooded with complaints about directors misusing their position to benefit firms run by their relatives. Due to the influence of directors, loans were allegedly given on the unflated value of the assets pledged as securities to the bank.

With the knowledge and blessings of the ministry of finance loan melas (credit camps) were organised in several places for promoting the ruling party's and its leader's electoral prospects. Although ministers sponsoring these melas say that they are meant for the 'uplift of the weaker sections of society regardless of which political party they voted for' these camps have often been used to serve political ends. In these camps, loans had been advanced to the Congress(I) supporters in violation of all banking norms. These 'loan melas' turned subsequently into 'loot melas'.

In September 1984, the loan camps in Bangalore city's banks caused great confusion when a circular was sent off requesting bank managers to 'fix the branch seal on ration cards to prevent multiple financing'. A subsequent decision required that branches should insist not only on stamped ration cards but passport size photographs of intending beneficiaries. Amidst conflicting instructions and their anxiety to fill up the initial quota from each branch, the mela camps enforced the stamping of all ration cards. As against a quota of 900 applications, Syndicate Bank's 18 branches had distributed to 1,981 applicants, loans worth Rs. 65.69 lakhs. But the idea spread that loans would be granted up to Rs. 5,000 upon production of ration cards. Although the Union Finance Minister of State Janardhan Pujari promised distribution of loans worth Rs. 3 crore to only 11,350 applicants, the number was far in excess. The worst that could happen in the confusion was a staggering 87,180 bogus ration cards were detected in the city during the mela. Many bank employees profited from the mela but in some branches protests surfaced among bank employees. Most of the loans remained unpaid as loans evaded payment and many could not be traced.

In Tripura, it was reported that Youth Congress(I) workers had submitted 60,000 loan application forms which were not procured from banks but printed by them personally, which, of course, did not confirm to bank stipulations. The effect this had on banking is obvious. The C.P.I.(M) had also printed loan application forms and distributed several lakhs of them among the party's supporters.

But what needs to be described is politicians delivering political speeches when loans in such numbers are distributed; as also local political elements having a significant role in the identification of borrowers. This had the highly pernicious effect of fostering a culture in which people tend to think that loans from banks need not to be repaid.

Political influence not infrequently pressurises bankers to deviate from norms and show favours. Even prime minister's office (PMO) is involved. A question by Prof. Madhu Dandavate on corruption and malpractice in various branches of the Syndicate bank and alleged involvement of the PMO generated a lot of heat in Parliament during the question hour on 6 December 1986 (The Times of India, 6 December 1986).

It is to be noted with regret the performance of the RBI has been far from being satisfactory. The Joint Parliamentary Committee (JPC) headed by Ram Niwas Mirdha on Securities scandals involving Harshad Mehta passed severe strictures on S. Venketraman, governor and Amitava Ghosh and R. Janakiraman, deputy governors.

The range of functions of the RBI has increased considerably. It has to act as an adviser to the government on financial and economic matters. Despite its statuary powers of control and regulation, it virtually functions under the direction of the banking division, ministry of finance. It has ceased to function as a 'watch dog' and converted into a 'lap dog' by the banking division.

The politicisation of banking was never the objective of nationalisation. In practice, however, public sector banks are required to serve the interests of the ruling party. As a result, the politicians in power have been utilising public money as though the banks have become their property by reason of nationalisation. Politicians have almost brought the banking industry to the brink of disaster.

The C.B.I. was able to establish links between Mehta and UCO Bank Chairman K. Margabanthu, between Mehta and Krishnamurthy and between Mehta and R. Sitaraman, from the SBI's securities division. Sitaraman got trapped because he had foolishly forgotten to remove fake bankers' receipts totalling Rs. 450 crore from his house. Besides this, the C.B.I. found evidence that Sitaraman had made foreign trips at Mehta's expense. While going through the records of 28 public sector banks the C.B.I. stumbled upon a racket in coupon rates, SBI apparently lost around Rs. 50 crore in one such deal. Sheer hard work had produced new leads to the C.B.I. Mehta admitted to have given Krishnamurthy Rs. 32.74 lakh because the latter asked for it.

Chairman and Managing Directors of nationalised banks had been involved in the Harshad Mehta securities and Urea scandals and Criminal cases had to be instituted by the C.B.I. against several of them. High flying bureaucrat V. Krishnamurthy of the finance ministry was arrested and put behind bars.

The C.B.I. charge sheeted a senior manager of a Vijaya Bank branch and three others accusing them of cheating the bank of Rs. 87 lakh on sanctioning credit facilities to a private firm. All the four accused including the manager were arrested by the C.B.I. In the charge sheets filed before designated C.B.I. Court, the C.B.I. claimed that the manager, N.B. Shetty 'conspired' with the owners of the R.K. Harbals Pvt. Limited to 'conceal' and 'misrepresent material facts' in sanctioning credit by the bank to the firm during 1987-90. The C.B.I. alleged that the accused R.K. Bhandari. Sanjay Bhandari, both directors of the firm and Mrs. Sonia Bhandari obtained the funds On the basis of bills of non-existent business concerns'.

Telecom Scam

A Division Bench of the Supreme Court consisting of Chief Justice A.M. Ahmedi and N.P. Singh and K. Venkataswami, JJ, dismissed nearly a dozen of petitions filed against the telecom department (DoT) and Sukh Ram, Union Minister of Communication on February 19, 1996. One of these petitions had been filed by seven Rajya Sabha MPs led by C.P.I.(M)'s Nilotpal Basu challenging the government's telecom privatisation policy, some what indirectly. The three judges disposed of the petitions on the ground that the court could not decide on policy matters. Finally, there was the issue of widespread corruption in the DoT.

Throughout December 1995 and January 1996, the Opposition had demanded Sukh Ram's resignation in Parliament charging him with widespread corruption in DoT. Even some members of the ruling Congress joined the opposition. Sukh Ram survived due to the protection provided by prime minister Rao and the whole matter was hushed up. Every time the Congress party and the prime minister Rao put up a strong defence for him.

The crux of the problem was prime minister Rao's son Prabhakar Rao was reportedly connected with the firm: Advanced Radio Masts (ARM) which secured contracts over crores of rupees from the Telecom department.

In 1992, the only member of the P.V. Narasimha Rao family Sukh Ram knew was Rajeswar Rao, the prime minister's third son. He supported Rajeswar Rao. However, he came to realise that Prabhakar Rao, the other son, was not happy with him. It was then that he met Sanjiva Rao, Prabhakar Rao's brother-in-law and a man called Pantula Ram Rao, the proprietor of Advanced Radio Masts (ARM).

Industry sources recall that Pantula Ram Rao visited the show-room of a business associate, who dealt with electronic goods. With him was a lady, who subsequently was known to the Runu Ghosh, Sukh Ram's accountant.

By then ARM, Runu Ghosh and Prabhakar Rao relationship grew. ARM had technology but no manufacturing set-up. Prabhakar Rao had the premises - and two companies, Sinclair and Goldstar - but no technology. Sukh Ram helped both. A contract for Rs. 80 crore was given to ARM which effectively sub-contracted technology to Sinclair. This was a perfect arrangement except that normally, stringent checks are carried out to see if the parties handed out the contract have the infrastructure. This was waived, allegedly, at the behest of the minister. By now, Sukh Ram had got wise to the game and when the question arose granting contracts he knew exactly what to do. After ARM, the Himachal Futuristic Communications Limited (HFCL) belonging to the Nahatas came into the picture. Nahatas were good friends of Narasimha Rao and Sukh Ram. Out of say four to five foreign companies wanting to do deals in India, Sukh Ram would only meet those which were brought to him by Nahatas. There were no deals in which the Nahatas were not involved.

From 1994, all purchases of Mahanagar Telephone Nigam Ltd. (MTNL) were made by Telecom department. This was inexplicable for MTNL is a public limited company. Out of 5 to 6,000 crore annually, a percentage was skimmed off because of bhi dena hai (we have to pay higher ups also). In the three clear years- 1994 to 1996 -in the area of purchases, Sukh Ram must have managed to arrange about Rs. 750 crore. This does not include the Rs. 500-600 crore from special deals. This made Sukh Ram worth about Rs. 1,500 crore besides some telecom officials very rich men indeed (Sunday 29 September to 5 October 1996 - The Jolly Bagman).

In one of the biggest raids conducted on 12 August 1996 under the United Front ministry, the C.B.I. recovered over crores of rupees from the residences of Sukh Ram in Mandi, Himachal Pradesh, Ghaziabad in Uttar Pradesh and New Delhi. A huge amount of cash, gold jewellery and incriminating documents, bank account books and papers relating to his acquisition of property in different places were recovered. A hotel in Mandi-Mayfair, owned by Sukh Ram's son Anil Sharma was raided by the C.B.I. and incriminating documents were found.

During C.B.I. investigation it was found that Sukh Ram had shown undue favour to ARM and HFCL. The total assets involved in the recovery of cash and gold jewellery only was reported to be at least Rs. 4 crore and his other immovable properties, accumulated through illegal fraudulent means, are yet to be valued. A strong suspicion was ventilated by the press and Opposition MPs that both Sukh Ram and prime minister Rao together were involved in the scandal. The assets illegally acquired by prime minister Rao could not be known as he has, throughout, been given protection by prime minister Deve Gowda and the C.B.I. was prevented from conducting any search to the residences of Rao or his son Prabhakar Rao who is deeply involved in almost all the scams.

The C.B.I. searched the residence of Ms. Runu Ghosh, a director in the finance wing of the Telecom ministry, who was deeply involved in the scandal. The search of Ms Runu Ghosh's residence led to the seizure reportedly of Rs. 1.32 lakh in cash, over a kilogram of gold, 20 expensive watches. She was arrested on 17 August, 1996 after registration of a FIR against her under the Prevention of Corruption Act for possession of assets disproportionate to her legal sources of income.

The accused Ms Runu Ghosh happens to be an officer of the Indian Audit and Accounts Service (IA & AS) of 1978 batch and reported to be close to ARM and Prabhakar Rao, prime minister Rao's son.

The Comptroller and Auditor General's (CAG) report on the Communications ministry for 1984-85, when Sukh Ram was the Union Minister, Communications, revealed gross irregularities and fraudulent transactions. The CAG's report mentioned specifically of a case where the Telecom department had placed an order for 500 multi-access radio relay system valued at Rs. 38.52 crore with Marine Communication Electronic Ltd, a Vishakapatnam based firm. An advance of Rs. 13.49 crore was paid to the firm but not a single set was delivered and the ministry made no efforts to recover the advance and the accrued interest of Rs. 8.90 crore. The matter was brought to notice of the prime minister but nothing happened and the whole matter was hushed up, allegedly, on receipt of kickback.

Sukh Ram has been arrested after the registration of a FIR under the Prevention of Corruption Act. His son, Anil Sharma, and MLA in Himachal Pradesh, who owns hotel Mayfair and Mayfair automobiles in Mandi, Himachal Pradesh and allegedly given a loan of Rs. 2.50 lakh to his mother besides holding several properties jointly with his father, is under C.B.I. investigation.

Medical Scam

The Union revenue secretary on 3 October 1996 apprised the Delhi High Court of the Customs authorities steps taken to recover the huge revenue loss in the Rs. 5,000 crore medical scam, allegedly involving Union minister, health, B. Shankaranand. N.K. Singh, Union revenue secretary informed the division bench monitoring the departmental probe into the scam that Customs authorities were proceeding to invoke bank guarantees worth over Rs. 72 crore of various hospitals in the prima facie case of fraudulent import of costly medical equipments. The bench comprising of Judges Y.K. Sabharwal and D.K. Jain after hearing the Union revenue secretary, N.K. Singh, Union health secretary, P.P. Chauhan, and the counsels for various parties, reserved its order till October 15 on the Constitution of two committees to probe into the scandal. A vigilance report by the Jt. Secretary, ministry of health, K. Chandramouli, had indicated several officials and former health minister, B. Shankaranand.

The Court, for looking into the action under the Customs Act, to recover the revenue lost in the customs duty exemptions and for the departmental action against erring and negligent officials, asked the revenue secretary to furnish the names of the revenue board, officials in the directorate of revenue intelligence and directorate general of health services. A petition by the People's Union for Civil Liberties had brought to the notice of the Delhi High Court that taking advantage of a 1988 notification of the Union government, which permitted charitable hospitals to import medical equipments free of duty, the officials in the director general of health services and Customs allowed import.

Corruption : Stock Taking in States

Corruption in high places is not an issue confined to the centre only. In States, crores of rupees are pocketed every year by political criminals in league with the bureaucrats. Not all States can be tarred with the same brush. It varies from State to State depending on the political leadership and high level of political corruption.

In North-East tribal ruled States the scale of corruption is unbelievable. For example, in Manipur, the C.B.I. investigations into corruption charges against non-Congress ministers, some years ago, did not yield much results beyond driving them into the fold of the Congress(I) party ruling at the Centre after which their looting became a forgotten history. It was no surprise that the two I.A.S. officers were arrested by the army.

In Nagaland, the special audit found that during Vamugo ministry Rs. 80 crore worth purchases made by the various departments between November 1991 and March 1992 were either 'bogus' purchases or purchases made at exorbitant rates. For example, homeless electrical section purves were purchased for Rs. 59,545 a price against an approved departmental rate of Rs. 4,400. There were atleast 32 items which were brought at inflated prices.

Though no longer in the post, after the President rule, Vamugo had ordered the release of Rs. 5 crore from the State treasury for payments towards several pending bills during his rule. The states financial commissioner, Raghu Menon refused to sanction the money on the ground that any allocation of funds after revised estimates of 1991-92 would be irregular. Menon's objections were overruled by the Chief Secretary, S.S. Ahluwalia and with the help of the latter Rs. 5 crore was released from the State exchequer and nothing was heard of the money"no bills, no record of payment and no department statement on the issue. The money vanished into the air (Sunday, 27 September-3 October, 1992).

Meghalaya, recently rocked by a Rs. 50 crore rural electrification scam under the State Electricity Board, is reeling under another Rs. 294 crore forest racket. About 120,000 valuable trees have disappeared from the Chimabanshi reserved forest in Garo Hills. The Meghalaya forest development corporation, an autonomous body reportedly sold timber, 1,777 teak and sal trees at Rs. 67.94 lakh, the market price being more than Rs. 2 crore. The Arunachal Pradesh Chief Minister Gogong Apang is allegedly involved in a Rs. 124 crore power department scam. The C.B.I. filed FIR against Mizoram Chief Minister Lalthanwala for alleged involvement in the multicrore Mizoram scam.

Bihar is today on the verge of a bankruptcy brought on by corrupt politicians, contractors and bureaucracy. Saibal Gupta, founder member of the Asian Development Research Institute (ADRI) says: Given the complete halt on development, Bihar will take 100 years to reach Maharashtra's current level of development. Bihar is turning into another Somalia'. This raises the question of what kind of life is possible when all the institutions that underpin a society have been so undermined that a reversion to some kind of nasty, brutish and short existence seems inevitable.

Corruption has brought Bihar to this pass. Taxes are not being collected and so the State has virtually no income. Citizens are not provided with even elementary services. Money meant for public projects is being embezzled. The staff in State Corporations are stealing hundreds of crores of the taxpayer's money. Police stations in the countryside are run by Mafia and antisocial elements and most police stations do not have the sanctioned staff. Cases are not registered.

Around 20,000 policemen turn up at their police stations only once a month on pay day. The rest of the month, they work as farm hands and domestic servants at senior officials houses. The revelation was made in a report prepared by a panel headed by the former director general of police, V.P. Jain. The report says some police officials, who are close to the politicians in power, have enrolled several men in the force and are using them as labourers, even though the constables draw their salary from the government. The Bihar Police association general secretary K.K. Jha says that it is a common practice to enroll policemen who are used by senior officials as labourer or domestic servants. About 14,000 policemen have been attached to I.A.S. and I.P.S. officers, ministers, and politicians as houseguards and bodyguards.

Corruption among policemen is widespread and even senior officers are involved. For instance, ten senior I.P.S. officers of the ranks of Inspectors General and Deputy Inspectors General have been directly accused of in the Uniform scandal relating to the purchase of uniforms and equipment running into lakhs of rupees, in a C.B.I. inquiry and they had to be arrested, cases registered against them and prosecuted. There was evidence that Laloo's government attempted to shield them for which their arrest by the C.B.I. was delayed.

The effect of corruption on medical services and academic spheres has been catastrophic. In Patna Medical College, the premier health centre in the State, there is such a dire shortage of funds that patients have to obtain written permission from the health commissioner if they want an X-ray done. Official sources say that although a cholera epidemic had broken out in many parts of the State, the public health department had no bleaching powder for the past two years. If one has the misfortune to need hospital treatment he avoids to visit the hospital because medicines are not available, not even bandages and cotton. Doctors, nurses and staff do not get their salary for months and there is no one to listen to their grievances.

According to the Bihar Pradesh Sanskrit Sikshak Mahasangh, the State's 45,000 Sanskrit teachers had not been paid for last 14 years. These teachers have survived by farming or working as farm labourers. Take the case of Patna University. The government released in 1994 money for salaries totalling Rs. 19 lakh only after the teachers and non-teaching staff went on a strike. Academic life on many campuses is controlled by politicians and criminals.

In 1994, the prison department warned the government that over 35,000 undertrials would starve to death unless immediate measures were taken. And they would die naked because the authorities had no money for clothes or food.

So appealing is the state of affairs that conversation amongst the people is littered with the acronyms of corruption: the politician-engineer and contractor nexus and the systematic loot and plundering by politicians in power. For example, an unfinished dam over the north Koel river in south central Bihar is one of the many projects ruined by systematic corruption.

Jagatanand Singh, Water Resources Development Minister told in the legislature that Rs. 40 crore had been siphoned off from the Durgawati Reservoir project in Central Bihar. Despite the government had spent over Rs. 80 crore on the project the farmers have not been benefited because the contractors, engineers and politicians had pocketed the money.

If irrigation projects are money-spinners for the unscrupulous contractors and officials involved, the Mahatma Gandhi Setu, Asia's longest bridge spanning the Ganga, has been a gold mine for those responsible for collecting the toll. It is believed that at the northern end of the bridge at Hajipur alone, an estimated Rs. 25,000 to Rs. 30,000 per day has been going into the pockets of engineers, district officials and local policemen. The method of looting is simple. And the scale enormous. The driver of every other car crossing the bridge is told to pay a few rupees less than the official amount and is then allowed to cross the bridge without receipt. So the money from half the drivers using the bridge fills the pockets of corrupt officials. Alternatively, since there are different rates for different types of vehicles, a heavily loaded truck which is required to pay say Rs. 60 is given a ticket designed for a mini bus, which pays only Rs. 24. The difference is pocketed.

In 1994, Raghunath Jha, food and civil supplies minister came across a file which revealed that nearly 1,700 employees of the food and civil supplies corporation had embezzled funds or misappropriated foodgrains worth Rs. 11.7 crore. He found that the staff had explained the shortfall by saying it had been eatenaway by rats in the godown or discarded as rotten.

All this and much more have combined to make Bihar bankrupt. The process began around 1980 when the Congress(I) ruled the State and has been continuing relentlessly ever since exacerbated by successive chief ministers who spent good money on projects which never materialised.

The fast unfolding scam in the Animal Husbandry Department (AHD) of Bihar can be understood from the following table which will show that nothing less than Rs. 1,800 crore had been fraudulently withdrawn within a span of ten years. The modus operandi was simple. The officials allegedly drew crores of rupees from the treasury against bills from fictitious suppliers of fodder and medicine. These withdrawals were found to be much higher than the funds allotted to the department in the budget but no questions were asked. For instance, against Rs. 225 crore allotted in the last five years, Rs. 568 crore was withdrawn from different district treasuries through fake bills for non-existent firms.

According to official sources, 43 FIRs have been lodged against as many as 275 persons - 125 private suppliers and 150 officials of the AHD and related departments like treasury and finance. Of the main accused 50 had been arrested and properties of absconds attached. Besides, 22 officials have been sacked and 115 officials placed under suspension.

Although Laloo's personal involvement in the scandal has not been established the proximity which some of the principal offenders enjoyed with the Janta Dal leadership casts some shadow of suspicion about his integrity. Moreover, the unnecessary belligerence with which he resisted a C.B.I. inquiry into the scam, convinced everyone, even his sympathisers, that Laloo had some skeletons in his cupboard which he feared would tumble down the moment the C.B.I. began probing. Laloo had failed to keep the lid on the enormous loot. Now it is becoming increasingly clear that despite rhetoric of social justice and upliftment of the poor and the oppressed the Janata government has been systematically plundering the funds that were meant for the development and welfare programmes for the dalits and the downtrodden.

Much before the fodder scandal leaked out, a House Committee in a report in 1990 had recommended a C.B.I. probe into the AHD irregularities and had named some bureaucrats. But the report was never tabled in the Assembly. The same year, the then agriculture minister Ramjewan Singh who was in charge of the AHD too recommended a C.B.I. inquiry but he was ignored.

Could all this have happened without high-level political connivance? That is the rhetorical question that opposition leaders are asking. As for Laloo, he announced that he had initiated steps to confiscate movable and immovable properties of the officials and contractors involved in the scam. But that did not satisfy the opposition which claimed that the government had not yet been able to lay its hands on the 'real culprits', the powerful contractors who provide election funds to the ruling politicians and the top level bureaucrats of the AHD and the finance department.

The only hope is that the inquiry is now in the hands of the C.B.I. as a result of the Patna High Court's direction and the Courts are beginning to stir in response to the hundreds of public interest litigation petitions which have been pouring in from citizens desperate to register their indignation over corruption. The Council for Protection of Public rights and welfare led by lawyer M.P. Gupta has been collecting cases and bringing them to the notice of the Patna High Court through public interest litigation petitions. C.B.I. sources said officers involved in the scam were granted promotions and extensions by the Bihar chief minister between 1992 and 1993.

The agency's special report to the Patna High Court said all original documents regarding Promotion, extension and cancellation of transfer' were signed by Yadav.

According to C.B.I., the following officers received undue favours from the chief minister:

Syam Bihari Sinha, the fodder scam kingpin, got a one-year extension as regional director of the animal husbandry department at Ranchi in 1993. This despite the fact that the finance secretary had said

Sinha's services could not be extended as there were inquiries pending against him. A Bihar legislative committee, the Nivedan Samity, passed severe strictures against Sinha, who finally retired in 1994.

Dr. Ram Raj Ram, who had a vigilance inquiry pending against him, was promoted, superseding other officials. Dr. Ram was made regional director of the department at Ranchi.

A police fraud case against Girija Nandan Sinha, an animal husbandry department official was overlooked and he was promoted.

Despite a state vigilance department inquiry, Inder Bhan Prasad, was re-employed for six months in the department.

R.K. Das, an official in the animal husbandry department, was also given re-employment though there was a vigilance inquiry against him.

A Rs. 1 crore fraud case against Shesh Muni Ram, district animal husbandry officer at Dumka, was suppressed and he was promoted. Ram had been named in the CBI's list of 33 persons involved in the scam.

B.N. Sharma, whose name also figures in the C.B.I.'s list to the High
Court, had a Rs. 52 lakh embezzlement case related to the fodder scam pending against him. But his transfer order was cancelled.

Sources said the officials involved in the scam Had the complete support, patronage and blessings' of Yadav. (The Telegraph 29 September 1996: Laloo backed officers named in scam.)

The C.B.I. allegedly seized seven registers on September 29, 1996 whose contents indicated the connivance between senior politicians and the fodder Mafia. The seizures were made during raids on the premises of Pataliputra Travel Agency. The registers revealed the accounts of J.S. Verma, a Calcutta based employee of Indian Airlines.

He has two firms in Patna and he used to supply air tickets to a large number of politicians, including Laloo Prasad Yadav, former Chief Minister Jagannath Mishra Congress Legislators Rajo Singh and Jagadish Sharma and the minister of animal husbandry Bholaram Tufani and several bureaucrats. Verma made payments for the tickers.

Verma had two firms dealing in medicine and animal fodder. He is alleged to have made false supply of medicine and fodder involving crores of rupees to the animal husbandry department. Verma on interrogation says that he himself paid for the air tickets either in cash or by cheques and the amounts were rarely reimbursed to him by the beneficiaries. Jt. Director, U.N. Biswas of the C.B.I. had submitted a progress report to the director C.B.I. (The Statesman, September 30, 1996.)

The report of the Jt. Director Biswas had listed 45 instances of Laloo Prasad Yadav 'aiding and abetting fraudulent dealings' in the multicrore Bihar fodder scam. Some of the charges highlighted in the report related to the period when Laloo Prasad Yadav held the charge of finance department also. Laloo was aware at every stage that the animal husbandry department officials were withdrawing in excess of budgetary allocation and committing various frauds. Even after the scam broke, he gave the main accused and former director of the animal husbandry department S.B. Sinha, a six months extension. Laloo cancelled 'in his own handwriting' the transfer order of B.N. Sharma, an animal husbandry official accused of embezzling Rs. 52 lakh, though a case was pending against him. On October 4, 1996 the C.B.I. seized a bank statement from the Patna branch of Canara Bank containing coded names of 300 people who made illegal transactions in the animal husbandry cell. (The Telegraph, October 6, 1996).

Biswas, Jt. Director, C.B.I. disclosed before Patna High Court on October 4, 1996 that his original progress report was tampered with by the top brass in the C.B.I. directorate itself. Biswas informed that Court that the report which it received from the C.B.I. directorate did not bear his signature, which he signed on every page of his report, and was a sketchy and truncated. The names of politicians involved, which he had mentioned in his report sent to director C.B.I. had been omitted from the report the C.B.I. sent to the Court. Jt. Director Biswas informed his boss that his report could not be changed by any one.

What had made Laloo's position untenable is the report of the Comptroller and Auditor General (CAG) indicting the Bihar government for financial mismanagement and looting of treasuries in full knowledge of the finance department.

Besides the fodder scam, Bihar government is knee-deep in other scams. Land scam is south Bihar, a preliminary State probe had revealed that 200 acres of government owned land, meant for the rehabilitation of tribals, was sold to a group of housing societies. The land at stake is estimated at Rs. 400 crore (Sunday 13-19 October 1996).

Bitumen Scam

Financial bungling of about Rs. 100 crore in the purchase of bitumen, used for carpeting roads. Bitumen had been purchased and entries recorded but it did not reach the PWD engineers (Ibid).
Forest Scam

Forest officials have figured in the bungling of State funds meant for afforestation. It is alleged that the timber Mafia in connivance with forest officials have swindled the State of anywhere between Rs. 50 and 100 crore (Ibid).

Medicine Scam

About Rs. 100 crore out of the sum sanctioned for the purchase and supply of medicine to various government hospitals had mysteriously disappeared and there are no accounts for this (Ibid). Notwithstanding the fact that Bihar is the ninth largest State in the country with an area of 1,73,877 sq. km. and ranks second in terms of population (86,338,853); vast fertile plains of north Bihar, watered by the Ganges, Gandak and Saraju and ideal for the cultivation of crops like rice, wheat, sugarcane, oilseeds and pulses; invaluable for the forest and mineral wealth in the south Bihar and in terms of mineral wealth Bihar is the richest State of the country which accounts for 40 per cent of the total mineral production in India; with two steel towns in TISCO's Jamshedpur and SAIL's of Bokaro which account for the large fraction of India' iron ore and coal production; and is practically the sole producer of cooking Cole, pyrites, uranium and the leading producer of coal and mica, Bihar is known today by its backwardness and dubbed as a lawless and highly corrupt State. For years successive governments have conspired to turn the richest State in the country into the poorest. Politicians who ruled the State, by and large, have been highly corrupt, casteists having close links with the underworld. Bihar's path to progress lies in having honest politicians who can ensure a clean administration capable of treating all caṣtes as equal and cleaning up the underworld activities.

Budgetary Allocations and withdrawals by Animal Husbandry Department over 15 years are provided below:

In Rupees Crores

Year	Budget Allotment	Amount Withdrawn
1981-82	10.21	10.47
1982-83	10.40	14.46
1983-84	15.63	15.14
1984-85	14.16	17.90
1985-86	17.84	22.26
1986-87	17.73	23.61
1987-88	19.48	28.10
1988-89	24.33	32.04
1989-90	34.23	44.01
1990-91	43.48	72.29
1991-92	46.24	117.60

1992-93	53.73	143.25
1993-94	62.41	191.27
1994-95	65.47	237.85
1995-96 (till Nov.)	48.00	156.55

Another development in the lawless State of Bihar has been the spectacular rise of cases of kidnapping for ransom. In 1993 the figure stood at 300; many more cases went unreported. The new cost-effective profession has an approximately annual turnover of Rs. 25 crore. Most of these cases arise out of politician-criminal and police nexus and the ransom amount is divided between them. The consequences has been disastrous for the economy of the State because businessmen and entrepreneurs, who are the main targets have been migrating to other States.

In Karnataka, some 200 officials of the income tax department swooped down on the offices and establishment of Karnataka's leading excise contractor, H. Dasappa and Co. What really shook the State's political circles was the fact that the Dasappas were linked closely to Bangarappa, Chief Minister. The raids, however, did not yield much result. Corruption during Bangarappa ministry was widespread granite, excise, land, captivation fee in colleges, bureaucratic appointments. Foremost of the charges against Bangarappa was his link with liquor lobby. Auctioning of excise operations fetched crores of rupees. While granting contracts, the excise commissioner violated the rules by encouraging rampant sale of loose and bulk arrack against the bottling rules in force, thereby sustaining heavy losses to the State exchequer. The Karnataka Legislature Committee severely criticised the government.

Corrupt and fraudulent housing societies had thrived during Ram Krishna Hegde's government. These societies ultimately proved to be one of the main reasons for Hegde's downfall. When Patel took over in 1989, the government appointed a Cabinet sub-committee to examine the working of these 100-odd societies. They were found to have been buying land with bogus agreements, enrolling bogus members, and collecting exorbitant site advances from members.

The scheme was put on hold. But at a meeting the Bangarappa government chose to overlook these developments and ordered the revenue department to speed up land acquisition. Surprisingly, the government order was issued, a week before the cabinet met to confirm its earlier decision. The government's action only invited speculation about massive pay-off.

The most prominent in Bangarappa's coterie was acting chief secretary J. Alexander who was raided by the Lok Ayukta two years ago for possessing assets disproportionate to known sources of his income. The Lok Ayukta recommended Alexander's suspension. Bangarappa closed the corruption case against Alexander and not only installed him to his original post of chief secretary but added several money spinning departments directly under him.

Bangarappa was investigated by the C.B.I. in connection with accepting bribe for approving the establishment of a dental college in Bangalore. According to the FIR filed in the Bangalore city Court Rs. 1 million was paid to Bangarappa and his secretary Suri Babu (The Asian Age, 8 July 1996 : I did not take any bribe: Bangarappa) (India Today, 18 September 1992: S. Bangarappa: A Last Ditch Stand).

In Tamil Nadu, corruption was widespread during the Jayalalitha's rule. Y.N. Sudhakaran, foster son of Jayalalitha was married off in Madras amid extravagance and controversy. A rough estimate of the marriage expenditure places the figure at 100 crore. It was called the mother of all weddings.

A 2-Km-long illuminated baraat route, 10 dinning halls, each seating a modest 25,000 persons, more diamonds than Elizabeth Taylor has seen, a 75,000 sq. ft. pandal, saris worth thousands of rupees and the entire State machinery on wedding alert. Tons of plywood, plaster of Paris and paints were lavish and used to erect arches and gates. The wedding pandal covered an area of over 75,000 sq. ft. The ostentation evoked public condemnation of the misuse of official machinery.

The Madras Municipal Corporation deployed hundreds of its staff to level the wedding site, widen approaches and blacktop roads on the VIP route. The Tamil Nadu electricity board installed transformers to supply power to the site; metrowater diverted water tankers to supply seven lakh litres of water; and government vehicles were employed to transport materials to the site.

The wedding hall and dining rooms cost Rs. 70 lakh; decorations, illumination cost Rs. 50 lakh, gift packets cost Rs. 50 lakh, VIP invitations including a silver plate with containers, a silk sari and silk dhoti-each worth Rs. 20,000. Over 1,000 VIPs were invited. Lunch for the VIP guests cost Rs. 100 per head; each VIP was given bottled mineral water and a fresh hand-towel. Food for the 1,10,000 Partymen cost Rs. 40 per head. About 1,000 rooms at Madras top hotels were reserved for VIPs, the average rent for each room about Rs. 3000. About 300 air-conditioned cars, rented at Rs. 1,100 per day were used. All figures are rough estimates. (India Today, 30 September, 1995).

VIP guests included Union Minister Sitaram Kesari, Chief Ministers, both present and former, included Laloo Prasad Yadav, Bhairon Singh Shekhawat, Deve Gowda, Ramkrishna Hegde, Biju Patnaik, S. Bangarappa and Sharad Pawar. Tamil Nadu Governor Chenna Reddy did not attend the wedding.

It raises one delicate question: How could the chief minister afford such a lavish wedding when she draws just only one rupee per month as official salary. Some lawyers filed petitions before the Madras High Court against the government spending crores of rupees from the public exchequer and disrupting of civic services. A prima facie inquiry revealed that no payments had been made and no meters fixed for the power drawn. The C.P.I. and C.I.P.(M) parties termed the event 'disgraceful' and 'criminal' and demanded an inquiry by the C.B.I. and the income tax department. Governor Chenna Reddy who did not attend the wedding had sent a report to the President of India and the prime minister was also informed about it. Since the matter involved abuse of power and there was public clamour and resentment over it, prime minister Rao should have ordered a C.B.I. investigation. Surprisingly, instead of taking action, prime minister Rao as president of AICC entered into an alliance with Jayalalitha and her AIADMK party in Tamil Nadu on the eve of the tenth Lok Sabha elections in 1996. Both AIADMK and the Congress lost the elections and the DMK ministry with Karunanidhi as Chief Minister came to power.

With the formation of the United Front Government, a joint C.B.I. and D.o.E. investigation was started against Jayalalitha for acquiring millions of dollars in violation of the provisions of FERA and other corruption charges.

There are several other allegations against Jayalalitha, namely (i) the accepted kickbacks of over Rs. 50 crore for coal imports. The company which secured the contract is said to be owned by Sasikala presently detained under COFEPOSA; (ii) her nephew Dinakaran booked under COFEPOSA for taking out from the country Rs. 65 crore and deposited the amount in foreign bank. His family floated 18 firms in the past five years; (iii) she did not refute charges of Rs. 11 crore being deposited in a bank account in Madras between 1991-96; (iv) she claimed she received Rs. 4.10 crore as gifts from Partymen between 1991-93 which was rejected by the income tax department; (v) Jaya publications received over Rs. 10 crore in 1991-95, most of it allegedly from the AIADMK account.

Jayalalitha was arrested on 7 December 1996 in connection with Rs. 8.53 crore colour TV purchase scam and remanded to judicial custody.

According to report in 1995 she and Selvaganapathy had entered into a criminal conspiracy to swindle crores of rupees in the supply of colour TV sets to the villages in a scheme ostensibly aimed at providing community education and entertainment through television to families below the poverty line.

It was discovered during investigation that much of the kickbacks routed through TV dealers and paid through cheques, stopped with a relative of Sasikala. But the investigating vigilance and anti-corruption officials of the Tamil Nadu government made no distinction between Jayalalitha and Sasikala. Sasikala was nobody in 1991. And Jayalalitha drew a salary of Re. 1 per month. So where did all the wealth came from?

The facts that Sasikala had given Jayalalitha's Posh Garden address as her own in all her dealings, that the two had at least three joint bank accounts and were partners in several Companies clearly established the link between the two and Sasikala was a front for Jayalalitha and her acquisitions.

When Jayalalitha became chief minister in 1991, she was among the most sought-after politicians in the State. She had impressed the corporate world with her quick comprehension of issues and readiness to give industrialisation a boost in Tamil Nadu. But it soon appeared to be a facade as the coterie around he made unreasonable demands for 'cuts', 'bribes' and 'percentages' thus ensuring that her tenure would be remembered as among the most corrupt that any State had known. Sycophancy evidently knew no bounds as ministers and other favour-seekers surrounded her all the time. Several ministers of Jayalalitha's cabinet were accused of corruption, namely E. Madhusoodhanam, former textile and food minister, charged with embezzlement in a Rs. 18 crore scheme to provide free saris/dhotis to the poor; R. Indrakumari, former welfare and handlooms minister charged in a scam involving a Rs. 11.5 crore scheme; K.A. Sengottaiyan, former transport minister, charged with causing Rs. 9 crore loss to transport department in the purchase of vehicles and spares and for disproportionate assets; K.P. Krishnan, former agricultural minister, accused of amassing disproportionate assets; and T.M. Selvaganapathy, former local administration minister, accused in a Rs. 83 lakh fraud in the Indira Awas Yojana and co-accused in granting illegal exemption to Pleasant Stay Hotel and in the Rs. 8.53 crore TV scam. They were all arrested some sent to jail and under judicial custody and some released on bail. Sasikala had been arrested.

The irony was that successive prime ministers had helped her. While Rajiv Gandhi ran to her rescue after she was assaulted by DMK

MLAs in the assembly house in 1989, Chandra Sekhar had, at her behest, dismissed the earlier DMK ministry of Karunanidhi. Narasimha Rao believed she could do no wrong and revived the political alliance which she had broken in spite of protests from Moopanar and Chidambaram. Even Deve Gowda restored the National Security Guard cover. Deve Gowda, allegedly, had soft corner for Jayalalitha as she had financed him and N.T. Ram Rao to fight assembly elections in their States when her relationship with the Congress(I) deteriorated three years back. And the power brokers, she had in her side persuaded Gowda to go soft on her, when they projected as the only opposition to DMK and Moopanar's TMK in Tamil Nadu.

Assam Scam

Assam chief minister Hiteshwar Saikia (Congress) is among seven political leaders against whom the C.B.I. reportedly found incriminating evidence in a multi-crore scam in the State's animal husbandry department. Late chief minister Hiteshwar Saikia had received a whopping Rs. 15 crore by cash and bank drafts carried by Dilip Bora in a government vehicle.

During 1988-90 the then AGP Veterinary minister Dilip Saikia Sonowal allegedly reportedly acquired assets amounting to crores of rupees. He purchased two flats in Andheri (West), Bombay in this period, one in his own name and another in the name of his wife. Besides he also owns another property in Bombay from where his brother-in-law Pranjal Chowdhury runs an ice-cream parlour.

Sonowal was one of the largest beneficiary of the Integrated Cattle Development Project (ICDP) drawing Rs. 7.12 crores, without a letter of credit (LOC), on November 23, 1990. Sonowal, reportedly also owns a large estate in Guwahati. The C.B.I. is inquiring into the siphoning of public money from treasuries running into crores relating to other departments, beside animal husbandry.

Uttar Pradesh Ayurveda Scam

Defence minister Mulayam Singh Yadav and ex-Chief Minister Uttar Pradesh enters C.B.I. drag net in Ayurveda Scam reports the Asian Age, 9 December 1996. The scam which actually began around 1990-91 when Mulayam Singh was the chief minister, was unearthed in 1994, again when Mulayam Singh was the chief minister. The scam was detected when it was found that payments of heavy overdrafts had been made by the State treasury. Against a sanctioned sum of Rs. 2 crores, the State treasury had paid Rs. 34 crores in an overdraft. According to the C.B.I. sources of the 150-odd firms that were supplying drugs to the Ayurveda directorate nearly 54 were fake. These firms mostly belonged to top-ranking politicians and did not exist, except on paper.

Maharashtra

In the 20 months of the Shiv Sena-BJP government in Maharashtra, thousands of transfers were effected, mainly in the agriculture, irrigation and public works departments. Only a fraction of them were valid. In the agricultural ministry alone, only 137 of the 1,681 transfers till August 1996 were legitimate. Indiscriminate transfers mean a rapid turnover of officials assigned to a project, delays and cost overruns.

Invariably, the 'price' for these postings was allied to the number of projects and villages that fell under its jurisdiction. In the department of agriculture, for example, the posting of a class III officer costs between Rs. 50,000 and Rs. one lakh, progressively rising to between Rs. one lakh and Rs. 4 lakh for a class I officer. Often ministers blatantly disregarded rules. Shashikant Sutar who was forced to resign as agriculture minister following social worker and Magsaysay Award winner Anna Hazare's anti-corruption crusade personally signed letters requesting transfers. Some who protested were blatantly asked: 'What other way is there to raise money for elections?' Besides being illegal, the transfers also cost the State exchequer a neat packet of Rs. 4,000 in each transfer as travelling expenses.

In some cases, ministers are directly involved in the scams. Agriculture minister Sutar allegedly usurped land earmarked for road and open space in Pune's Gujarat colony. But the most outrageous instance is of Mahadev Shivankar- the other casualty of Hazare's crusade - sanctioning Rs. 30 crore for 'canal repair and flood control' in 1995-96 as irrigation minister, when most of Maharashtra suffered drought conditions. The BJP finds three of its ministers Shivankar, Shobhatai Phadvavis and Nitin Gadkari charged with corrupt practices. This had hit BJPÕs attempt to portray itself as an incorruptible party (India Today, 31 December 1996).

Hazare's crusade began over a year ago when volunteers of his Bhrashtachar Samiti (an anti-corruption body) compiled a list of 2,000 cases, with details, of corruption across the State in various departments. Hazare put together 400 cases and handed over the list to chief minister Manohar Joshi and Sena chief Bal Thackeray. For two months the matter was shelved but subsequently departmental inquiries revealed that in 50 per cent of cases the charges of corruption were true.

Lokpal

In its interim report on the 'Problem of Redress of Citizens' Grievances' submitted in 1966, the Administrative Reforms Commission recommended, inter alia, the setting up of an institution of Lokpal. To give effect to the recommendation of the Administrative Reforms Commission, a Bill called the 'Lokpal and the Lokayuktas Bill 1968' was introduced in the 4th Lok Sabha in 1968. The Bill was considered by a Joint Committee of the two Houses of Parliament and the Bill, as reported by the Joint Committee, was passed by the Lok Sabha in 1969. While this Bill was pending in Rajya Sabha, the 4th Lok Sabha was dissolved and consequently, the Bill lapsed. Fresh Bills were introduced in the Lok Sabha in

1971, 1977, 1985 and 1989 without any results. The Bill was put up again before the Lok Sabha in 1996 and has been under discussion.

One wonders whether or not the politicians are at all serious about tackling the problem of corruption in high places. It appears the Congress(I) was opposed to the idea of bringing the chief executive within the purview of the Lokpal. In 1989, the Janata government viewed such exclusion as the negation of any 'accountability'. The Bill is still to find a place in the statute books. This raises doubts about the sincerity of politicians in tackling the problem. The existence of the institution of Lokpal will no doubt act as a Democle's sword hanging over their heads but its effectiveness is questionable when we consider the fact that the Lokayukt institution in States has not been of great success in the eradication of corruption.

Conclusion

India has plunged into the worst political corruption crisis in its history with the disclosures of the hawala and other scandals. From the prime minister, his sons and his cabinet colleagues, high-ups in the political parties in the opposition, except the left parties, chief ministers in States, businessmen and bureaucracy - all have been caught red-handed. What a difference from the Nehru era when we were justly proud of our political class - Nehru, Sardar Patel, Kidwai, Gobind Ballav Pant, Lal Bahadur Shastri, Moulana Abul Kalam Azad, etc. and held our heads high and felt proud to be Indians. We urgently need to reform our political system, good governance and a State that enjoys moral authority.

One wonders whether or not the Indian State is at all serious about tackling the problem of corruption to ensure anti-corruption values and behaviour among highly placed political functionaries. An attempt was made, as early as in 1969, to establish an ombudsman type institution - Lokpal. But the Lokpal Bill is still to find a place in the statute books.

CORRUPTION IN HIGH PLACES

When the hawala bomb exploded the public reaction to it was expressed in the following words: ALL ARE THIEVES. It is a sad commentary on Indian political elite. It never occurred to them that the crores of rupees belong to the people of India and that by pocketing "a couple of crores" for themselves they are stealing from the people.

It was during Narasimha Rao's rule political corruption came to the fore and Rao by his, pick and choose method filled his cabinet with persons with dubious integrity; and who' as subsequent events disclosed, dropped to the ground from the corridors of power like apples which rot upon the tree before they are knocked off their pedestals in this manner. The political system itself may never be corrected, but, atleast one set of unsavory politicians are being strained out. There are doubts, real doubts about the final outcome of the cases because of several escape routes. There is very real and deep suspicion in the minds of many that the CBI charge sheets in hawala and other cases contain a number of loopholes.

Every morning we read in newspapers of thousands of millions disappearing into the pockets of ministers and their relations. They are named by the CBI their houses are searched, property recovered, FIR registered, they are arrested, some go to jail, most released on bail - and then we forget all about the affairs. We do not care whether or not these felons are put behind bars but we must get our money stashed away in foreign banks into India. Confiscation of property acquired through dubious means to enrich themselves must be given high priority. The CBI must ensure this so that atleast they should not be allowed to enjoy the spoils of corruption.

Beginning with the Rs. 3,500 crore securities scam in 1992 in which several ministers were indicated by the JPC to the Rs. 300 crores telecom scandal which led to the arrest of former Union Minister of Communications, Sukh Ram and his son Arun Sharma; from the illegal allotment of 8700 government houses by former Union Urban

Development Minister Sheila Kaul and her deputy P.K. Thunggon, who were arrested, to the infamous Jain hawala case. But no scandal created pandemonium sweeping across the country as the Jain hawala pay-off have done. Every major party except the Left parties has been rattled.

Almost all prominent leaders from the ruling Congress including Rao, the highest executive in the country were brought down from their high position and denounced as thieves. The entire affair is the perfect example of the criminal-politician-businessmen nexus. The involvement of the prominent leaders belonging to the BJP and Janata Dal is the message to the voters that there are no clean parties or clean politicians.

Over the years, the people have been fooled by the ministers, pledge of *Garibi Hatao* (Get rid of poverty). While thousands of people die almost daily for want of shelter, food, medicine and clothes, Indian Ministers including the Prime Minister have no compunction to amass money through illegal means turning their pledge *Garibi Hatao* into a sham. Rarely one can find a minister who has not acquired property in houses and land, and accumulated jewelry and cash and invested money in shares, debentures, *etc.* Since independence the country has had around 50,000 Central and State ministers. None, so far, has been punished in a court of law for corruption. They are all above the law. Looting money is their inherent right.

Corruption is nothing new in the Indian polity. Yer, the frequency with which it is now appearing in the press is out of the ordinary. One example is the recent incident at the Indira Gandhi airport — a minor incident, but a representative one. Ms. Shakuntala, an honest customs official, slapped duty on the baggage of Kamal Nath, Union Minister, amounting to Rs. 125,000. She was immediately transferred on the charge that she did not know how to treat VIPs. Narasimha Rao did not say on this occasion that the law will take its course. Interestingly, this incident occurred a few weeks after several customs officials at the same airport had been caught accepting bribes by the CBI. Most customs officials had gone on strike protesting against "harassment". Ms. Shakuntala was one of the few who reported for duty during the strike. The episode proves that rules are meant only for ordinary mortals. Kamal Nath is one whose name appears in Jain's diary.

When Jaipal Reddy tried to raise the issue in Parliament, fellow Members of Parliament, cutting across party lines, did not wish to pursue the matter arguing that "such things happen". This is hardly remarkable considering the customary treatment accorded to VIPs. Figures provided by the public works department minister in Madhya Pradesh show that the State government spent Rs. 220 million on minister's perquisites in 1995. The Chief Minister's bungalow alone required Rs. 2.5 million for its renovation. This took place at a time when the government had undertaken pro-austerity drive (The Telegraph, February 11, 1996 - Pure Dairy Product by Alok Ray).

The nexus between criminals and politicians is known, over the years and hawala scandals have surfaced from time to time. Political donations have been accepted on the ground that they are permissible under the Companies Act. In the recent cases, the money involve is ill-gotten in the first place, reportedly, to finance the Kashmir terrorists and the Vishwa Hindu Parishad.

Political leaders belonging to the Congress, Bharatiya Janata Party (BJP) and Janata Dal have been besmirched by the scandals and have been caught almost red-handed. The mighty have fallen in general disgust at the corrupt ways of the rulers of this ancient land. In the hullabaloo, however, several aspects have escaped attention. Let us concentrate on those relatively untouched by the scandal, the likely impact of the hawala scandals on politics as it unfolds along with the prosecution of those charged.

First, the scandals have principally hit the national leaders. Politicians in the States have, by and large, remained untouched. This is not to say that politicians in States are not corrupt. On the contrary, serious charges of corruption and other misdemeanors have been leveled against State leaders too. But, for the moment, when attention is focussed on the hawala cases, the leaders of the periphery can stand by and watch the show like ordinary citizens. Thus, Laloo

Prasad Yadav, Mullayam Singh Yadav, Digvijay Singh, J.B. Patnaik, Sharad Pawar, H.D. Deve Gowda and others afford to snigger at the discomfiture of those who strutted Central stage.

A second aspect of the hawala scandals also concerns those who have remained outside them. Of these, only the Left Front has seen the reputation of both its leader Jyoti Basu and that of its political parties remain in tact. The enigmatic leader of the National Front, V.P. Singh has also retained his reputation for personal probity. But, he faced two problems. First, he had distanced himself from his organization. Secondly, the Janata Dal had found its president, S.R. Bommai and its parliamentary leader, Sharad Yadav dipping his hands in the hawala scandal. The Congress had suffered because of the indictment of its leading lights as well as the shadow the scandal had cast on the party organization.

In the wake of the recovery of Jain's diaries, Prime Minister Rao asked Hawala tainted ministers to resign and then denied them tickets for the Parliament elections in 1996. At the time, Rao took the line that anybody who was even accused of a crime could not be considered fit to occupy high office. Although Rao had been accused in the JMM bribery case and a FIR had been registered against him by the CBI, Rao did not apply to himself the same standards that he applied to the charge sheeted ministers. Rao had been accused of in two other cases too and in the St. Kitts case, pending investigation, Rao had been named. Rao continued in office to manipulate investigations against him and his son. Meanwhile, witnesses are gained over or they die, documents are destroyed. There are hundreds of such cases gathering dust and finally dropped or withdrawn in Court for want of evidence. Since the CBI functions under the control of the prime ministers this can be easily manipulated. There should, therefore, be no surprise that during the last 50 years not a single minister, even charged with serious crime, has been sent to jail. All are hushed up in PMO. The CBI has been misused so often that the people believe the worst about it, even when it is in the clear.

The practice of post-independence, after the Nehru - Shastri era, reveals that ministers and powerful politicians invariably, had enjoyed an immunity from prosecution. Classic examples are the cases of HKL Bhagat and Sajjan Kumar involved in Anti-Sikh riots in the country's capital in 1984. The case of Bhagat has been reopened after 12 years due to public clamor and he is now under-going trial. Sajjan Kumar has been evading prosecution due to political support and he was elected to parliament in the Parliamentary elections from Delhi in 1996. In the recent Rs. 133 crore Urea case one of the main accused was Prime Minister Rao's son. While in the cases of other accused their houses were searched and they were arrested, Rao's son remains untouched. Rao assured that the law will take its course. But, then why does not the law take its course when he and his son is involved. The question is asked: Is Prime Minister and his son above the Law?

Until recently, the CBI in what critics believed was a strategy aimed at absolving Narasimha Rao, held the view that the Prime Minister could not be subjected to scrutiny because the CBI's investigation were based on the entries in Jain's diaries alone and not on the oral statement of S.K. Jain in which he was implicated. But nowhere the Supreme Court stated that the CBI should limit its inquiry to any single source. On 22nd February, 1996 Justice J.S. Verma of the Supreme Court told the CBI. "Be clear that your investigations should not be conducted in water tight compartments. You cannot close any case against anybody". And Justice S.P. Barucha emphasized "you have to keep on trying and getting fresh evidence. No case to be closed by you". The Supreme Court finds no logic in the answer that oral evidence does not constitute proof unless there is something in writing. It is true that under Section 162 of the Criminal Procedure Code (Cr. P.C.) a statement made before the police may not be regarded as evidence during a trial. But it is a pervasion of justice to assume that the police cannot register a FIR and submit charge sheet on the basis of oral testimony. In any case, if S.K. Jain makes the same statement under Section 164 Cr. P.C. before a magistrate the evidence is treated as admissible for the purpose of a trial.

What the Supreme Court of India is doing for the first time is not without international precedent. In 1993 Italian judge ordered the arrest of about 3000 people including Cabinet Ministers to a kickback scandal involving organized crime. Similarly, heads rolled in France, Germany and Spain. In 1995 former South Foreign President Rah Tae Woo was jailed on charges of bribe taking. In Japan, more than one Prime Minister were unseated when they were charged with bribery. Peoples' movements' backed the judiciary when the latter took the executive to task.

The judiciary has played a major role in overhauling the executive. It has also served a warning to the rulers that corruption in the corridors of power cannot be overlooked. As Justice Verma observed "keep the top clean and whatever trickles down will also be clean".

The hawala case has thrown the scum among Indian politicians and the scum has to be thrown out. It has to be swept away by citizens who have been duped by their double standards. Test lies with the next government, irrespective of the party in power, in cleaning up the rot. How far it will succeed is a matter of doubt because of its inherent weakness in depending upon Congress President, who is under investigation for survival. However, the only hope is that the Supreme Court is now busy in cleaning up the system which till recently gave wide powers to the Prime Minister to shield his favorites or to take revenge on his opponents. One of the Supreme Court's most significant contributions is that through a string of decisions it has sought to make judiciary stronger and more accountable. Now the corruption issue will be more sharply focussed than it was in the Bofors case. According to the previous order issued by the PMO the CBI could not investigate public servants of and above the rank of Joint Secretary, without the consent of the Prime Minister, Justice Verma of the Supreme Court viewed this order as a procedural formality that was clogging up the process. He directed that "no concurrence of any authority would be required by the CBI for this purpose". But for this order the CBI would not have been able to initiate investigations against any Minister without first taking the permission of the PMO. This order helps the CBI to act indecently, without fear or favor. But then much depends on the director CBI.

He should succeed if he keeps in mind that he is a public servant of the Prime Minister.

Several politicians and bureaucrats who had been charge sheeted by the CBI in the Jain's Hawala scandals have been accused of doling out contracts to companies either owned by Jain brothers or for which they acted as middlemen. Among those who are facing such charges are former Power Ministers Kalpnath Rai, Arif Mohammed Khan; Railway Ministers C.K. Jaffer Shariff and Madhav Rao Scindia and a number of bureaucrats who held key positions in public sector undertakings. The hawala scandal has shown that a large number of public sector undertakings were milked by politician-chairmen and unscrupulous bureaucrats working as managing directors.

A look at the charge sheet against Kalpnath Rai in the TADA case registered against him shows the brazenness with which men in power misuse public sector facilities. Rai was accused of not only providing shelter to some hardcore terrorists in the guest house of the National Thermal Power Corporation (NTPC) but writing off bills during their stay there. For several decades now it is an open secret that Union ministers blatantly misused guest houses, transport, telephone and other perquisites belonging to public sector undertakings, most of which are in the red. And the Indian tax prayer has been subsidizing this kind of profligacy. The charge against Kalpnath Rai only go to reinforce a fact long known.

Allegations of corruption had been brought against C.K. Jaffer Shariff, Minister for Railways in the controversies of locomotive and wagon deals and against Santosh Mohan Dev, Minister, for Steel and Mines, in the leasing out of the Bailadila mines to a private company.

While the charge sheeting of politicians is welcomed by all those who are serious about a fight against corruption, there has been selective targeting. Why several ministers close to the Prime Minister and other ruling party politicians named in the Jain's diaries have been left out requires an explanation? Recipients of the illegal payments in black money cannot be allowed to enjoy immunity. It was a stroke of luck for the anti-corruption cause that Jain's diaries opened the Pandora's box and in rare instances corruption offences involving politicians, ruling the country, are uncovered.

The Jains categorized the payments broadly in three departmental expenses, other expenses and political expenses. Departmental expenses refer to payment to officials. Other expenses included payments made to friends and business associates. Political expenses involved money paid to politicians. The single largest beneficiary group consists of politicians who were paid in total Rs. 30 crore. Not all payments were made in return for a consideration; in several cases money was paid not for immediate gain but as an investment for the future.

It remains to be seen whether the Income Tax Department takes action against all the recipients of the black money under the Income Tax, Wealth Tax and Gift Tax laws and prosecute them, besides taking action against Jains and their close associates. Jains will also be liable to prosecution for violations of the provisions of (Foreign Exchange Regulation Act) FERA.

And most important, the government must set up special courts to deal speedily with cases filed under the Prevention of Corruption Act; as now the trials of these cases take an average of about 10 years, if not even more.

All politicians who profited from Jain's largesse cannot be tarred with the same brush. Those who spent the amount for accumulation of personal assets like Kalpnath Rai and Arif Mohammed Khan stand on a different footing compared to those recipients who used the money for public interest. And in the cases of the former category the charges become graver. The spending patterns and investments of Arif Mohammed Khan and Kalpnath Rai are highlighted here.

Arif Mohammed Khan : Received 6.5 crore

Since May 1988, when first payment was shown against Khan, he and his relatives staying with him started accumulating assets in the form of land, houses, flats, cars and jewelry. Khan had only a Premier 118 NE prior to May 1988. Soon, he and his relatives purchased as many as 12 cars, one van and a truck. Though some of these were sold off, the flow was extraordinary. Between May and August 1990 when he was a minister he purchased two ground floor flats and two basements in Mayfair Gardens, Delhi; purchased 14 vehicles, besides cash deposits and investments. He made 12 visits with his family abroad to U.K., Debai and France besides other countries between 1990 and 1991.

Kalpnath Rai : Received Rs. 71 lakh

During the 1987-1991 period a total of 11 projects of the NTPC and the National Hydro Power Corporation were given to the Bharat Industrial Works (BIW) owned by the Jains. Again, several works awarded to the Bharat Heavy Electrical Ltd (BHEL) by the NTPC were sub-contracted to the Jain firm. All this helped the BIW made an earning of Rs. 34 crore during this period. Significantly, Kalpnath was Minister for Power from June 25, 1988 to December 2, 1989 and also from June 20, 1991 to January 18, 1993. He was an MP during the remaining period.

Kalpnath and his wife Sudha made major investments after July 1988. These included a flat worth Rs. 25.47 lakh of Hailey Road, in Central Delhi; four flats in Ghaziabad in Uttar Pradesh; fixed deposits of Rs. 3 lakh in the Punjab National Bank; land worth Rs. 1.41 lakh in Bakwal and two farm houses worth Rs. 16 lakh and 9.49 lakh at Dera Mandi and Mehrauli. They built a house worth Rs. 7 lakh at Simri Jamalpur in Uttar Pradesh. While the farm houses were in the name of Sudha, the flat was in the name of Sidharth, son. The fixed deposits in the name of Vaishnavi, daughter. Besides, Kalpnath formed a Vande Mataram Trust involving mainly his relatives, and placed fixed deposits for Rs. 26 lakh in the Union Bank of India. Agricultural land worth Rs. 2 lakh was purchased in the name of Sudha, wife.

The first essential prerequisite for rooting out corruption from the country is to put clean men at the top in the political leaders are the mainspring of corruption. Many high-ups who are now sermonizing against corruption and exploiting the "Garibi Hatao" pledge are those who are making money through corrupt practices by defrauding the poor. The havoc wrought by the personal example of Narasimha Rao has made things worse over the years. By patronizing shady characters like Jains and Chandra Swamy, to name a few, ministers changed from being men of character to being characterless and became deeply involved in corruption. The Prime Minister paid no attention to the growing corruption among his ministers.

The sincerity of the ruling Congress party to weed out corruption can be judged from the fact that the question of establishment of a Lok Pal has been shelved for the last 30 years. Asking MPs and MLAs to declare their assets before and after holding office is particularly a sick joke while active protection is extended where accumulation of assets disproportionate to known sources of income is established. The painstaking report of the National Police Commission recommending independence of the police and insulating them from political interference is gathering dust since last 30 years. A depressing conclusion that suggest itself is that not only the Congress but the BJP and Janata Dal are full of thieves and criminals involved in major financial scandals. Prime Minister Rao says the process of "cleansing" has started in the wake of Jain hawala scandal. It is rather late in the day to ask Prime Minister Rao why he did not remove Kalpnath Rai from his cabinet when the latter was investigated on as serious a charge as harboring terrorists carrying explosives or why he did not ask Sukh Ram to resign when MPs in Parliament made allegation of corrupt practices in Telecom Ministry.

The entry of so many names of politicians in high places in Jain's diaries and the dramatic disclosures made by S.K. Jain in his statement before the CBI released by the press, stunned the nation. They, however, have no evidentiary value unless supported by other evidence such as expanding personal assets with Jain's largesse. With Jain's background you cannot trust him. He may have been instigated by someone to make entries in his diaries to besmirch his enemies.

Narasimha Rao's talk about "cleansing" the system after the hawala cyclone as been a mockery. How can be the system be "cleansed" it first being reformed — politically, administratively, electoral and judicially? Contrarily, how can reform occur if the system is not first "cleansed" and transfused with reformers. Sumir Lal in his article : Shaken but not stirred (The Telegraph, January 31, 1996 that reverberations from the "mother of all scandals" will result in nothing more than a game of musical chairs between sets of Tweedlums and Tweedlees.

One wonders whether or not the Indian democracy is at all serious about tackling the problem of corruption. It needs to be stressed that institutional and legal changes by themselves are unlikely to bring out the condition in which corruption will wither away. Conditions need to be created to sustain anti-caption values and behavior. In a democracy, the most effective watchdog are the people and the press.

The hawala racket exposed by the press is about a crisis in the elite's mutually agreed way of running Indian politics. Jain is not only one individual source of such funds. The quid pro quo racket in the grant of contracts is the major problem that has seriously affected the economy and development of the country. Public sector banks had loaned crores of rupees to unscrupulous brokers to speculate on the stock market. Remember the size of the Indian parallel economy. That is not an aberration. Reforms that do not touch that, merely preserve and polish the system it creates, the politics it breeds. However, important reform of election funding may be, it cannot in itself even begin to address this larger reality. There are other dimensions, too, to the hawala scandal. Some whose trials lead all the way to Kashmir insurgency and Bombay blasts.

List of persons mentioned in S.K. Jain's diary as recipients (names the CBI has decoded)

Politicians (Ruling party)

Rajiv Gandhi (Cong.)	March 1991	2 crore

Bhajan Lal (Cong.)	Feb. 88-June 90	1 crore
Balram Jakhaar (Cong.)	March 88-April 91	61 lakh
N.D. Tiwari (Cong.)	April 88-April 91	25.8 lakh
Kalpnath Rai (Cong.)	July 88-April 91	54.7 lakh
V.C. Shukla (JD, Cong.)	July 89-April 91	65.8 lakh
R.K. Dhawan (Cong.)	September 89	50 lakh
Madhavrao Scindia (Cong.)	Jan. 90-April 91	75 lakh
K.K. Tewari (Cong.)	April 91	30 lakh
P. Shivashankar (Cong.)	July 88-Dec.90	16.94 lakh
C.K. Jaffer Sherief (Cong.)	Nov. 88-Aug. 89	10 lakh
L.P. Shahi (Cong.)	July 89-Aug. 89	35 lakh
M.L. Fotodar (Cong.)	Sept. 89	10 lakh
Kamal Nath (Cong.)	Feb. 90-April 91	17 lakh
Arjun Singh (Cong.)	April 88-90	10.5 lakh
Motilal Vora (Cong.)	April 88-March 90	10 lakh
Krishna Sahi (Cong.)	April 88-March 90	2 lakh
Tajdar Babbar (Cong.)	April 88-March 90	1 lakh
Giani Jai Singh (Cong.)	April 89-Dec. 89	5 lakh
Pranab Mukherjee (Cong.)	April 91	10 lakh

Digvijay Singh (Cong.)	April 91	10 lakh
Jagannaath Pahadia (Cong.)	April 91	5 lakh
Chandulal Chandrakar (Cong.)	April 91	5 lakh
M.J. Akbaar (Cong.)	April 91	5 lakh
Buta Singh (Cong.)	May 89-Sept. 89	75 lakh
Politicians (Opposition)		
L.K. Advani (BJP)	April 89-April 91	60 lakh
S.R. Bommai (JD)	Sept. 90-April 91	52 lakh
Arif M. Khan	May 88-April 91	7.5 crore
Chimanbhai Patel (JD)	Dec. 89-Jan. 91	1.9 crore
Yashwant Sinha (SJP)	March 90-April 91	21 lakh
Devi Lal (SJP)	April 89-March 90	50 lakh
Kalyan Singh Kalvi (SJP)	Dec. 90-April 91	95 lakh
Ashok Sen (SJP)	Dec. 90-Jan. 91	20 lakh
Ranjit Singh (son of Devi Lal)	November 90	15 lakh
Sharad Yadav (JD)	April 88-March 90	5 lakh
M.L. Khurana (BJP)	April 86-March 90	3 lakh
V.K. Malhotra (BJP)	April 88-March 90	1 lakh
Harmohan Dhawan (SJP)	April 91	10 lakh

Lalit Suri (Industrialist)	1988-1991	10.5 crore

Bureaucrats

P.S. Bami (NTPC)	March 88-April 91	34.5 lakh
B.S. Ojha (Agriculture)	April 88-March 90	50 lakh
M.P. Narayan (Coal India)	Feb. 90-Oct. 90	25 lakh
V.K.	April 89-Dec. 89	90 lakh
K. Padmanabhan (Power)	March 90-Oct. 90	58 lakh
J.S. Bedi (RAW)	June 91	20 lakh
V.K. Khanna (Power)	Sept. 89	5 lakh
M.L. Malik (?)	May 90	1 lakh
V. Sunderrajan (NTPC)	May 90	1 lakh
C.N. Swami (NTPC)	Nov. 88	3 lakh
Anil Baijal (NTPC)	Sept. 88	1 lakh

Secretary in Madras in 1956 had a tiff with a minister and he was transferred to the charge of the smallest district from which he resigned. This may sound to be a record of rebellion, but it was less than what I felt was my duty says Lobo Prabhu. I cannot claim that I was the only martyr because many other members of the I.C.S. have resigned perhaps for stronger reasons. What is important is that the I.C.S. had bred in may a sense of sacrifice for its principles. Like me, they may not have done well by themselves, but they have done their best for the country.

Gone are the days when in the Nehru era the civil servants were asked to record their unbiased opinions in files. Sardar Patel, during a Constituent Assembly debate, had said 'My secretary can write a note opposed to my views. I have given that freedom to all my secretaries. I have told them, 'If you do not give your honest opinion for the fear that it will displease your minister, please then you had better go. I will bring another secretary'. He followed this principle as long as he ruled. This policy was changed and civil servants were caught unaware when ministers changed from being men of character to being characterless.

Efficient and honest civil servants were discarded like an old pair of shoes and the administration was filled with men who could pander to the whims of venal ministers like Kalpnath Rai, Sukh Ram to name a few. There are stories about civil servants with personal integrity who refused to toe the lines of these venal ministers and either resigned or suffered, even physically.

The classic examples are C. Umashankar, who had been about six years in the I.A.S. in the Tamil Nadu cadre was transferred four times because he refused to please ministers and MLAs by distributing relief funds to non-existent persons or undervaluing government land for private purchase or overlooking irregularities in such schemes as the Jawahar Rozgar Yojna or Integrated Rural Development Programme.

Madhav Godbole, a competent and upright officer, quit the post of Union home secretary following differences on the handling of the Babri Masjid issue. He has recently, published a book on inside account of the political inaction, intelligence failure and administrative lapses that led to the demolition of the Babri Masjid.

K.R. Vanugopal who worked N.T. Ram Rao's mid-day scheme, met his nemesis in the prime minister's office where he ran afoul of A.N. Verma of the PMO. He was a brilliant officer who could not be bent.

M. Shankaranarayanan, one of the Karnataka's finest Chief secretaries was removed by the Chief minister S. Bangarappa and later placed under suspension. The marketing of IMFL had been nationalised by Bangarappa's predecessor, Veerendra Patil and Bangarappa set about reversing it under pressure from the liquor barons in the State, and Shankaranarayanan had resisted this. Bangarappa also exonerated several officers indicated by the Lok Ayuta and Shankaranarayanan had protested it.

Ms. V. Chandralekha, a young I.A.S. officer and Chairman, Tamil Nadu Industrial Development Corporation was severely burnt when acid was thrown on her face. She had refused to oblige Chief minister Jayalalitha in a deal connected with the Tamil Nadu I.D.C. Several I.A.S. officers of Tamil Nadu were horrified by the acid attack on Chandralekha.

Unaccounted money and property valued at several crores of rupees was unearthed by the income tax authorities in state-wide raids on offices and residences of about half-a-dozen senior bureaucrats and technocrats in Uttar Pradesh.

About 35 teams of income tax officials from Uttar Pradesh and Madhya Pradesh swooped down on offices and residences of bureaucrats and technocrats on 21-1-97. Officials whose houses and offices were raided include Brijendra Yadav (1971 batch IAS officer), Padam Singh (1974 batch IAS officer), B.P. Neelratna (1993 batch IAS officer), R.P. Tyagi (PCS officer). Yadav who owns rice mills in Haldwani, was one of the first officers to be raided.

These developments are fraught with danger to the administration. They have given rise to politician-friendly, casteist and corrupt civil servants. Several of them figure in Jain hawala scandal. In most of the States, I.A.S. cadres are deeply afflicted with corruption. The only silver lining in the dark cloud is barely 20 per cent of the I.A.S. are corrupt and the majority honest and upright.

The decline in the country's civil service has been attributed to the decline of democracy itself. The size of civil service has grown faster than our population. The explanation offered is that a larger number is appointed in a socialist system than in a non-socialist system because of large scale nationalisation and implementation of various types of development projects. A telling example is provided by what happens when there is a growth in the number of automobiles. The vehicles may be private. The plants that produce them May also be private. But the government has to appoint more traffic policemen, more men to maintain more roads, and more emergency services to deal with road accidents.

In connection with civil servants I read a lecture by Dr. P.C. Alexander, governor of Maharashtra. Dr. Alexander is not only one of the most distinguished civil servants that independent India has produced but a historian and scholar. The theme of the lecture is : Challenges to Democracy in Multiparty Democracies in SAARC. It was delivered in 1996 at the Administrative Staff College in Kathmandu, Nepal. Because it was delivered on foreign soil, Dr. Alexander had dealt more with the problems common to all South Asian countries.

Dr. Alexander begins his lecture by dealing with most important features of well-organised civil service system: selection on the basis of merit, literacy and promotion based on seniority plus merit, permanency of tenure, political impartiality and anonymity. In speaking of hierarchy he deplores the proliferation of levels in our country, through the creation of posts of additional secretaries and special secretaries, mere to accommodate more of the aspirants, leading both to duplication of work and dilution of responsibility. If he were speaking to a home audience Dr. Alexander would certainly have given instances of how small divisions which used to be looked after by a joint secretary have been blown into full departments under wholesome secretaries and ministers as a mere employment devise.

The relationship between ministers and secretaries is a vast field in itself. Dr. Alexander does not want officials to be too closely identified with ministers. At the same time, he wants civil servants to put forth their best to carry out the policies of the government of the day. Is this possible? To show that it is,

Dr. Alexander cites the testimony of the British Labour prime minister Clement Attlee, who said of the officials he had inherited from the Conservatives, I always found them perfectly loyal. I never had complaints. That is the Civil Service tradition. They carried out the policy of government. They were all anxious to do the best they could by the Labour Government. If he had wished to reach back into our own history, Dr. Alexander could have given the example of Amatya Rakshasa, who was the prime minister of the Nandas and whose services Chandragupta Maurya sought after defeating the Nandas.

Dr. Alexander is rightly critical of ministers who think laws and regulations are not for them but only for bureaucrats. He is equally severe on Civil Servants with a flexible conscience who come up with notes to suit their ministers wishes. He pleads for the return to the time-tested principle that all decisions should be recorded on the files and ministers written orders should be obtained. With Ivor Jennings he believes that it is the duty of Civil Servants to prevent ministers from making mistakes.

But what about ministers who are not inclined to believe they can ever make mistakes and who think that whatever they do or say is right? Would they be too ready to tolerate what they regard as bureaucratic unhelpfulness or impertinence? This difficult question has not received adequate treatment at the hands of Dr. Alexander. He does not hesitate to disapprove of ministers who carry with them their own favourite civil servants to whichever ministry is assigned to them. He is critical of prime ministers and chief ministers who make large scale changes in senior positions for toning up the administration which is but another name for punishing the inconvenient officials and rewarding the helpful ones. He has suggested one remedy for the widely prevalent political meddling into appointments, and that is the posting and promotions should be entrusted to Civil Service Board as in Britain and other democracies like Sweden, Switzerland, France having most efficient, clean and courteous permanent Civil Service.

The crux of the matter is to nurture administrative leadership of the kind that, because of its intrinsic ability and reputation for unpurchasability will make the politicians think twice before bypassing it. We have fewer civil servants who are strong personalities in their own right. We used to have them in the early years of freedom. If we do not have them now, the reason is not that the I.C.S. was superior to the I.A.S. The reason is that earlier men of character and ability stayed longer in the senior posts like cabinet secretary, secretary to the prime minister, home secretary and foreign secretary and were able to leave their imprint on all who dealt with them. Some names that come to my mind are N.R. Pillai, Vishnu Sahay, B.K. Nehru, Dharam Vira, L.P. Singh, V.P. Menon, B.G. Rao, R.N. Banerji, Subimal Dutt, P.N. Haskar, B. Sivaraman to name a few.

Top officials today are changed too frequently. There should be a convention that any cabinet secretary, home secretary, foreign secretary at the centre will stay for a minimum period of four years in his post. It is this assurance of longer tenure vis-a-vis other senior officials that partially accounts for the power of the prime ministers secretary. Dr. Alexander has also made many useful observations on the role of Civil servants in development and in the management of the public sector.

On the subject of deterioration of standards he is forthright. He welcomes the spotlight that a vigilant press, alert public opinion and watchful legislature focusing on the performance of ministers and civil servants. He has somehow overlooked another great deterrent, perhaps was most potent them all, namely an active and independent judiciary. While conceding that the salaries of civil servants are inadequate, Dr. Alexander rightly observes that increase in salaries and perquisites will not by themselves inhibit corruption. The possibilities of getting rich quick at the public expense are so vast and tempting that any increase in pay will appear only a pittance. More effective will be quick and condign punishment.

We cannot have a democracy without politicians and we cannot have any kind of civilised government without civil servants. To imagine that we should abolish the whole lot of civil servants because so many of them are rotten would be like believing that we must get rid of our body just because the body is subject to so many ailments. The solution to the problem lies in taking measures to combat the evils associated with our civil service. The task is difficult but not impossible.

Conclusion

The Civil Service in India (ICS) had filled an important role in the government of the country. A civil servant occupied a unique position in the administration. Lord Macaulay did not exaggerate his importance when he declared in Parliament that the character of the Governor-General is less important than the character of the administrator by whom the administration was carried on. The Parliament may enact laws and rules, the ministers may issue orders, but if the executive lacks the will or the freedom to act, little will be achieved. A cynic might well remark I will tell you what the law can achieve, if you will tell me also who are the men who will enforce it.

Look back to the Partition days when the civil service and the police kept India united and maintained law and order when everything else was falling apart. Ministers, untrained in the art of administration depended on the Civil Service for sound advice and it newer failed them. In a fighting speech Sardar Patel frankly told the Constituent Assembly that he had tested the Service and found that the members of the service were worth their weight in gold. Strong leadership of Sardar Patel and civil servants, mostly firm, but not rigid, co-operative but not subservient, honest but not difficult will be remembered in Indian history for having consolidated the India of today.

The mantle of the ICS fell on the Indian Administrative Service (IAS). It consisted of a body of men who could be compared very favourably with those in any service organisation in the world. They are the pick of the universities. During the last 50 years of independence they have, by and large, served the country with dedication.

However, the standards of the service deteriorated sharply, over the years, and a new class amongst them sprang up. Instead of devoting their time and energy to the work entrusted to them, their sole aim was to please their ministers. Corruption entered the service in a big way in collusion with ministers. Far more serious was another factor which I call 'intellectual dishonesty'. Some members of the Service were clever enough to find out which way the minds of their ministers were working. They would record notes contrary to their dictates of their conscience to ingratiate themselves with the ministers, with a view to improving their prospects. This king of intellectual dishonesty, though difficult to detect, became quite common.

The young trainees are so aware about the need for political patronage that they are seen in politicians residences developing the necessary links and lobbying to be selected for postings in their home States. Corruption, favouritism, transfers and postings are all linked and every politician in power built up its own set of favourite officials. Those who were sent to Coventry by previous government are pulled out by the present government and installed in positions of power and influence. It happens all the time. Corruption flourishes and today even political flunkies, not necessarily legislators, determine the transfers and postings of senior officers.

With a view to prevent political pulls and pressures and a suggestion was made to have a three member board to effect transfers and postings within the State. I do not know how far this board will solve the problem when we consider the fact that even the chairmen and members of the State Public Service Commissions are not free from political influence. The solution lies in strengthening the IAS associations with members having high reputation, not amenable to political pulls and pressures.

In most States, political leaders have completely crippled the Civil Servants and made them subservient to their whims and fancies. Phoolan Devi declares she will not visit her constituency in Uttar Pradesh until the district magistrate was transferred. In Dhanbad, Bihar the transfers and postings of district magistrates and superintendents of Police were decided by Suraj Deo Singh, MLA, a Mafia leader against whom several criminal cases are pending in Court.

Conclusion

India is a corrupt nation. Corrution is all pervasive and eating away the vitals of the nation. The Indian system operates on corruption. The constable on the beat, or at traffic point, or at check posts; bankers granting loan to customers, patwari dealing with land records in villages, teachers admitting students in schools, colleges and universities. Almost all government departments e.g. telephone, electricity boards, income-tax, house-tax etc. etc. Just name which department is not corrupt in India?

12

POVERTY, POPULATION, POLLUTION AND CORRUPTION

Corruption is a global phenomenon, as is poverty. Even the mighty USA has poor citizens, although the abysmally poor are still the monopoly of the Third World. Fully one third of the world population of 5.2 billion is too poor to manage two meals a day. What should the governments do to end this unspeakable condition? Don't' fret counsels the World Bank - IMF duo; economic growth will take care of them. And the growth will be robust as long as every country sways to its mantra of globalisation, it says. Globalisation, the report warns, has made the Third World Vulnerable to attacks by finance capital while investment capital is hard to come by. The reason is simple. Market forces are propelled by profit motive, and there is more profit in deploying money to make more money (for instance, by heavily betting in currency and stock markets) than in building asset-generating plants. Even where capital is employed in setting up manufacturing units, the unhidden desire is to exploit low-paid labour. In both cases capital is not used to increase output, productivity and wages; quite the contrary. The end result is to keep productivity and wages low and transfer jobs from the mother country (where the plants have their headquarters) to the adopted country. This way, the globalisation drive is spreading unemployment and sustaining poverty. Analyses by well-known American economists, published in a leading newspaper, bring out another damaging effect of globalisation-cum-technological advance. New technology is necessarily labour-saying, and drives up existing jobs. Also, the days of the small man, as an active or passive player in economic activities, are over. One perceptive commentator has warned that he world is fast moving towards establishing "the dictatorship of the rich". And the bad news is that this process is more or less irreversible. Belyign the Bible, the rich are about to inherit the earth.[1] Greed and not the need has led to corruption.

---

1 "Globalising the Poor", The Tribune, September 19, 1997, p.10.

"Greed is good, Greed is right Greed works. It terrifies and captured the essence of the revolutionary spirit. Greed, in all its forms has market the upward surge of mankind... it will save the malfunctioning corporation called the USA." The words of Ivan Bosky, a Wall street financier, soon backfired. Shortly after his statement, he was in jail with $ 100 million fine. Greed has been the grim reaper of many souls. Desire makes the world go round, and money is desire's way of organising itself. Whether it be the paparazzi bounding Princess Diana for a big fast buck or a woman claiming to be bill Cosy's illegitimate daughter, greed has no shame. It is by definition ravenous, gluttonous, avaricious, eager and intensely desirous. In the "90 rhetoric, greed has gone global. Global Greed Inc. can seek out low wages areas for super profit exploitation. It is a virus infecting addicted gamblers, stock speculators, real estate flippers and more recently, the over Rs. 1200 crore industry - Bellwood [2]

The vast bulk of our population is uneducated and are poor with the alarming growth of population, the constraints are on natural and publicity utility, services, causing environmental degradation. The environmental degradation is at the very centre of interaction between demographic growth and economic developments, between man and what he consumes and produced; because whatever be contributes to greater production and productivity and distribution has an in built negative impact on environmental degradation. The problem of environment degradation is the outcome of ever increasing pace of rural to urban migration. The problem is even more accentuated by the vast scale of very short duration, seasonal migrations, especially to the slums of the city and their cyclical concentration in the districts which are among the most poorly endowed by way of natural and land resources the upward souring of poverty the inordinately heavy concentration of wealth and privilege among a very small proportion of the population, leads to environmental degradation corruption.

---

2 Neelam Matthew's and Anusha Samir Gill, "Money makes the World Go Wrong", The INFOTAINMENT, The Hindustan Times, Weekly, September 19, 1997, pp 8-9.

Corruption was rampant in the UK at both the national and local levels. In France, at least three ministers had been embroiled in financial scandals. There were kickback scandals over arms sale in Belgium which implicated the secretary general of the North Atlantic Treaty Organisation (NATO). In West Asia, a political corruption scandal in Histadrut, Israel's largest labour union discredited the Israeli government. The Saudi Arabian monarchy is getting shakes as wasteful public spending and kickbacks come to light. Financial scandals have been reported routinely in countries with divergent political systems—Italy, Japan, Korea, China, the USA, the UK and former USSR. The Furze trial reported in Izvestia (July 22, 1962) and Sovetskaya (January 9, 1962) was one of the most important events in the history of the USSR. The number of accused was as high as fifty four. They included ministers and officials, who were sentenced to various terms of imprisonment with confiscation of property. Leaders of the plundering band were sentenced to death.

On March 17, 1981 the special branch of the Italian police in charge of financial probes raided the residence of Licio Gelli. The documents they seized sparked one of the worst scandals in Taly's recent history. The list of 962 members included cabinet ministers, Generals and journalists. Gel's secret organisation had penetrated the nerve centre of Italy's political and financial institutions. The government tried to stall a probe. But the magistrate's forced publication of the list Gelli fled to South America. None of those whose names appeared in the list was spared.

The Lockheed Aircraft had paid bribes to Japan and other countries to boost the sales of its planes. This information exploded all on a sudden in February 1976 during hearings of the Sub-Committee on Multinational Corporation of the U.S. Senate Committee on Foreign Relations. In July 1976 the former prime minister of Japan Kakui Tanaka was arrested in Tokyo. Many a head rolled thereafter.

In the USA and Japan heads of government have been removed for corrupt practices. The French minister of industry had been jailed for corruption under public pressure. A president and prime minister had been imprisoned in Bangladesh on Corruption charges.

In Italy, a prime minister found guilty of corruption was imprisoned. Colombian president is awaiting his impeachment by Parliament for receiving massive contributions from drug-traffickers.

In all democracies, the most effective watchdog is free press which is free to comment and criticise as they feel inclined and the vocal public opinion against declining norms of conduct in public life. Most of the countries have enacted harsh laws to ensure purity in the corridors of power. For example the United States Ethics in Government Act 1978 enacted by the US Congress at President Jimmy Carter's instance in the wake of the Watergate scandals and the United States Independent Council Reauthorization Act 1994 apply to the President, vice-president, members of cabinet, judges of the Supreme and Federal Courts, senators Congressmen and officials serving them. We shall revert to the details these laws later. In the UK, the Court has the power to ask a political functionary to appear before tribunals in order to testify about government's functioning.

Rudra Datt in an article "Population, environment and Development" justifiably wrote unless the development is geared for taking care of the population, more especially the weak and down trodden, the mere talk of environmentalists to diminish pollution will have no meaning to the poor masses. However, for the creation of a healthy society, it is necessary that the resource base of the poor should improve and unemployment among them should decline.

It is generally believed the poverty breeds over-population and as much there is need to tackle and cure over population. A frontal attack, as such, needs to be made on the basic problem of poverty. However, poverty is another name for the existence of widespread unemployment and underemployment and, therefore, unless underemployment and, therefore, unless development strategies focus on the provision of employment as the central objectives of planning and wave other objectives like maximising production, modernisation of techniques and institutions round the central objective, the problem of poverty will defy solution in a global perspective. Poverty and sub-standard living conditions have direct impact on environment. The urban poor because of the compiling circumstances, their habitual has a deteriorating and unhygienic style of living has eventually caused congested and inhuman environment.

Meditations

P.D Shastri in a write up, "Poverty - a curse at all times", explains:

RELIGIONS generally have sung the praise of poverty. Blessed are the poor and the meek, for they shall inherit the kingdom of heaven. One remembers God in poverty not in plenty. Jesus Christ says: "Sooner shall a camel pass through the eye of the needle than a rich man enter the kingdom of heaven!"

Wealth breeds pride and sin, wine, women and gambling and other concomitants of opulence. Says Tulsi Ramayana: Whom God wants to favour, he takes away his wealth.

All religious command the virtue of or charity. The Sikh Gurus preach Vand-Chhakna—share what you have, little be it or much, with others. The Muslims call it Zafat.

Our saints and sages, whom we worship, shunned earthly assets. The Jain Munis beg for their bread, to cast off ego. The greatest Indian of our times, mahatma Gandhi, was above the bread, clothing, and machine civilisation : "Bread I have not taken for 40 years, clothing, and I don't wear and go naked, of shelter or other possessions I have none. Yet emperors envy my peace of mind and real happiness!"

The motto of his ashram was: voluntary poverty. Prince Siddartha bade farewell to regal glory and wealth, when on that fateful night that changed the history of world, he embraced life of a mendicant. He was on the road to becoming the Buddha. P.D Shastri.

Undoubtedly, the incidence of unemployment is inversely related to the economic conditions of the household. The economically better off families are able to secure and corner employment for their members, but the poor, the landless and the slum dwellers are always worried about their next day's bread. As such, the poor families are forced to live in most unhealthy conditions, very poor housing and many have to go without shelters event hey have to travel several kilometres to procure drinking water. Diseases and consequently death visit them frequent. Traders, money lenders and small businessmen exploit the poor in variety of means and quite a large number among them become bonded labourers. Such an economic environment gives them a feeling of insecurity. They see people rolling in luxury and the spectacle of palatial mansions coming up just near the slums, huts colonies only kindles the seething anger among the poor.

Moreover, a feeling is generate among the poor that conditions in jail are better than the environment Huts- and they feel that living in slums without amenities of pure drinking water, sewerage, drainage and unhygienic conditions etc. is an open Jill for them. This even encourages crime and gives birth to social evils like prostitution. The rich employ many hardened criminals of course, drawn from the poor strata, to protect their illegitimate wealth or black money. This further reinforces the idea in the minds of these poor that honest methods do not promise them even a simple and reasonable living. It is this kind of a social and economic environment that is polluting the very fabric of the society.

Unfortunately, the ecologists and environmentalists are worried about the outer physical environment, but more important than that is the creation of employment opportunities which holds key to the creation of a healthy social environment that can provide for the well-being of a large mass of the people.

The rapid growth of population imposes a variety of hardens, considerably organisational demands and besides disturbing the social structures, make the country's political and administrative apparatus perpetually off the balance. If further creates an imbalance between population and resources resulting in deforestation, soil erosion and other ecological changes leading to a deterioration of the natural environment which if unchecked, will obviously threaten the very existence of human being. Environment does not necessarily concerns land, air or water is ultimately all about resources. However degradation is closely related to the pattern of resources use permitted within a society in a country like India, with a high population density and unbearable a high level of poverty, virtually every ecological niche is occupied by some occupational or cultural group for its sustenance. There is a close correlation between population growth and its specific concern with poverty. Thus, the low health conditions cause poor, unhygienic living environment which leads to a threat to very human survival.

India is the second largest populated country in the world only next to China with the total population currently estimated at around 950 million which is about 25 percent., of the making. India is having only 2.4 percent of the total land area of the world. Compared to this the United States of America with only about 6 percent of the population of the world is having 7 percent of the total area of the world. But what is more alarming is the growth rate of 1.9 percent population per annum of our country. This rapid increase of population is a threat to the national development as it will neutralise our economic achievements, social political and cultural targets set forth in our Five Years Plans. No problem of our country may be suitably and satisfactorily slogged if our population goes on multiplying in this manner and we will have more slums, malnutrition, and starvation. Ultimately this will further, erase the rapidly dismembering of social values and serious threat to a congenial environment and threat to the very survival of the family. Thus, a small family is a happy family, which besides a boon to the family itself, helps to build up a systematic social organisation raising the standard of living, peace, cohesiveness, and a good economic and political system in society. Whereas growth population creates problems to the Government for obtaining financial resources for delivering medical services, education, drinking water, housing and sanitation to its citizens. Unlimited population leads to fundamental structural change, fundamental decisions concerning implications on fundamental programmes and inextricable part of economy.

Population is increasing in an alarming proportion and the situation needs a revolutionary immediate action, when one considers the fact that it is so called third world with two third of the world population that on a average population doubles every 18 years, while the world population doubles every 23 years. Asia is the most heavily burdened as a whole continent with total population of approximately 56.7 percent of the world total and second largest populated area is Europe. With 12.6 percent of total population in both cases minus the USSR. All over the world the population explosion is a serious threat to congenial environment. Further, the population pressures are leading to destruction of forest in an alarming proportion in a global perspective. Besides, the population explosion exerts considerable stress on the Earth's limited resources. Further, the population phenomenon is a world-wide perspective has given rise to an enormous constraints on natural and financial resources. It has eventually given rise to forest destructive, excessive urbanisation and industrialisation has ultimately resulted into a serious threat of air, water pollution and is turning most parts of our cities a heap of garbage. This is particularly true in regions where population growth is fast and natural resources are scare.

The relationship between population explosion, poverty and natural resources could be illustrated by continued population growth in the developing countries at the rate of 2.1 to 2.2 percent a year, which would require an increase of food supplies available to them by at least 4 percent annually. This could be achieved through either massive imports of food or greatly stepped up agricultural production. Both have their socio-economic technological and environmental impacts, some of which could be negative. Expanding population, uneven distribution of wealth and slow income growth in combination with generally inadequate technology is causing over-exploitation of land resources for food and fuel in many developing countries and resulted in making poor the poorer. The result is a deteriorating human and natural environment in a world-wide perspective.

The gap between the developing and developed countries is likely to widen still further unless some concrete steps are taken. It is apparent that per capita income in developing countries will be reduced by population growth and more and more public will go down the poverty line, leading to the hazard living conditions in slums and squatter conditioning particularly in the Third World.

At the national level, rapid population growth translates into a steadily worsening employment future, massive city growth, pressure on food supplies, degradation of the environment, an increase in the number of "absolute poor", a stimulus to authoritarian government, coercive national policies restricting the freedom of the individual, and brutal family practices. All are rightly viewed by Governments as threats to social stability and orderly change. Even under the vigorous economic growth managing this demographic expansion seems to be difficult, with a faltering economy it is all but impossible. Perceived political threats, actual anticipated, elicit a strengthening of administrative control over the population. This contribution is especially evident where population growth is associated with ethnic or communal differences. Many communal tensions are rooted in expectations of adjustment in political representation as demogration change occurs. Population explosion, large backlogs in terms of shelter and essential urban services, growth of slums and squatter settlements and above all the increasing deprivation of environment quality for a majority of the city dwellers are the common characterises of most of India's large cities particularly metropolitan cities. Fighting property, population explosion, pollution and corruption is not just a question of moral imperative. It is highly practical necessity for a political system to function in a democracy. Behind the growth of social violence, terrorism, secession, social disharmony, the spectres of corruption is corruption vitiating public life has always played a riots and mass disturbances are often the signs of the malaise of the times. Today anger against over-growing corruption is mounting. It is likely to manifest itself in new and unorthodox forms.

The modern technology as developed mainly in the west is considered even more desirable object for adoption by poor countries. It is often suggested that developing country have a special advantage in being late-comers as they can jump over the intermediate stages of technological development and can now go straight to the highest level of technology to produce affluence without exploitation. The idea of great jumps from bullock cart to jet engine can remove several bottlenecks from the path of development of the third world. In fact the very success of science and technology has generated to some extent a backlash. There is a great debate among the economists and technologists about the danger of unlimited application of science and technology for accelerating industrialisation leading to the exploitation of natural resources and the anti-life impact of technology on human existence itself. The techno-maniacs fail to see that the human life span is the unchanging yardstick in future also, and it is not the man who must adapt to the storms generated by science, but science and technology must adapt to man and their adaptation means more than a simple limitation of scientific activity. There is a growing feeling among many that we are going too far and the vastly increased power, that technology has placed in the hands of man, has not been matched by his ability to use it wisely. We are on consumer spree.

Society has come to realise slowly that earth unimaginably rich in natural resources is limited in the amount of abuse that it can bear without disastrous effects on the biosphere. Perhaps we failed to perceive this earlier because we have been so busy enjoying the benefits of the technological advancement that we had not had time to think about tomorrow. Dr. (Mrs.) Rashmi Sharma & Dr. Jai Narain, Department of Gandhi Study, Chandigarh, in an article "Environment as Human Problem" writes :

Earth, the planet we inhabit, is a single living, pulsating entity and the human race an interlocking extended family. The land, water and the atmosphere which constitute its environment, support come from some 0.36 million species of plants and more than a million species of animals. The unprecedented human interference into the environment has upset the delicate ecological balance of our planet. Ruthless exploitation of non-renewable natural resources has created havoc and if allowed to continue can result in a series of major ecological disaster that can disrupt life on this planet. Some of the most dramatic cases of tempering with the environment are man made fires, slash and burn agriculture, mineral mining, dumping of sewage and industrial wastes, introduction of new transport system into natural areas, persistence of nuclear testing and disposal of nuclear wastes, the danger of global warming and the attenuation of our ozone shield, the menace of deforestation leading to destruction of many species of flora and fauna, devastation of landscape by herbicides, introduction of pests into new areas, over population, overgrazing coupled with drought, extensive air and water pollution, and the poisoning of food chain, the malign underworld of drugs and the alarming spread of communicable diseases. All these problems which the human race share in common, and in order to solve them people must try to attain as complete as understanding of their environment as possible.

The survival of man depends on how judiciously he manages the earth and maintains the quality of his over all environment. One fact we must bear in mind is that our genetic make up can not adapt to a changing environment such as rise of carbon-dioxide, or to reduce oxygen content in the air we breathe, all due to too much of fossil fuel burning and destruction of vegetation, too much of toxic substances in our air and water etc. We can not develop resistance to toxic effects of many poisonous materials we are pouring out in the atmosphere, water bodies and soil. It is indeed a wonder how we are bearing the onslaughts of ecological backlashes in our environment. We are reaching the limits of tolerance on most fronts and any greater onslaught might result in major catastrophes. Man has no option other than to seriously fight for the cause of sustained quality of his environment and natural resources and this flight has to be united and concentrated at all levels—individual, communities, villages, towns, districts, stages, governments and inter-governmental bodies, continental and global. In this endeavour short term personal or regional interest must be subordinate to the global and long range interest. This can be achieved through mass education, enacting uniformly standard laws etc. To save our environment, all nations, all religions and all human races have to stand united on a common platform guided by sound ecological principles alone. Simultaneously we have to control the human population or at least ensure a zero per cent rise level. If these are not handled on a war footing, our biosphere will be in danger of a major catastrophe.

Regarding prospectus of science and technology advances, Philip Hander, President National Academy of Sciences, USA describes that at some unspecified date in the future, "The bulk of humanities will be gathered in megalopolis, dwelling in huge buildings surrounded by park lands perhaps covered with domes within which the atmosphere will be maintained rather constant. Each individual will have a private pocket-two-way television instrument and immediate personal access to a computer as his news source, privately programmed educational medium, memory and personal communicator with the world at large—his bank, broker, government agents, shopping services etc. The bulk of the labour force, then, will engage in activities currently classified as services rather than productions goods." He continues that most of us held such a dream in common and the most important thing one can say about that dream is that it may well be feasible. He believes that biological and physical research can refashion ourselves and our world and there is really no question whether man can live with his technology. However, he ponders over the real question whether man can learn to live with himself. The answer he provides is that man can not learn to live with himself in a technologically obsessed society, therefore, we have to limit technology.

Actually man does not know how to be a truly modern man. Other species do not have similar failings. A swallow has learned what it takes to be swallow. A tiger knows how to be a tiger. By the use of natural wisdom, these species are continually readjusting and refining their survival qualities, adapting them to the modification of their environment. Their success is proved by their very existence as the present day end product of age long evolution. Now they are in danger because man moves more against them. Already at the dawn of history, he began to forsake his natural capacity to adapt and survive, finding it expedient to trust his lot more and more to his brain, that is to his technological capacity and, by it, to modify the environment instead. While the animal adapt themselves according to the environment man tries to modify the environment according to his requirements. The club of Rome has termed it the predicament of mankind.

In a commentary on the report, "The Limits to Growth—A Report to the Club of Rome", the Executive Committee of the Club expresses this view.

"We are convinced that realisation f the quantitative restraints of the world environment and of the tragic consequences of an overshoot is essential to the initiation of new forms of thinking that will lead to fundamental revision of human behaviour and by implication, of the entire fabric of the present day society.... We affirm finally that any deliberate attempt to reach a rational and enduring stage of equilibrium by planned measures, rather than by chance or catastrophe, must ultimately be founded on a basic change of values and goals at individual, national and world levels. And they did not hesitate to use highly dramatic language, such as the following:

"The concept of a society in a steady state of economic and ecological equilibrium may appear is to grasp, although the reality is so distant from our experience as to require a Copernican revolution of the mind. Translating the idea into deed, though, is a task filled with overwhelming difficulties and complexities. We can talk seriously about where to start and only when the message of 'the limits t growth' and its sense of extreme urgency, are accepted by a large body of scientific, political and popular opinion in many countries The transposition in any case is likely to be painful, and it will make extreme demands on human ingenuity and determination. As we have mentioned, only the conviction that there is no other avenue to survival can liberate the moral, intellectual and creative forces required to initiate this unprecedented human undertaking."

The concept of earth's flintiness is by no means now. But its corollary expounded in the report, that due to the plant's finite dimensions, there are necessarily limits to human expansion, was growing against the grain of growth culture prevailing in the world. The success of the material revolution had made this culture arrogant. It was and is the culture of a civilisation of quantity which neglect quality, and which couples its arrogance of the real life supporting capacity of the planet with the extravagant exploitation of its resources and the insufficient erratic use of human capacity.

The growth syndrome which has developed is well known. When no remedy of society's ill in sight, faith in growth takes over. Growth is considered as a super medicine. By producing abundantly one can try to meet all wants and satisfy demand or if demand is lacking, it can be created artificially. But now it is apparent that a policy of bounty can solve some problem indeed and alleviate others, but is something just a palliative and not a permanent solution. Indeed it is not being realised that this syndrome may mean the tragic end of earth resources and consequently the growth itself.

Alvin Toffler, in his best seller, 'Future Shocks' has well described the inexorable price we are paying for this technology which we are told is being developed or our benefit.

"Our technological powers increase but the side effects and potential hazards also escalate. We risk thermos pollution of the oceans themselves, overheating them, destroying immeasurable quantities of marine life, perhaps even melting the polar ice caps. On land we concentrate such large masses of population in such small urban technological islands, that we threaten to use up the air's oxygen faster than it can be replaced, conjuring up the possibility of new Sahara's where the cities are now. Through such destruction of natural ecology, we may literally in the words of biologist Barry commoner be destroying this planet as a suitable place for human habitation."

Similarly the major findings of the Global 2000, Report to the President of United State of America are :-

"If the present trends continue, the world in 2000 will be more crowded, more polluted less stable ecologically, and more vulnerable to disruption than the world we live in now. Serious stress involving population resources and environment are clearly visible ahead. Despite greater material output, the world's people will be poorer, in many ways than they are today. The average gross national product per capita is projected to rise substantially in some L.D.Cs. (especially in Latin America) but in great populous nations of South Asia it remains below $ 200 a year. All the happens because of materialism, consumerism & non-contentment.

Thus the cumulative impact of this growth syndrome is now being felt like shock waves in rising disillusionment, thickening frustration and mounting fear. The nature of this predicament lies in the fact that science and technology which emerged as a system promising to liberate human beings from the bondage of poverty and misery etc. are opening ever-new frontiers discussed above. It is amply evident that the primary motivating force of such technologically induced economic growth is the satisfaction of ever-proliferating material wants. In such a system, the quality of life is measured primarily in terms of material well-being which is sought to be insured even at the cost the degradation and defilement of the echo system.

Like the club f Rome or Alvin Toffler etc., Gandhi did not employ nor did he require a computer to arrive at his conclusions. Common sense told him that this western-style industrialisation for the whole of mankind could never be implemented. He wrote as early on in 1928. "God forbid that India should ever take to industrialism after manner of the west. If an entire nation of 300 million (the figure has now risen to more than 900 million) took to similar economic exploitation, it would strip the world bare like locusts." Gandhi attacked western industrialisation craze on many grounds. Unmindful exploitation of natural resources leading to destruction of ecological balance is one main ground among them.

No single factor, according to Gandhi, has contributed more to the phenomenon of world wide erosion of natural resources than the greater possibilities that have been opened up of getting rich quickly with the help of new powerful machines. Nineteenth century economy, particularly in the British empire with its expanding power industry, colonial system of rule and huge overseas financial investments by the European powers, gave rise to a heavy, ceaseless drain of food and raw materials from the countries affected by it. Vast regions of earth were as a result depleted of their soil fertility. In the words of Jacks and White, "The new World acquired in a few years the fruits of the old world's thousand years struggle with nature." Western nations achieved a meteoric burst of prosperity and power for themselves without straining their own resources within their own borders but only by robbing other countries of their natural resources that had been maintained for thousands of years. In the exploited countries, as in India, population increased, roads and railways were built, there was rapid expansion of trade and industry, new cities sprang up, higher living standard were achieved for privileged class, forests were cleared, pastures brought under cultivation insects and vermin `which hold the balance between the organic and inorganic forces were annihilated.' But all this outward show of progress in the exploited country was paid for in progressive deterioration of natural resources, silted up rivers, recurring floods, droughts, dust-storms and famines and diseases due to the deepening poverty and lowered stamina of the masses.

So long as food and raw material continue to be produced in one region to be consumed in another in bulk in pursuit of the philosophy of unlimited material wants in limited world, nature's equilibrium can not be maintained. There are certain things found in nature apparently have no life and do not grow or increase, and so get exhausted or consumed by being used. The world possess a certain stock of such material as coal, petroleum, ores or minerals like iron, copper, gold etc. These being available in fixed quantity may be said to be 'transient'. 'While the current of over flowing water in a river or the constantly growing timber of a forest may be considered permanent as their stock is inexhaustible in the service of man but only when the advantage of this flow or increase is taken in a calculated manner.

In animate life, the secret of natures permanency lies in the cycle of life by which the various factors functions in close co-operation to maintain the continuity of life. A grain of wheat falls from the parent plant. It gets buried in the earth, sends out roots in the soil and through them absorbs nutritive elements with the aid of moisture and heat of the urn. It sprouts up into a plant by this process. The plant shoots out leaves which helps to gather nourishment from the air and light, as the roots do from the soil when some of these leaves die, they fall to the ground and are split up or decomposed into the various elements which the parent plant had absorbed from the soil, air and light. This is again used to nourish the next generation of plants. The bees etc. while gathering the nectar and pollen from these plants for their own food, fertilise the flower and the grains, that are formed in consequence, again become the source of life of the next generation of plants. When ready, these seeds fall to the ground and come to life with the help of soil that has already been enriched by fallen leaves of the previous generation of plants.

Insects and worms and same of the rodents and burrowing animals play an important part in the restoration and maintenance of nature equilibrium. Earth worms are known to turn and aerate the soil to a depth of from 4 to 6 feet. Some animals though not directly useful to agriculture, 'fit into complicated ecological scheme as one of the links in a food cycle. They provide food to other species that are useful to agriculture by living upon insects, plants, animals that are destructive of crops. The system is interdependent here. Thus a fresh cycle of life begins once again. In this manner life in nature goes on, and as long as there is no break in this cycle, the work in nature continues endlessly, making nature permanent.

Human life rarely reaches even a hundred years while the unit to reckon the life of nature will run into astronomical figure. The problem arises when this life of hundred years start playing with the life of astronomical figures and exhaust both the transient and permanent in nature. Nature functions in a pattern and that pattern keeps the fertility o nature intact.

Civilisations come and civilisations go but the nature remains. "If a civilisation is such that it degrades the nature, then it is the civilisation and not he nature that comes to an end." Sooner than later, we have got to come to terms with nature and start building afresh from the start. The struggle for existence that has hither to principally been a struggle for markets is bound in not very distant future to become a struggle for maintaining ecology. Civilisation will then have to set about to base itself on a new, symbiotic relationship with nature. In that set up it is obvious that farming cum small scale and cottage industries will have to be the way of life for the bulk of population. The social and political ascendancy of the town will end. The power of the country in relation to that of towns will increase. The men who rule the river according to the way and manage the land, will rule the nation. The may not have the wealth but collectively they will have the power now in the hands of captains of industry. Industry will become the handmaid of a balance and fruitful agriculture upon whose enduring prosperity the fate of towns depends.

Conservation of industry in big towns is not good for industry itself. By breaking up big industrial units into a number of small ones and removing them to villages, it is claimed, industrialism will be cured of most of its glaring evils and the conflict between industrial and agriculture will be resolved. Geographical dispersion of industry and its location in the countryside is, however, as different form the decentralised economy that Gandhi aims at 'as chalk is from cheese' As an economic and social policy, industrialisation can be effective only on the basis of individual production and individual production is not mass production on a reduced scale. Individual handicrafts production and mass production in the villages represent two rival systems of economy. When henry Ford hit upon the idea of the assembly line taking jobs to the workers instead of the workers having to walk to various jobs in different parts of the workshop it was unquestionably a more economic way of factory management. It cut down costs but it did not mean any abatement of either the profits or the power of the industrial magnate. Dispersion of the industry and its location in the countryside to facilitate mass production in the vicinity of the homes of the country folk, by taking the assembly line right into the countryside, might provide to the industrialist a more thorough and efficient means of the economy and biological exploitation of the material and human resources of the countryside. It turns the farms into an adjunct to the factory and the countryside. It turns the farms into an adjunct to the factory and the countryside into a larder for the non-producing industrial city proletariats to draw upon, but the means absolutely no lessening of the political and economic control of industry and high finance, rather the reverse. The revival of the village is possible when it is no more exploited. The city must get off the back of the village. But industrialisation on a mass scale, as Gandhi pointed out would necessarily lead to passive or active exploitation of the villagers, as the problems of the competition and market come in. The Charkha and the allied industries alone, maintained Gandhi could stop exploitation of the villages and abolish all inequalities both social and economic between the urban and the rural. "The rising consciousness of the strength which non-violence gives to the people and their intelligent refusal to co-operate in their slavery must bring about equality."

He described the spinning wheel as, 'science reduced to the terms of masses'. In its economic aspect, he looked upon it as the means par excellence of overcoming the mental inertia of the masses and of quickening their intelligence and inventive faculty. At the beginning of non co-operation movement, when million had taken to the spinning wheel and the allied processes, and everybody from the oldest village dame to the tiniest tot playing his "Talkie" was busy thinking how to improve them. He once exultantly remarked, "Never has the spirit of invention been more briskly at work among the common people than now.

Henry Ford in his personal memoir, 'My Life and Work, 'has recorded how once when he received an order for tractor from one country, he sent trucks instead. "It was to make the people speed minded", he explained. "Once they became time conscious he could count upon their wanting many more tractors". And the result proved that he was right. In the wake of trucks came a much bigger order for tractor than he had originally received." It was Gandhi's anticipation that the resuscitation of the spinning wheel with all that it implies would inaugurate a new revolution in technology which would give birth to a series of invention as marvellous as those that made the industrial revolution but of a different order. They would reverse the evil effects of the industrial revolution. It was Gandhi's aim to bring down science and technology from the mountain tops to the plains where common folk dwell, so as to give to the masses—the small producer, the tiller of the soil and the handicrafts man plying his craft in his cottage their full benefit. This approach is more human, gentle and not based upon exploitation of natural resources but on their proper use for the benefit of the whole humanity.

To Gandhi, essential human requirements are food, shelter, clothing, health and individual freedom. To take up food only in spite of all the wonderful discoveries that have been made in the science of agriculture, labour saving machines which enable one person to do work of many, new fertiliser and insecticides, and new hardener strains of crop which thrive on soil and in climates that were formerly considered to be uncogenial—our food supplies are not keeping pace with the increasing population taken the world over, and the danger of world starvation can by no means by dismissed.

Population control is undoubtedly the ultimate solution. But whatever may be the method of choice for population control, one thing is clear. It must go hand in hand with a system of economy that would enable the maximum population to be maintained on the available acreage in health and reasonable comfort for the longest period of time without impairment of soil fertility. It can be shown that the system that is best suited for this is that of intensive individual farming based on cattle and human economy, as a way of life, supplemented by cottage industries as against large scale, collective mechanised farming ancillary to heavy industrialisation.

Prince Kropotkin has in his 'Fields, Factories and Workshops Tomorrow' showed on the basis of experiments which he himself had conducted, what unbelievable result could be achieved by individual intensive small scale agriculture. F.H. King, the great American authority on Agricultural Physics and Soil Management has similarly recorded, "In China, Korea and Japan conservative economy in agriculture has made it possible after twenty and perhaps thirty centuries for their soils to produce sufficient for the maintenance of such dense population as are living in these countries." He and his colleagues, were 'instructed surprised and amazed' at the conditions and practices which confronted them which ever way they turned; 'Instructed in ways and extent to which these nations for centuries have been and are conserving and utilising their natural resources, surprised at the magnitude of the returns they are getting from their fields.' Similarly, Gandhi too was of the confirmed opinion that given a proper land system, 'conservative subsistence farming could enable us to maintain out of our own resources all our population even with the present rate of increase for a good long time to come, provided we are prepared to forego for the time being some of the trimmings of progress and to put first things first.' He accordingly made the proper disposal of night-soil by composting the foundation of his reconstruction schemes beginning with his Ashram. The erection of trench or pit latrines and scavenging was an essential part of the daily Ashram routine and of the apprenticeship which ever novice went though.

There are two well known approaches to life. One is embodied in the well-known dictum of the famous German Professor William Roscher. "Every advance in culture made by man finds expression in an increase in the number and in the keenness of his rational wants. The other summed up in the Indian spiritual ideal of a watchful self-restraint.

The nature sets limits. It requires a person to contain himself with in its capacity. Thus the emphasis is on self-control and limitations of wants. Mechanised industry knows no such limitation. Its law is one of progressive increase. Those who laid down the pattern of India's ancient culture could not accept the notion that culture increases with the increase in the number of man's wants and their satisfaction.

Gandhi advocated a solution of this problem in the form of wantlessness, meaning thereby that let us voluntary reduce our wants to genuine level. Professor J.K Mehta, distinguished economist has suggested a process of killing of wants. Wants can be killed by wants only. Hence stronger wants must be employed to kill the weaker wants. And when such a battle is fought in the human mind all the interior wants get ultimately killed and one is left with superior wants only. The better among them can, in their turn, be employed to kill the other wants. In this way we can ultimately reach a stage in which only the most superior (in other words most genuine) wants would be left to satisfy and it is only when this stage is reached that we can with impurity satisfy the wants. "The remain unsatisfied … Our ancestors, therefore, set a limit to our indulgence.. Our fore-fathers knew that, if we set our hearts after such things, we would become slaves and lose our moral fibre. They, therefore, after due deliberation decided that we should only do what we could with out hands and feet. They saw that our real happiness and health consisted in a proper use of our hands and feet. If we follow this it can conserve a lot of natural resources for us which will be sufficient for generations to come.

The propensity to accumulate commodities cramp the soul and degenerate into the morbid desire to make a fetish of external goods of life. The luxury of the ascendant classes therefore, make them morally deprived. The monopolisation of the things by a few men at the top is unjust. Moreover accumulation is condemnable because it is not possible to be practised by all. "I venture to suggest", he observed in one of his earliest speeches in India, "That it is the fundamental law of nature, without exception that nature produces enough for our wants from day to day, and if only every body took enough for himself and nothing more, there would no pauperism in this world." He did not want to dispossess anybody, he went on to say, "I should then be departing from the rule of non-violence.. But ... I do say that ... you and I have no right to anything that we really have until these... millions are clothed and fed better. You and I... must adjust our wants, and even undergo voluntary starvation in order that they be nursed, fed and clothed."

Men by virtue of his ever unsatisfied desire for more and more has made a hell of this planet. Increasing ecological imbalance, environmental degradation, vanishing flora and fauna, unhampered population explosion and deteriorating human values all are the outcome of this greed of the modern Homo-Sapiens.

Gandhi without consciously attempting at systematic theory explained the phenomena of the exploitation of natural resources through alienation also. He was of the opinion that the more nature was overpowered, the more alienated man will become from nature. He simultaneously wanted to focus on the relationship between man and his natural environment which would end exploitation, which in turn is the very cause of exploitation of nature. But this alienation of man from nature has also paved the way of alienation from himself also. His true-self is what man can discover through the search for truth following the path of non-violence. Gandhi had a full view of man, his spiritual, cultural and social aspects as much as his economic needs. This led him to advocate that man must adjust himself to The nature and not the other way round. He would not permit imbalance to be created between man and his environment.

Similar views are expressed by two highly experienced ecologists, Tom Dale and Vermin Gill Carter, "Civilised man was nearly always able to become master of his environment temporarily. His chief troubles came from his delusions that his temporary mastership was permanent. He though of himself as master of the world, while failing to understand fully the laws of nature. Man, whether civilised or savage is a child of nature—he is not master of nature. He must confirm his action to certain natural laws if he is to maintain his dominance over his environment. When he tries to circumvent the laws of nature, he usually destroys the natural environment that sustains him. And, when his environment deteriorates rapidly, his civilisation declines."

The problem is how to conduct affairs in a manner that is compatible with Gandhi's approach. The problem gains real urgency, from the strenuous attempts all over the world to develop at any cost. This development is generally conceived along western lines. Yet it is easy to see that the western way of life can not be permanent and will be incompatible with peace if it spreads to all mankind.

The western way of life, even in a much more modest from than its American modal, requires the annual use of several tons of 'fossil fuel' per person. But the world's resources of fossil fuels, obtainable at reasonable cost, are strictly limited. It follows that a civilisation based on fossil fuel can be only an episode in the history of man—and when measured against the life of nations, a very short episode. By suing coal and oil, we live on capital instead of income. This is quite legitimate under certain conditions. When a young man has his education financed out of capital funds, but if he is wise he does two things; (a) he voluntarily limits his annual drafts on capital so that it will last at least until he no longer needs it, and (b) he never loses sight of the fact that he must quickly learn to subsist an income, without further substantial drafts on capital. His principal task is to find a way of life that is self supporting.

The 'Limits to Growth' report produced by Massachusetts. 'Institute of Technology, among other material contains, an interesting table which shows U.S. consumption as percentage of world's total. Some of the important figures are as follows;

Table 1

Aluminium	42%
Coal	44%
Copper	33%
Gold	26%
Iron	28%
Mercury	24%
Molybdenum	40%
Natural Gas	63%
Nickel	38%
Petroleum	33%

Having calculated when each of these commodities will be exhausted, the authors give their general conclusion, "Give present resource consumption rates and the projected increase in these rates, the great majority of the currently important non-renewable resources will be extremely costly 100 years from now." In fact they do not believe that very much time is left before modern industry `heavily dependent on a network of international agreements with the producing countries for the supply of raw-materials might be faced with the crises of unheard proportions.'

Professor E.F Schumacher gives the world a timely warning of the three crisis engulfing the world. They are: the crisis of resources, the crisis of ecology and a very deep human crisis of alienation and disorientation.

These crises occurred because every body strives hard to have more and more. Schumacher focuses his attention on one important natural resource 'fuel', taking it as the representative of all other sources. More prosperity, according to him, means a greater use of fuel. He shows the prosperity gap between the rich and poor in their respective fuel consumption in the following table using data taken from United Nations Reports.

Table 2

1966

	Rice	(%)	Poor	(%)	World	(%)
Population (millions)	1060	31	2284	69	3384	100
Fuel Consumption (million tons c.e.)	4788	87	721	13	5509	100
Fuel Consumption per head (tons c.e.)	4.52		0-32		1.65	

The average fuel consumption per head of the poor is only 0.32 tons—roughly one-fourteenth of the rich (4.52), and there are very many poor people in the world. If the poor suddenly start using as much as fuel as rich, world fuel consumption would treble right away. But this can not happen as every thing takes time. And in time both the rich and the poor are growing in desires and in numbers. So, professor Schumacher makes an exploratory calculation. If the rich populations grow at the rate of .25 per cent and the poor at the rate of 2.5 per cent a year, world population will grow to about 6,900 million by 2000 AD If at the same time the fuel consumption per head of the rich population grows by 2.25 per cent, while that of poor grows by 4.5 per cent a year, the following figure will emerge for the year 2000 AD.

Table 3

(2000 AD)

	Rich	(%)	Poor	(%)	World	(%)
Population (millions)	1617	23	5292	77	6909	100
Fuel Consumption (Million tons c.e.)	15588	67	7588	33	23156	100
Fuel Consumption (per head tons c.e.)	9.64		1.43		3.35	

The total result on world fuel consumption would be a growth of 5.5 milliards tons. in 1966 to 23.2 milliards tons in the year 2000—an increase by a factor of more than four, half of which would be attributable to population increase an half to increased consumption per head. This half and half spilt is interesting enough. But the spilt between rich and poor is even more interesting. Of the total increase in the world fuel consumption from 5.5 milliard to 23.2 milliard tons., i.e. an increase by 17.7 milliard tons, the rich would account for nearly two thirds and the poor only a little over one third. These statistics given by Professor Schumacher nearly three decades ago still hold good. In the light of our present knowledge of fossil fuel reserves world stock will not survive for a loner period. And what is the future of this civilisation based on fossil fuel?

"I have taken fuel merely as an example to illustrate a very simple thesis, "writes Professor Schumacher, "That economic growth, which viewed from the point of view of economics, physics, chemistry and technology, has no discernible limit, must necessarily run into the decisive bottlenecks when viewed from the point of view of the environmental sciences. An attitude to life which seeks fulfilment in the single minded pursuit of wealth—in short, a materialism—does not fit into this world, because it contains within itself no limiting principle, while the environment in which it is placed is strictly limited. Already, the environment is trying to tell us that certain stresses are becoming excessive. As one problem is being solved ten new problems arise as a result of the first solution. As Professor Barry Commoner emphasises, the new problems are not the consequences of incidental failure but of technological success."

Schumacher not only points out the defects and drawbacks of the system, but also suggests positive remedies. "If the road is leading us into a crisis of survival, we may consider whether new guidelines may be called for, which would point in opposite directions."

towards smallness rather than giantess;
towards simplifications rather than growing complexity;
towards capital saving rather than labour saving; and
towards non-violence, in a rather generalised sense.

Findings of Professor Schumacher and a host other technologists and ecologists have reinforced the basic validity of Gandhi's approach. Mulling over these points time and again, one becomes progressively convinced that the present ecological crisis is a direct consequence of man's inability to rise to the level of understanding and responsibility demanded by his new power role in the world. The problem is within man, not outside him, and so is any solution. And this is precisely what Gandhi emphasised. To quote him, "The world will live in peace only when the individual composing it make up their mind to do so." Human beings will have to realise that a way of life that rapidly depletes the power of earth instead of sustaining it piles up more insoluble problems for each succeeding generation can only be called violent. Man's urgent task is to follow a non-violent way of life in economics. It is a concept that needs to be widened out to combat not merely the violence of man against man, but also the violence of man in his dealing with living nature around him and with the limited and finite resources of the earth.

Entirely new approach would be required to redirect the human society involving a supreme effort of understanding, imagination and political and moral resolve. There is no

the concept of inter-dependence of nations has penetrated and permeated the stratum of human consciousness with unusual speed and strength. It is only four decades since the last World War ended. Yet the international institutions symbolising the inter-dependence of nations, started after the war, have become as firmly rooted in the human psyche as any of the centuries-old organisations. The World Bank and the International Monetary Fund have served the Third World well. Their annual meetings are milestones along the road to global growth.

The picture of inter-assistance, especially aid by the North to the South, is again, not one of unrelieved gloom. "Nothing is here for tears, nothing o wail or knock the breast." Ours is a perfecting world, but its progress is painfully slow, sometimes by the millimetre. The famous anthropologist Margaret Mead concluded that it takes about a generation, say three decades, for a new idea to strike roots in the public mind. The impatient dialogue between the North and the South started only thirteen years ago. We must be reconciled to the inevitability of gradual's. Brand's passionate plea has begun to work. More and more people of the North realise more clearly, that the economically desperate of today are the international flashpoints of tomorrow. There is a growing consciousness that, as Rabindranath Tagore reminded us, the weak in their weakness can do no less harm to the strong than the strong in their strength to the weak.

The greatest gift the North can confer on the South is the gift of knowledge. Transfer of technology can be the most fruitful type of assistance. An old Asian adage says, "Give a boy some fish to eat and you will assuage his hunger for a day, but teach a boy to catch fish and he will never by hungry." Shared responsibility should beget a shared programme for development and an adequate, collective response.

The South has to abandon its wild rhetoric and engage in conciliatory negotiation. And the North has to realise that the search for solutions is not an act of benevolence, but a condition of mutual survival. In the historical perspective, that search has had a good start and must continue with redoubled vigour. In the words of Arnold Tony, "Our age will be well remembered not for its horrifying crimes nor its astonishing inventions, but because it is the first generation since the dawn of history in which mankind dared to believe it practical to make the benefits of civilisation available to the whole human race." The insight of Nanny A. Palkhivala, in his book, "We, the Nation, is meaningful, when he writes:

If mankind is to live in minimum comfort as a single family and the internecine tensions and strains are to be avoided, population control is not only desirable but necessary.

There can be no doubt that the frightening growth of world population is one of the strongest forces shaping the future of human society. It took mankind one million years to reach the first billion.: that was the world population around the year 1800. By 1900—in just a hundred years – a second billion was added. The twentieth century by itself has already added another three billion. The present world population is five billion. According to the Global 2000 Report to the American President, "three-quarters of the people who have ever lived since life on earth began are alive today." The number is expected to increase to 6.3 billion by 2000 AD The nine-tenths of the increase will be in developing countries. Every five days the world population increases by one million. Fertility falls as incomes rise, education spreads and health improves.

The rich get richer, and the poor get children which helps to keep them poor. More children does not mean more workers but more people without work. The World Bank's World Development Reports rightly suggest that population control is one of the first imperatives of development, since economic advance is so severely diluted by rapid population growth. It is not suggested that human beings should be treated like cattle and compulsorily sterilised. But there is no alternative to family planning at a human level without introducing an element of physical coercion. The choice is really between control of population and perpetuation of poverty.

No one familiar with the conditions of the South would have any doubt that the hope of the people there would die in their hungry hutment's unless population control is given the topmost priority.

"CONFUCIAN CONSUMERISM

Perils of China's market march", Profile Bawdier in an article writes:

China look like after the conclusion of the 15th Congress of the Community Party (CPC). The hazy, dusty air with a quarter of the city being rebuilt into chrome-and-glass structures – is full of expectancy and foreboding. One the surface, people seem content to leave the nation's fate to the wisdom of the 344-strong Central Committee and to policies driven by the "DEng Xiaoping Theory" of combining market-driven growth with a one-party state.

Mr. Jingo argued in a new elaboration and extension of the "DEng Theory" of "socialism with Chinese characteristics", is necessary because China is in a "primary stage of socialist development." The "primary stage", presumably analogous to Marx's notion of primitive accumulation of capital – with gross inequalities and unethical practices – necessitates private and mixed ownership. This will turn China's industrial economy into a quasi-capitalist sector, undermining public control over means of production. This is not a creative use of the market, but capitulation to it. It is founded on Confucian consumerism.

In China, you do not see poverty on a scale even remotely comparable with India's. You certainly do not see many crippled or blind people. But there are beggars, and poor people without work permits who labour in China's own black economy.
Contrary to what is imagined by many, and despite rapid growth, China still remains a fairly poor and extremely unevenly developed country with a capitalism that fits Charles Dickens' description.

Nation-wide, 81 percent of household own a bicycle and 40 per cent posses a colour TV set, but only 9 per cent have telephones. Most families live in 240 sq. ft. tenements. The craving for the Three Big Things - the colour TV, the washing machine and the refrigerator – has been quenched only in big cities.

In China today, income disparities between the top 5 per cent and bottom 20 per cent of the population can be as great as 1000 to one. The average factory worker's wage is less than 400 Juan ($ 50) a month – the daily, rent of a modest hotel room. True, housing only claims 7 per cent of household spending, but rents of new apartments are rising. The practice of levying fees in schools is spreading. For every "success" story – e.g. the 34-year-old Shanghai wheeler-and-dealer who started business five years ago and owns two Mercedes-Benz 600s and a Ferrari – there are 10 stories of failure: social immobility, suppression of labour rights, forced relocation, 180 million illegal migrants.

Under the "DEng Theory", the state is losing leverage over economic processes, and instruments of intervention are being discarded. In their absence, China faces uncertainties. It has much potential for convulsions and eruption of tensions between rival centres of power. But is has hardly any safety valves. Democratisation would have been a great moderating influence a healer, an instrument of mediation between the state and the people. But the 15th Congress has firmly rejected this option China has undoubtedly been a success story in dealing with mass poverty, one we should learn from. But it is far from clear it China can deal with problems of wealth produced by iniquitous, environmentally unsound and unsustainable growth.

No society is altogether free from corruption. Indian society is particularly prone to it. Since the last five decades, we Indians have no limit in mechanism for providing automatic correctives. State functionaries and politicians get away with the violation of law against corruption; the law being rarely enforced and even when enforcement is threatened, the threat is seldom carried out and its culmination in punishment is non-exist. According to Edward Gibbon: Corruption is, the most infallible symptom of constitutional liberty.

India is not the only country engulfed in corruptions' deadly embrace. It has equally alarming proportions in Pakistan & Bangladesh - as the people their are no different; and corruptions magnitude in Indonesia has been disturbingly high. However, we Indians cannot comfort ourselves with the thought that other countries are sailing with us in the same or similar boat with Roles of Corruption. At a centenary celebrations of the then ruling Congress Party in India, the then Prime Minister of India, late Mr. Rajiv Gandhi minced no words in cordially criticising the Congress leaders as brokers for power and influence, who had lost touch with masses. They are too preoccupied with their own private welfare at the public expense & live no time to worry about public weal. Corruption, undoubtedly is a double edged weapon that cuts deep into the revenues of the State and strikes hard at the income of the ever growing poor population and polluting environment. Its cumulative effect is felt in soaring prices; low and slow tax-returns. The bureaucrats, businessmen and industrialists alone are its real beneficiaries. And it tend to widen the disparity between plenty for the rich influential class and scarcity for the poor.

India, one of the poorest of the poor country of the world is world-wide known as the most corrupt country. The governments both Centre and at the State levels are recurred by the Sugar scam, Telecom, Bofors, Hawala, Medical, St. Kitts Forgery; Harshad Mehta, defrauding Lakhubhai, Urea Scam, Housing Scam, Fodder Scam, JMH Bribery case and earlier Jeep scandal; Huddle Episode; Mundhra deals, Kairon case; Serajuddin affair, Challenge Tubes, Kerala Rice Enquiry; Back scams; Forest scam; Bitumen scam, Ayurveda sac, so on & so forth.

13

GLOBAL RAMIFICATIONS OF CORRUPTION

"The Second World War was a watershed point in bringing about a change in the age-old value system based on religion and fear of God. It had been declared by Nietz Che German philosopher, that God was dead. The old value system was being replaced by one based on reason, secularism and scientific outlook. The holocaust of a senseless wholesale destruction of human life and civilization had raised a number of questions in the conscious and unconscious mind of man. Fear of God and belief in divine punishment for wrongs were deemed unreasonable and without proof. Fundamentalist forces became stronger and more ruthless than before. Fundamentalism of one community, group or faction provoked and activated the fundamentalism of the other. But God as the source of higher values and ideals and the fear of offending sin had suddenly disappeared from the man's moral and intellectual horizon. It was replaced by a faith in material superiority as a goal to achieve power and happiness.

The end of the Second World War saw the devotion of self-rule on most of those countries which had been under foreign domination for a long period. Most of these had learned patriotism and nationalism from their rulers. Rigid boundaries of the nation-state had come about only recently in many parts of the world and the societies based on tribal affinities had not yet accepted them as ground reality. These people, therefore did not realise the huge responsibility of self government which fell on them after independence. Need for self-discipline, self-examination and self-correction is essential in a democratic society, but people were not mature for democracy either by training or by a firm faith in its efficacy. Democracy was accepted for either want of a better alternative or as a fashion of the day. Democracy grows out of individual and his faith in his own judgement. In the new democracies, most people lacked in these qualities and note, were cast in groups based on communal, religion, caste, sectarian and other considerations. The leadership lacked national outlook and farsightedness and looked for immediate gains for themselves and their communities or constituencies.

Democracy is a costly form of government. Political parties required huge funds to be able to propagate their programmes and fight elections. This money could not come from the poor. It come from who had a lot of unaccounted spare money made by illegal means. These people needed political protection and patronage to be able to legitimise this money and to further increase it. Though political parties needed this money very badly, they did not realise that this would compromise their ideology and in the long run criminals politics

This coming together of illegal money and politics converted the latter into commercial activity. The ideals of patriotism, nationalism and social service associated with it became suddenly irrelevant. The men with money came to power to have their own men in the corridors of power instead of working through their political affiliations. A new generation of politicians arose who had no commitment to the welfare of common man and development activities. They tried to grab the major share out of governmental spending and corrupted the public officials to their best financial advantage. They had no respect for the law of the land but had the power to influence the process of law making. This made crime a socially accepted reality, if not respectable. Dishonesty, bribery and anti-social economic activities were no longer reprehensible.

The majority of the people in India and other colonial countries were poor before independence, but they were not ashamed of it. They were honest and feared God. Those who gained money through bribery or other illegal means were looked down upon and they knew that they were morally in the wrong. In the post independence era, religion lost its hold in the name of secularism and scientific attitude. Political leaders pushed out other leaders of the community or made them powerless. There was no one to check the politician indulging in corruption or corrupting others to extend his influence.

Corruption in politicians was accepted as a necessary evil to provide for their needs both personal and political.

Corruption has many ramifications. It is not only that some people use social resources out of turn and to the detriment of others, they gradually come to control political power. Criminalisation of politics is not conferred to some pockets of India. It is a national curse in some African and Latin American countries. It damages the law and order situation of a country. It demoralises the law-empowering agencies when they repeatedly fail to bring punishment to the corrupt on technical grounds even when the truth is blatantly apparent to everybody.

Political power against through corruption means it is subservient to the interests of the corrupt. The economic activities are so affected that they go against the national interest. Quality of products and services goes down and nation is forced to accept what is offered. There is a slow down of nation's endeavour to achieve intellectual superiority or supremacy. Disparity increases both in economic conditions and in social relationships among different groups. Few people become immensely rich and majority becomes very poor. Exploitation of different groups excavates. Material gains being the only objective, means used are considered amoral. Propagation of drugs and other evils in the society and making profit out of it do not appear wrong to this amoral and secular leadership.

Fall in social and ethical values gives rise to violence used by the man in power to extend their hold on it and by the men who are exploited to fight against this exploitation. Consequently, there is every likelihood that weapons will proliferate and terrorism will grow. Already there is ample evidence that the use of terrorism by the state on the one hand and by the rebel groups on the other is making the life of common man miserable. The greatest achievement of the British Raj in India was that it took weapons out of the hands of the common people and, thus, brought violence substantially down both in rural and urban areas.

With the advances in science and technology, the criminalisation of politics can lead to strong and ruthless dictatorships. Initially, dictatorships might appear to be a blessing after the rampant run of criminal politics but sooner or later absolute power corrupts absolutely. Democracy with all its problems is by far the best system of governance evolved by man. The ramifications of corruption on the moral and material life of the individual and society are far reaching the implications of which simply cannot be foreseen.

14

INDIAN ECONOMY AND NRI's

The Indian economy had been fast sinking into the quicksands of rising prices, balances of payment, mounting internal and external debts, increasing unemployment and poverty. The liabilities of the Union Government in excess of its total assets had increased from Rs.77,518 crores in 1991 to Rs.2,15,753 crore. The failure of the government to restrain revenue deficit and spare more funds from investment on infrastructure and weakened the fundamentals of the economy. The fiscal deficit of 1993-94 has been projected at 4.7 percent Rs.36,959 crore of the GDP which went upto 7.7% whereas it should have been 3% in terms of original targets. To improve its economy India need not beg, borrow or steel as its own. NRIs can generate and pour into India the foreign remittances to meet its financial needs; provided the NRIs are convinced about the honest utilization of funds in India. Generally speaking NRIs are sentimental and loyal to Indian soil, the country of their origin.

The situation of the internal debt was not better. There had been an increase of over 700% in the internal debt over past five years. The GDP growth rate between 1991-92 and 1995-96 had been only 4.6% as compared to 5.8% between 1985-90 and 5.7% from 1980-85: Need is for the protection to the Indian industry for some more time so that it could improve the quality of the products and was in a position to face competition from multinationals.[1]

Abani Kumar Dash[2] in an article, "caution needed on external debt front" explains: In economics, as they say, there is nothing like a free

---

1 Atal Behari Vajpayee, "Indian Economy Sinking", The Tribune, March 28, 1996; P.

2 Abani Kumar Dash, "Caution needed on external debt front", The Hindustan Times, March 30, 1996; p.11.

lunch. And foreign debts, as they come, must look like unpaid launches until the bills arrive. Even as countries need to borrow from abroad, there comes a point when one should begin worrying about the accumulating weight of the debt. The critical point is reached when a country earns just enough in foreign exchange to keep its external debts serviced. That is the classical case of the debt trap. One prudent ways of staying out of a debt trap is to start worrying about it well before the critical point is reached. On December 21, 1995, the Finance Minister, Dr. Manmohan Singh, released a white paper, which came after a gap of two years, and which admitted that the volume of foreign debt had grown to $99.04 billion as March 31, 1995 and may have crossed the century mark in the he intervening months. In the document, Dr. Singh has observed that the level of India's external debt is a matter of concern to the Government. While the Finance Minister was right in voicing the government's continuous concern" over the rise in external debt, it needs to be followed up by measures that strengthen the inherent capacities of the economy.

A good part of the debt, especially that relating to multilateral institutions excluding the International Monetary Fund (IMF) and bilateral debt has a large degree of concessionality. Basically, such borrowings must be kept within prudent limits so that the country does not get into a debt trap. The paper entitled "India's external debt - a status report" significantly pointed out that of the total increase in external debt during 1994-95 as much as US $5.61 billion or about 88% of the rise was due to exchanged rate changes alone. It was underlined that had the exchange rate between the US dollar and the other international currency basket remained unchanged. India's external debt would have increased in dollar terms by only US$ 794 million in 1994-95. The White paper points out the share of commercial borrowings in total debt declined marginally from 13.3.% in end-March 1994 to 13.1% to end-March 1995[3].

It may be recalled that since the mid-1970s the high level of foreign

---

3 Ibid.

borrowing by many developing countries has led to debt crisis. Foreign borrowing is useful source of finance for economic development. The burden of foreign debt is the need to pay the interest and principal in foreign exchange that is obtained from export earnings or by reducing imports. The OIL CRISIS of 1974 led many developing countries to increase their borrowing to pay for their imports of oil. This borrowing was largely achieved through a recycling of the oil revenue of OPEC countries through EUROCURRENCY markets. The second oil crisis of 1979 was more difficult to cope with as interest rates had increased the prices of many of the primary exports of developing countries had fallen, growth in the world economy and trade was sluggish and many existing loans were coming to maturity. Many countries were unwilling to deflate their economics, in order to reduce imports and free foreign exchange to pay for the servicing of debts and the greater cost of oil imports. By 1983, many countries were in a very insecure financial position and began to attempt to renegotiate with private international banks the structure and terms of their debts. These banks, concerned about these countries and their own financial insecure position, formed consortia and insisted that the debtor countries first apply to the IMF for further funds and accept the IMF's conditions on the future conduct of economic policy. The world financial system has managed to cope with most of the short terms problems of the debt crisis and world economic system can be solved is a matter of importance and speculation"[4].

It must be clearly understood that a debt is a present obligation to pay an ascertainable sum of money, whether the amount is payable in praesenti of ruin futuro: debitum in praesenti, solvendum in futuro. But a sum payable upon a contingency does not become a debt until the said contingency has happened[5]. The word "debt" is applicable

---

4 M.P. Todaro, 'Economic Development in the Third Word (London, 3rd ed. 1995)

5 Kesoram Industries & Cotton Missals Ltd. V. CWT (Central), AIR 1996 SC 1370.

to a sum of money which has been promised at a future day as to a sum now due and payable. When there is an obligation to pay a sum of money at a future date, it is debt owing but when the obligation to pay a sum of money at a future date, it is debt owing but when the obligation is too pay sum money in presenti, it is a debt due. A sum due would, therefore, mean a sum for which there is an existing obligation to pay in praesenti, or in other words, which is presently payable[6]. "Debt" includes any liability in respect of any obligation to repay capital sums by ways of annualities and any liability under any guarantee, and 'debt charges' shall be construed accordingly[7].

The question arises as to why the interest rates sky-high at a recent Indian Econometric Society seminar, Dr. Urjit Patel[8] of the RBI offered several explanations, and one of them being that the banks are unable to liquidate their huge surplus holdings of securities in the absence of a debt market.

Many co-operatives planned projects on the assumption they could raise unlimited sums from the capital market. When this turned out not to be the case, they used working capital from banks as a substitute for long-term funds, driving up interest rates. N.J. Jhaveri[9] in a lead published article, "Glorious past, hazy future", while cautioning writes: Remember how Clinton, in electoral campaign, capitalized to his advantage the 'lacklustre' performance the American economy during the last months of the Bush presidency. When the final data became available the American economy had performed far better than what preliminary estimates indicated. But Bush lost and Clinton won".

The task ahead is much more formidable than it appears now, and the legacy not as health as this government seems to leave behind. Truly speaking, growing centralization has weakened the federal

6 Union of Indian v. Raman Iron Foundry (1974)2 SCC 231.

7 Art. 366(8) of the Constitution of India.

8 Interest puzzle, The economics Times, March 25, 1996; P.4

9 N.J. Jhaveri, "Glorious past, hazy future", The Economic Times, March 8, 1996; P.9

structure. Most of our problems economic, political and social stem from a top heavy and highly centralized political and administrative system,, the concentration of power, resort to unprincipled means, have resulted in inefficiency, and corruption and the undermining of democratic institutions. After Independence, the size of administration and expenditure and expenditure incurred on it, has gradually increased, occasionally to save and strengthen the individual's government. It has given birth to a vicious circle leading to corruption. Corruption is no longer the monopoly of any individual or to particular party. Undoubtedly, rampant corruption had seeped at every step of the government structure. Public servants, whether politicians of bureaucrats, irrespective of their creed, ruling class, as also the opposition crowd, all are accountable and answerable for such state of digression on account of which the whole nation hangs its head in shame. Actually, democracy has been prevented by the small men from bestowing its full benefits upon the people, due to corruption, opportunism,, power lust, greed, and other such ills in the political system. And what is more depressing is that the woes of the common man to get ordinary routine thing, done in normal way, and without loss of much time, have remained unremedial, and their sufferings go on unabated. The vagaries of officialdom at the lower level or "grass roots" level are hardly on the wane. Something very drastic is required to be done so that developmental benefits percolate to the lower levels, and the public life is cleansed of huge accumulated and mounting silt and slush, and solution is found to solve the genuine problems faced by the society. J Krishanamurti is right when he says, "if, we can really understand the problem the answer will come out of it, because answer is not separate from problem".

The country at the moment is being forced to run virtually by judiciary because of the failure of democratic institutions. The CIA has already published a document that India is on the verge of collapse. The road ahead is not easy. Criminal gangs,, vested interest of those in power for their own vested ends would not yield easily and so soon. But then the battle has to be fought out by reason as well as by the clarity of ideas along with sharpness and efficiency of action. If men and women of wisdom and sincerity lie low and want to escape the hardy road ahead no future lies for the nation. Modern technology had given India new vision and new outlook but the gains will be negated if power direction is not given to them.[10]

Part XVIII of the Constitution makes provision for three kinds of emergencies which have different incidents. (A) Proclamation of Emergency: (B) Financial emergency. The expression instates; (c). The expression "Proclamaton of Emergency" means only a proclamation issued under clause (1) of Article 352. Accordingly, wherever the expression "Proclamation of Emergency" occurs, it should not include the two other emergencies, namely, the emergency arising out of the failure of the constitutional machinery in a State or the financial emergency.

Article 360 has never been involved so far. But, if the President is satisfied that a situation has arisen whereby the financial stability or credit of India or of any part thereof is threatened, he may make a proclamation or make a declaration to that effect. During the period the proclamation is in operation, the executive authority of the Union shall extend to the giving of the directions to any State to observe such canons of financial propriety as may be specified in the directions, and be deemed necessary for maintaining financial stability and credit of the State. Under these directives, any State may be required by the Union to reduce salaries and allowances of all or any class of persons employed by the State and reserve all money or financial Bills for the consideration of the President after they are passed by the legislature of the State[11]. As amended by the Forty-fourth Amendment, a proclamation, of financial emergency shall cease to operate in two months from the date of issue unless it is approved by both House of Parliament. If the House of the People is dissolved, it has to be approved within thirty days from the reconstitution of the House. Once the proclamation has been approved by Parliament it will continue to remain in force unless revoked by the President.

---

10 Arun Mitra, "Intelligentsia's role today", The Tribune, March 27, 1996 ; P.10

11 V.N. Shukla's Constitution of India, Ninth Ediction (1993) p.872

Further, during such financial emergency, it shall be competent for the President to issue directions for the reduction of salaries and allowances of all or any class or persons, including Judges of the Supreme Court and High Courts serving the Union. The constitution of India is unique in the respect that it contains a complete scheme for speedy readjustment of the peace-time governmental machinery in moment of national peril. These provisions may appear to be harsh, particularly in a Constitution which professes to be built upon an edifice of fundamental rights and democracy. But the provisions must be studied in the light of India's past history. India had her inglorious days whenever the Central power grew weak. It is well that the Constitution guards against the forces of disintegration. Events may take place threatening the very existence of the State, and if there are no safeguards against such eventualities, the State, together with all that is desired to remain basic and immutable, will be swept away[12]. It is worth consideration what Professor Milton Friedman, the Nobel Prize Winner for economics, concluded in the Tyranny of the status quo that no elected head of the state has more than six to nine months to initiate major policy changes. Thereafter, the force of status quo take over.

A person shall be deemed to a person of Indian origin if(I) he, at any time held an Indian Passport, or (ii) he or either of his parents or any of his grand parents was an Indian and a permanent resident of undivided India at any time. A wife of a citizen of India, or a person of Indian origin shall also be deemed to be on Indian origin even though she may be non-Indian origin . The three based of citizenship in Article 5 of the Constitution are thus citizenship of persons of Indian origin residing outside India. This is a proviso to Article 5 and aimed at certain type of citizenship. It requires that a person of Indian origin can be registered as an Indian citizen while residing in the foreign country itself and without the necessity of having any Indian residence. It does not require any qualification except the Indian origin. It does not require residence in India. The registration is a recognition of citizenship by being a person of Indian origin.

---

[12] Ibid

Chapter Xii-A of the Income Tax Act, 1961 in Section 115(c) defines non-resident Indian as follows:

Non-resident Indian means an individual being citizens of India or a person of Indian origin who is not a resident. Explanation: a person shall be deemed to be of Indian origin if he, or either of his parents for any of the grandparents, was born undivided India.

Indians and persons of Indian origin numbering about 15 millions are spread over in all corners of the world. They include all sorts of People such as skilled, unskilled and semi-skilled workers, scientists, professors, students, entrepreneurs and petty traders. Many left the shores of their motherland during the last 150 years. Although a large number of them, particularly those of the second and third generations, are coming under western influence and submerged in a local culture, they still continue to maintain emotional links with India and look towards it for cultural and religious inspiration. Unfortunately, India and its missions working all over the world have done precious little to inspire them. At present Indians are those of Indian origin are found in as many as 142 countries spread over all the continents. Their number varies from few persons in Guinea (2) and Cuba (5) to more than one million in Nepal and Malaysia. Of these 14 countries have more than one lakh Indians each and 39 countries have more than 10,000 Indians each. A large number of them are either nationals of these countries or have taken citizenship of the countries of their adoption.

According to Jayant Patel, it is an irony indeed very sad to note than the Indian government's list of Indian abroad does not include about 800,000 of Indians in South Africa. For blind political support to anti-apartheid movement and to appease the black African government does not recognize even the existence of these Indians in South Africa. It is a shame that Indian government has disowned eight lakh Indians and refuses to guide them, inspire to help them, and satisfy their cultural and emotional needs. Indian migrants, like migrants from other countries have been having their own problems. They have their distant culture, habits and taboos. Although some of them have become westernized and adapted to local two levels this exclusiveness serves as a self-preservation function. In the pre-Independence period, overseas India's exclusiveness was a matter of pride to Indian nationalists and as a result, on India's independence in 1947, an even stronger sense of consciousness of being Indian arose among them. But the response from the parent land was poor.

Barrister Jayant Patel on NRI is of the view that the negative role played by the Indian Government and near total silence of our members of Parliament and Indian intellectual and other groups is most disappointing. Parliament and Indian intellectual and other groups is most disappointing. The relevant question is this: what is India, the champion of victims of while racism, going to do about this unconstitutional and named racism in Fiji? It is sad commentary on the upside down priorities of our government to note that it sent a high power parliamentary delegation headed by Mr. Sat Pal Malik to countries to Europe to muster support for the anti-apartheid movement and sanctions against South Africa on 17th May, 1987 (three days after the coup of Fiji). Surely the need of the hour was to send high power delegations all over the world to muster support against the undemocratic and illegal coup in Fiji. It is depressing to note that at this crucial juncture, the Foreign Minister Mr. N.D. Tiwari went to Japan and Korea. Was this not the time to ask Arab and African friends - whose cause we supported for the last 40 years come out openly against the coup in Fiji? It is also sad to note Ministry for External Affairs lived up to its reputation of doing too little - too late and adopted the principle 'wait and watch. The governments of Australia and New Zealand came out immediately, categorically and forcefully against the coup in Fiji and so did Mr. Sridhar Ramphal, the Secretary General of Commonwealth Secretariat. But alas; The Indian government let the things cool off, lost the initiative and came out with guarded statements much too late. Mr. Natwar Singh was sent to U.K. and Mr. Edward Falerio to Australia, New Zealand nearly ten days after the coup took place. By then Col. Rabuka was firmly in the saddle, and now it is clear that Fijians of Indian Origin, though in majority will never acquire what is due to them - political power. Thus as usual, Indian government allowed the initiative to slip out of Indian hands and the victims are Fijians of Indian origin. Time and again, the Indian government shouts from the roof top for the Arab and African cause; but when the victims are Indians and people of Indian origin, it keeps mum and refuses to speak out. This encourages potential Iddi Amins as is proved by the emergence of Col. Rabuka.

The International Monetary Fund has brought out a report on the debt financial of the power economics and related issues. The report gives an idea of how to determine a safe level of external debt stock for any country. It takes into account the discounted present value of the total debt rather than the nominal value of the debt stock. The present value of debt essentially discounts the confessional component in the total debt. Indian policy makers will have to decide in future whether they should look at country's debt stock in isolation or view it in the context of the growth such inflows can generate.

It may be recalled that the General Agreement on Tariffs and Trade (GATT) is a multilateral treaty world trading system. In July 1944, the Bretton, Woods Conference had decided to establish three international institutions, namely (1) the International Bank for Reconstruction and Development (World Bank), (ii) the International Monetary Fund, and (iii) the International Trade Organization. However, while the first two institutions came into existence on December 27, 1945, the International Trade Organisation could not be established, owing to the resistance from the US senate. Instead of protocol of provisional Application was signed in late 1946 by 23 original members, which became effective on January 1, 1948 ushering in the GATT. It is engaged in "calling for non-discriminatory treatment of trading partners and setting rules intended to counterprotectionism and the 'law of the jungle' in international trade". During the period 1947 to 1993 the Contracting parties successfully conclude eight rounds of trade negotiations. This was the seven years of intense and procrastinator deliberation on contentious trade-related issues, the Uruguaary Round of Multilateral Trade Negotiations, which started at Punta del Este, Uruguaary in September, 1986, was finally endorsed by the contracting parties on December 15, 1993. The 500 page bulky agreement was formally signed in Marrakesh, Morocco in April 1994, after individual contracting parties presented their final tariff reduction formulae in February, 1994.

Most developing countries impose certain conditions on foreign investors referred to an 'investment measures'. These impose obligations on raw material for components, local equity participation and export operations of foreign investors to protect local industries from unfair competitions, to safeguard countries balance of payments conditions and to curb unethical MNCd practices like pricing. Developed countries argue that these measures are not less than protective tariffs and should, therefore, be removed. The electorate has mandated a critical review and drastic revisions of the government, whatever may be its completion or composition, will not be able to evade or side-track. A minuscule section in society which has stake in the so-called structural adjustment of the Indian economy initiated in 1991 has tried to spread the notion that the electoral contest was devoid of any policy issue. This is far removed from the mass mood and sentiments. The popular masses decisively voted the Rao government out for its economic policy and its disastrous impact on their lives and living conditions. Balraj Mehta, in a published article, Economic Challnges Mandate for policy review, writes: In the name of rapid growth and modernization, integration of the Indian economy with the global economy rather than autonomy of the Indian economy and its development became the siren song of the Rao government. India after gaining political independence, however, did not become autarkic and has never shut its doors to the inflow of foreign capital.

Foreign investors, in particular multinational corporation, and their political patrons have found a wide opportunity for a well-planned softening up operation in India. They have made a calculated bid to turn the balance of social and political forces in the economy and polity of India in their favor. The foreign investors, the powerful transitional corporations in particular, have enlarged their demands backed by political strategic pressure and sanctions of the governments of the developed countries through international financial institutions the World Bank, the IMF and GATT as well as on a bilateral basis, for the dismantling of any protective or regulatory framework to safeguard national interests, economic, social, cultural and political strategic. The new government must put a halt to the process of erosion of India's sovereignty and undermining of economic independence.

The manner and terms on which India has been made to accept the membership of the World Trade Organization is a stark case of the surrender to foreign pressures under false pretences. The autonomy of the government of India of decision making in critical matters has been circumscribed. The spreading WTO tentacles are assuming menacing features and dimensions. The latest move of the USA on patents, which the new government had to contend with at once after its formation, was ominous. But there can be no real economic progress, nor social cohesion and political stability without the assertion of the sovereign rights of the Indian Republic to curb the rapacious claims of foreign business interests, especially those operating as transitional corporations of India and technological enterprise, labor and consumer are the first obligation of the government of the sovereign republic of India. Local-made must not be derailed but become the guiding principle of economic policy of the government.

C.H. Prabhakara Rao and S.C. Srivastava in a published article on incentives for Foreign investment in India by non-resident Indians and persons of Indian origin conclusively concludes, that the Government of India is really keen to invite foreign investors in the present day economic scenario of India. It has taken several measures to encourage the non-resident Indians and Persons of Indian Origin to invest to the optimum and thereby play a very important role in the development of Indian economy as compared to the past. From the view point of NRIs and PIOs there appears to be number of hurdles and bottlenecks as discussed in Part III of this chapter. While the issues raised by the NRIs and PIOs require due examination at the end of those who are charged with the responsibility of inviting and attracting foreign investments by NRIs and PIOs, certain other issues also require adequate consideration for the purpose of making foreign investment more attractive and lucrative for the NRIs and PIOs. It is a naive to mention that the economics of the developed countries appear to be more secure and more attractive in terms of foreign investments as compared to the economics of the developing countries. Thus, creating a sense of security in the minds of NRI and PIOs is of prime importance for the purposes of foreign investment in India.

Secondly, the NRIs and PIOs may not be able to meet the challenges and competitions posed by the giant multi-national foreign investors which are running in the forefront for foreign investments in those developing countries whose economies appear to be bright and fruitful in the future. The Government of India, therefore, may consider some kind of most favored national treatment to NRIs and PIOs for foreign investment. In the third place, it is also worth considering that the south-south co-operation has an important role to play in the development of Indian economy. While the contribution made by the NRI and PIOs of the north are certainly appreciable, it would probably be an additional source of foreign investment in the NRIs and PIOs of the south block are given a preferential treatment for foreign investment in India. This would probably open the doors for better export of Indian products to the markets of south which has been potentiality and larger consumption as compared to the northern countries.

According to Bhamumathy . several reasons have been attributed for the inadequate investment by NRIs. Some NRIs consider that "even now the Indian Government treats them as milking cows, and the India bureaucracy's attitude is daunting". The NRIs want further liberation of economic policies and better conditions for investment. NRIs want further liberation of economic policies and better conditions for investment. NRIs abroad are asking for dual citizenship which they say, will act as an investment incentive. Also they feel uncomfortable about the export policy current convertibility and industrial policy.

Arun Ghosh has given further reasons which have contributed to the inadequate investment by NRIs. India is "a country of social tensions" for justifiable reasons and the present atmosphere can be described as anything but ambient. NRIs and PIOs consider that massive cuts in Government investment. According to them there is a scope for improvement of infrastructure functioning even without investment, but the effect of the cuts in expenditure may begin to surface in three to four years. Political uncertainty and instability of coalition governments is a contributory factor for lack of confidence in investments. Further liberalisation is also required.

In order to appreciate the contribution of NRIs and PIOs to the foreign investment in India, it is desirable to examine the scope of "non-resident Indians and Persons of Indian Origin". non-resident Indians means: A citizen of India staying abroad for employment or for carrying on business, or vocation or for any other purpose in the circumstances indicating period of stay outside India, or a citizen of India proceeding abroad for higher studies, touring, recreation, training or medical treatment, etc. He is treated as non-resident Indian from the time he takes up job abroad, or government posted broad on duty with the Indian Missions and similar agencies set up abroad on an assignment with foreign government or Regional/International agencies like WHO, ESCAP, IBRD IMP etc., or an official of a public sector undertaking or an autonomous organization deputed abroad on temporary assignment, or posted to its branches or offices abroad.

Swaraj Paul, asserts: we have changed our stance towards NRIs often enough. First, it was the fear of "brain drain". There was no love for people who took advantage of Indian education and opted to work for others countries, whatever be the reason. But this was not the case with the lakhs of unskilled and skilled workers who went over to the Gulf. They starved off the employment crises. What was more, they sent regular remittances to the mother country. In 1994-95, remittances stood at 56.2 billion. Barring exports, this was the largest source of India's receipts. There are about 18 million NRIs around the world. But only 2.5 million, living in the affluent West, are vocal. But they speak a language different from that of other NRIs. Their concerns are different. Rich NRIs must realize that without forgoing strong links with India, they have no future. If NRIs want to play a global role, that suits India has much need of the experience of NRIs to promote its MNCs. The choice is before the NRIs.

Indians are always fond of basing in the glory of ancient Indian civilization and its so-called :moral values". But corruption has totally changed its set of values. Corrupt public servants were social outcasts till the sixties, they started gaining acceptance during the servants and acquired respectability after mid-eighties. Corruption has become a part of Indian life now and a daughter' father is occasionally seen to be searching for a son-in-law in a post which has the potential. The irony is that the received if illegal gratification is the most aggrieved one when it's his turn to give. A friend once casually remarked that corruption received acceptability at the national level when Mrs. Indira Gandhi once remarked that it was a global phenomenon. It has got institutionalized now.

UN 1990 there were 1,559 cases of bank frauds, resulting in a loss of Rs. 65 crore. But after the advent of economic liberalizaton in 1991 the curve of bank frauds has been going up. In 1995 there 1,890 cases, leading to a loss of Rs. 116 crore. Last year saw detection of 1,954 cases, amounting to a loss of Rs. 320 crore.

It is difficult to explain why bank frauds have been increasing because economic liberation has not been accompanied by any loosening of banking procedures. On the contrary, the Reserve Bank of India constituted a Board of Financial Supervision (BFS) in 1994 which is expected to exercise integrated supervision on the banking system. Earlier also measures were announced by the R.B.I. to prevent bank frauds which include issuance of comprehensive guidelines for strengthening of the control mechanism, snap inspections in fraud-prone areas and on-site and off-site inspections. The increase in bank frauds obviously shows that neither is the BFS functioning effectively nor has the RBI bothered to ensure that the anti-fraud measures announced by it have been implemented seriously by the blanks. It is also indicative of the existence of corruption in the ranks of bank employees as well as limitless ingenuity of the crooked mind. Data on frauds detected in the nationalized banks shows that the worse-affected ones are the State Bank of India, Bank of Baroda, Bank of India, Central Bank of India, Canara Bank and Syndicate Bank. The chief modus operandi of perpetrators of bank frauds, who also include a fair sprinkling of NRIs and foreigners, is to draw money either by hoodwinking bank employees or in collusion with them, through forged drafts and cheques.

In 1996 the State Bank of India topped the list of banks which lost money through withdrawal of funds by foreigners on the basis of forged drafts. It lost Rs. 60.48 lakh. The private sector Federal Bank was next, losing Rs. 51.69 lakh. As distinct from these common frauds, there are the high-level scams involving misuse of loan-sanctioning discretionary power by senior bank executives, sometime at the behest of powerful politicians. The most notorious is, of course, the Indian Bank scam. It is alleged that senior executives of the Indian Bank in collusion with loaders of the Tamil Manila Congress - to which Finance Minister Chidambaram belongs - caused a loss to the public exchequer to the tune of Rs. 1,300 crores. Since the Indian Bank is having difficulty in finalization of its balance-sheet which should be done by September 30th, Mr. Chidambaran, the Finance Minister, is reportedly arranging release of Rs. 1,600 crores as recapitalization fund for the scam-scarred bank.

On August 20, 1997 the CBI court in Chennai (Madras) hearing the Indian Bank scam ordered arrest of K. Subramaniam, Chairman and Managing Director, Indian Overseas Bank, in connection with a scam-ridden loan of Rs. 3.6 million (Rs. 12.6 crores) he had authorized during his tenure as General Manager of the Indian Bank in favor of Greenseas Shipping Corporation, a Singapore-based company, without proper collateral security. Two months ago the CBI had sent a letter rogatory to the Singapore Government seeking help in investigating accounts of the Indian Bank branch in the nation-city. But the request was turned down.

15

WORK ETHICS

There is no service in Indian Government which is totally "clean'. Modes of corruption, to take the broad view, may be grouped into two categories: practices involving the public, and those internal to the administration.

The practices involving public may include bribery over tender contracts, and licences; acceptance of substandard stores; forgery and conniving at false assessments of claims and income-tax; irregularities in transport bookings; intentional delays in order to obtain "speed money" bribery for performance of what should be normal duties or for performance acceptance of gifts to use influence; misuse of power; and carrying on private business under the cover of official duties.

Corrupt practices internal to the administration cover misappropriation of public money and of stores; production of false medical claims, false claims of allowances and reimbursement, and of forged certificates of ages, community educational qualifications etc., abuse of official position or powers; acceptance of illegal gratification and favours in recruitment, posting, transfers and promotions, misuse of government employees for private work; misuse of advances sanctioned for purchases and leave travel concessions; cheating in connection with the sale and purchase of land; and unauthorised occupation and subletting of government residential quarters. Ways and means have been involved by taxation authorities. Custom and Excise; Defence, legal services; Medical services, Indian Administrative services, Forest and Revenue services; Public undertaking, Banking officers, etc. to grab the money. Opportunities for corruption are always there for those who seek them. But for the satisfactory performance of duty some seek inspiration from lofty spiritual philosophies like the selfless working preached in Gita which ordains: "Thou are entitled to work but not to its fruits which you have to surrender to the Lord". By way of an ideal nothing could be taller an order. The people do endeavour to work the ideal. An Indian Saint when he was serving an engineering firm in Spain, on issue of enhancement of wages reacted: "I am already overpaid and under worked". That is the spirit needed to be cultivated. The ideal is undoubtedly worth the while of every human life. Others seek incentive in the social concept of a good Samaritan or just a good citizen. Those in disciplined walks of life perform duty by sheer instinct because sense of discipline has got imbibed by them in their mental make-up. Whatever the driving force, all these categories bear a healthy mentality and generally a dutiful attitude and performance. There are of course those specimens of humanity who would rather specialise and excel in malingering and striking work harvesting nevertheless bumper crop of benefits and profits, thereby degenerate and corrupt vitiate the whole system. Perhaps the most widely accepted definition and the meaning of the term "corruption" is the use of public power for private profit.....in a way that constitutes a breach of law..."This covers the case not only of an official who receives bribes either to act or not to act, but also of the one who takes none, but uses his office to enrich himself illegally. The term 'private' is to be understood as not limited to the official, but also including a group or a class with which he identifies, while profits should be taken to cover all forms of advantage or benefit, not merely financial. The offence in corruption lies in the destruction or perversion of integrity or fidelity. It is not only the immediate employers who may suffer loss of fidelity. The general public as ultimate paymasters are made to suffer, when those holding public office, are corrupt.

Trade Unionism was a historical and ethical necessity. The weak united to resist exploitation by the strong and united they stood on equal terms with their oppressors on the platform of justice & fairplay. The tragedy of human frailty is that everything good tends in course of time to degenerate. Gandhi taught us how to fight the British. Eschewing violence, he advocated direct action. There was to be a peaceful defence of law. Given that violent rebellion was not to be attempted, it was the only way by which a people could successfully deal with an alien government. Whilst we have forgotten to use direct action. Whilst Gandhi recommended it against a foreign ruler, we see instances of it, in support of one or the other mundane issue, more often for ultimate selfish gains. This is happening even after more than four decades of independence and it is more concerning when we have a democratic system with full franchise.

Indians are not living in a very idealistic age. Indians have already suffered a lot of oppression and discrimination for thousands of years not only at the hands of foreigners but by them own people. It is time to make the rule of law and rule of life run closer, so that springs of social justice may arise. In this perishable world one should live like a fish, which lives in water but never drowned. This is an important message for the civil services, which owes a lot to the society for status, authority and privileges conferred on them. The civil servants are seated at the steering wheel. The very purpose of civil services is to serve others; to serve the society. In a welfare State, the concept of common good makes the public employment a mission, as well as a challenge, the entire machinery of the government works and functions for the common public good. The posts are created, filled and held, to achieve the objective of common good. Even the pay and emoluments of an employee are not merely personal to him but bear an element of public good and welfare.

A welfare state would simply promotion of individual welfare and realisation of the collective aims of society. It is imperative that the state must allow for the just and fullest possible development of the creative self - a free expression of its people its policies, plans and actions, all must enable the citizens to realise the best that is within. It is expected ultimately to enrich their happiness, promote spiritual uplift and ensure general welfare. However, welfare and all growth depends upon an energetic activity. Development without effort is not possible and effort means work - and hence work ethics.

N.A. Palkhiwala very aptly says: The country can do with dirtier finger nails and cleaner minds. Work and positive activity itself will clean and purify the minds, like the Ganga water which is self purifier. Thomas Carlyle was right in saying: "Blesses is he who has found his work. Let him ask no other blessedness." To some people work is success and hardwork is next to godliness. To quote a proverb: "It is better to be Socrates dissatisfied than a fool satisfied. It is better to be a human-being dissatisfied than a pig satisfied". The contribution of an individual civil servant and administrator within his own functional and territorial limits can make or mar a system. Change yourself and you have done your part in changing the world. Enlightenment starts within the individual.

To do good to the employees the emoluments are paid to them. The people are vitally interested in the payment of emoluments to the employees. The emoluments are paid out of the exchequer. The public pays for the emoluments of the employees in consideration of what the employees give in turn, through their service. The fairness of the payments has therefore, to satisfy the double test. It has to be fair both to employees and the people they serve.

The object and purpose of the State evolved in this country from time immemorial has been, that it is the permanent duty as the State to ensure that individual enjoys wealth - Artha - and every kind of pleasure kama without transgressing the Law - Dharma. The ideal placed before the State under the ancient Indian Constitutional Law - Rajadharma - is, that the State must strive for the happiness of the people. In the happiness or his subjects lies the happiness of the Ruler; in their welfare, his welfare; whatever pleases him, the Ruler shall not consider as good but whatever pleases his subjects, The Ruler shall consider as good. This directive enables the enforcement of law for ensuring the upliftment and welfare of the people. For the efficient administration of the affairs of the state and implementation of the above directive, elaborate administrative set-up with numerous departments were required to be created. Provisions regarding the qualification for appointment to important posts, for taking disciplinary action against civil servants who are found guilty of misconduct, including provision to punish individuals who make false complaints against civil servants, were made. The duties and responsibilities of heads of departments were laid down

in precise terms. And one of the duty is maintenance of discipline. Discipline is the foundation on which the structure of any society or institution rests. The administrative techniques pursued by the government are the same as were cast in concrete mould more than a century ago. Files and minutes still go perpetually from official to official and from ministry to ministry. Lord Curzon the Viceroy noted, "like the diurnal revolution of the earth went the file - stately, solemn, sure and slow". Decades later, Mal Colm Muggeridge observed the same phenomenon: "It was government pure and undefiled; endlessly minuting and circulating files, which like time itself, had neither beginning nor end, but just were." Even today the situation remains unchanged - only the number of files has increased thousandfold. Millions of man-hours are wasted every day in coping with finance bureaucratic regulations and a torrential skate of their amendments.

The basic lesson of all history, Barbara Tuchman concludes, "Philosophers of government ever since Plato have devoted their thinking to the major issues of ethics, sovereignty, the social contract, the rights of man, the corruption of power, the balance between freedom and order. Few-except Machiavelli, who was concerned with government as it is not as it should be - bothered with merely folly, although this has been a chronic and pervasive problem. More recently, Woodrow Wilson warned, in public affairs, stupidity is more dangerous than knavery'. Meanwhile bureaucracy rolls on impervious to any cry for change, like some vast computer than when once penetrated by error goes on pumping it out forever.

There is always need for discipline and the only effective method of introducing and maintaining discipline in any institution is by following a code of conduct, whether it is written, unwritten or self-imposed. The discipline may be broadly divided in different categories. It may be self-imposed, as is done in case of private individual where the principles laid down in holy scriptures by our great prophets and teachers are followed. Again there is the unwritten code of conduct, which in view of the institution is expected and followed by its members or employees and any deviation therefrom is apt to invite dispels are from those in a position of authority so as to ensure that there is no repetition. The Government Servants (Conduct) Rules purport to describe the various kinds of misconduct which a civil servant may commit and for which departmental proceedings may be launched against him. But in the very nature of things, these conduct Rules cannot be exhaustive of every conceivable kind of misconduct that may be committed by a civil servant. Any lapse from the character or integrity expected of a civil servant may be regarded as misconduct even though it may not amount to commission of an offence.

The code of discipline which is binding on a Government servant has necessarily to be both written and unwritten. In addition to the code of conduct specified in conduct Rules for employees, there exists what is known as an "unwritten Code of Conduct" which must be observed by every Government servant. The unwritten Code of Conduct has been partially incorporated in Rule 3 of the Central Civil Services (Conduct) Rules, 1964. Lord Justice Lopes observed: "If a servant conduct himself in a way inconsistent with the faithful discharge of his duty in the service, it is misconduct which justified immediate dismissal. That misconduct, according to my view, need not be misconduct in the carrying on of the service or the business. It is sufficient if it is conduct which is prejudicial or is likely to be prejudicial to the interests or to the reputation of the master. The unwritten Code of Conduct is broadly determined by the behaviour that is expected of a Government servant in his dealings even outside the normal sphere of employment.

An improper act of conduct is likely to give rise to disciplinary proceedings, Tambe J. emphasised: "It is true that the misconduct in respect of which disciplinary action is taken against a servant must have reasonable relation to the nature of service, but it need not necessarily arise in the course of employment. When a person accepts an employment by necessary implication he agrees to conduct and behave himself as would not be inconsistent with the nature of his service. By unwritten code of conduct is meant those self-evident or established principles of conduct and behaviour which are universally recognised and are to be followed by civil servants. If they fail to observe certain standards of decency and if the

Government were to tolerate its officers to commit any outrage in their private lives the result may be a catastrophic fall in the normal prestige of the administration. The unwritten code of discipline has always been there for Government servants. A reference to this may be found in the report of the Board of Enquiry, appointed by the British Government in 1928, wherein it was observed: "The Civil Service like any other profession has its unwritten code of ethics and conduct for which the most effective sanction lies in the public opinion of the service itself and it is upon the maintenance of a sound and healthy opinion that is value and efficiency chiefly depend. The report (1928) of Board of enquiry further postulated: "A Civil Servant is not to subordinate his duty to his private interest, but neither is he to put himself in a position where his duty and his interests conflict. He is not to make use of his official position to further those interests, but neither is he so to order his private affairs as to allow suspicion to arise that a trust has been abused or confidence betrayed.

For every enlightened profession and calling there exists a code of ethics. Such a code has no legal sanction in the sense that it is not embodied in legislative enactment. It is self-imposed compilation of restrictive conditions drawn up by the representatives of the profession or the challenge as the case may be. In addition to the Government Servants Conduct Rules, one of the traditions of the Civil Service is that a civil servant shall not only be honest in fact, but beyond, the reach of suspicion of dishonesty. Apart from the strict observance of the discipline as enjoined by the Government orders, the Government has a right to expect that every Government servant must observe certain standards of decency and morality in his private life as otherwise the reputation of the Government which is based on the conduct of the Government servant in public as well as private life, may be at stake. Even the conduct rules enjoin a Government servant at all times whether in office or outside to do nothing which is improper or inappropriate or unsuited to his position as a Government servant. The Government has, therefore, in exercise of their powers conferred on them by various enactments framed rules to regulate the conduct of their employees.

Generally speaking Government Servants have to be obedient, faithful, careful, honest, punctual, well-behaved and reasonably competent to discharge their duties. But in view of the falling standards of honesty, integrity and growing tendency on the part of the public in general and the Government servants in particular not to observe either any self-imposed or unwritten code of conduct, the stringent conduct and for ensuring compliance thereof, the Central Civil Service (Conduct Rules), 1964 based on the report of K. Santhanam were enforced. The Government Servants (Conduct) Rules purport to describe the various kinds of misconduct which a civil servant might commit. Such conduct rules cannot be exhaustive of every conceivable kind of misconduct that may be committed by a civil servant. "Rule 3(1) of the Central Civil Services (Conduct) Rules 1964 requires every Government servant to maintain at all times absolute integrity, devotion to duty and prohibits the doing of anything "which is unbecoming of a Government servant. "Integrity" is uprightness, honesty or purity. Devotion to duty is faithful service and not failure to discharge duties properly or dereliction of duty. Misconduct in discharge of duties includes dereliction of duty. Code of Conduct as set out in the Conduct Rules clearly indicates the conduct expected of a member of a service. It will follow that conduct which is blame-worthy for the Government servant in the context of conduct Rules would be misconduct.

It is said when politics gets in through doors, justice escapes through the windows. Thomas Jefferson is right when he emphasised: Politics is such torment that I would advise everyone I love not to mix with it.

A public office is a public trust. Every employee on accepting government employment assumes a special duty to be fair and impartial in his dealings with the public; and must completely subordinate his self-interest to public service in all circumstances in which there might be, or appear to be, the possibility of any conflict of interest. He should do a full day's work for a full day's pay. But the people wish to become rich overnight and that creates problems. People want quick results and short-cuts in success. This human frailty of minimum effort and maximum results' has encompassed all fields of Indian national life. The path of honesty which implies sincere, hard labour has to yielded to means, foul and unfair. A greedy man is tempted to think in terms of short-cuts to become rich; and if he could become so overnight, he is prepared to descend to any low level. The people become enamoured of such short-cuts involving to sacrifice and quick results believing that political power is the panacea for all the ills, unmindful that short-cut means of state power would really lead to creation of an immoral national life of a country. The Apex Court in appeals by three nationalised banks: - State Bank, Syndicate Bank and Canara Bank - seeking a finality on whether employees were entitled to waves for strike period if it had been declared unjustified but legal by a statutory machinery under the Industrial Disputes Act, declared that even when the strike was legal, Employees would loss their salary but would not be subjected to disciplinary proceedings. A five Judge Constitution bench headed by Mr. Justice Kuldip Singh, while noting that old balance between the management and workmen had undergone a qualitative Change" with the emergence of organised sector, felt that labour had "acquired even the power of holding the society at large to ransom." The court identified two situations in which a strike or Lock-out could be resorted to. First as a weapon it should be sparingly uses for redress of urgent and pressing grievances when no means are available or when available means have failed. Or it should be last resort to compel the other party to dispute to "see justness of the demand", In any event strike should not be "utilised to cause hardship to the society at large so as to strengthen the "bargaining power" the judge said: Employees were entitled to salary for strike period if it was both legal and justified. The court ruled: strike or lock out should not be resorted to "because one has a superior bargaining power or requisite economic muscle to compel the other party to accept its demands," The Judges warned: such an action would be nothing but an assertion for "might is right". The judgement of the Apex Court is the beckon light on work ethics.

Throughout the world there is an acute crisis of confidence in integrity and fairness. There is gradual but wider realisation though the impact of actuality and the intensity of immediacy are wanting in our actions. Unfortunately the idealism which prevailed when we became independent has since evaporated. The consciousness which had been generated when the fruit of struggle for independence was about to materialise is no more found. In the post-independence era we have not been able to sustain the requisite element of patriotism. The famous saying that 'eternal vigilance is the price of liberty' appears to have been forgotten and the country has taken a turn leading us away from what we were looking for at end of the struggle for independence. Indisputably law is a regulator of human conduct but it is difficult to achieve noticeable social reform through law. The voice of reason is more readily heard when it can persuade but no coerce. It is high time to remember and practice the prophecy of Fourteenth Dalaii Lama: Work in harmony with one another, and do not aspire to do what you cannot. Consider what is proper to do and not to do and carry out your task without doubts, as all knowing Master's will, as if everything was happening under his eye. Act in this spirit and all will be well.

Inspite of some minor and not patent pilferages, the man may still be termed as a honest one. The acts of omission and commission may not be visible to and detectable by normal people. We refuse to see red even as we are sitting on a veritable mine-field. Despite the fact that the normal people can get around does not wean that they are seeing and hearing. David Schuman opine : Both healthy minds and healthy bodies may be crippled. The fact that "normal" people can get around, can see, can hear, does not mean that they are seeing and hearing. They can be very blind to the things that spoil their happiness, very ideal to the pleas of others for kindness: when I think of them I do not feel any more crippled or disabled than they.

N.A. Palkhivala described the rare species; we are surrounded by too many persons who are willing to compromise. We have in our midst far too many "bone-less wonders". There exists a huge class of people who have neither industrial nor commercial capital and yet live like real masters. They own neither land nor factories nor workshops but they enjoy a robber's income. They do not have their own enterprises, but spend their whole lives free from manual labour. They are commanders just like the capitalists and proprietors, having all the rights and privileges but no corresponding responsibilities and duties. The enormous wealth that they possess is perhaps due to the new 'Indian dharma' of private good at the expense of the state. Such people have over the time won wider acceptability and it no more excites passion. The top brass of the country look upon the State as the private property and use it for their private enrichment. Peter Drucker elaborates Civil Services depends, entirely on Government money. So do the health care, education, the universities - even the churches - in most countries. And one institution that most depends on the Government for its income is the civil service.

A problem of ethics in public service may be said to exist whenever public servants, individually collectively, use positions in a way which compromise public confidence and trust and because of conflicts legalities or values, or as result of attempt to achieve some form of private gain at the expense of public welfare or common good. The civil servants now work for self-interest and attempt to maximise their utility. The people who preach high, themselves practise low. The craze for easy money, evidenced by the monumental bank scams, is symptomatic of the breaking down of ethical values. Accused involved in Bank Securities Scams, behind the prison bar, are silently questioning the people of the country as to whether they are not corrupt the difference may be that they are caught and they are undetected or that they got the opportunity to commit fraud and they could not get the opportunity. If given an opportunity and capability they too may commit the frauds may be of much bigger dimension and higher magnitude.

One may kill the mosquitoes in a room by spraying flit but many more will come inside from the breeding ground, the hole needs to be plugged, breeding ground generating the corruption deserves to be culture and the cause has to be located and removed by socio-economic operation. In the context of present day country's conditions. However, well designed a building, its strength basically lies in its bricks. However, well conceived any institution its future ultimately depends on the human material running it. The tragedy of these closing decades of twentieth century is the declining values.

The brick kiln is sick. The quality of the civil services is on the decline, quote a large part of the blame lying squarely at the door of the politician. Politics is not an open game. The games the bureaucrats play remain undisclosed. Politics these days is not based on morals.

The unholy nexus between the civil service and the political leadership makes the deviation from rules and law possible, resulting in the politicians getting away with their excesses. The healthy functioning of the administration depends not only on the competence of its personnel but also on the maintenance of a high standard of personal conduct and the observance of discipline. The word 'discipline' has a wide connotation, it is a way of life as well as philosophy of life. Discipline is the foundation of any orderly society or State. The efficiency or otherwise of the Government depends not only on the conduct and behaviour of its servants in the discharge of their duties and responsibilities but also on their conduct and character in relation to the public with whom they have to deal and whom they are employed to serve; because ultimately it is the public that is affected by any misconduct or misbehaviour on the part of a government servant. Since any misconduct on the part of a government servant would reflect on the government itself, it is essential that the Government should be in a position to regulate the conduct of its servants in order to uphold the interest of the Government, and to serve the interests of the common man. The Government servants have thus not only to conform to a system of rules of conduct enjoined on them by the Government but they have also to observe certain standards of dignity, discipline and decorum in their dealings with the public. It would not be correct to say that a government servant is answerable for misconduct committed in the course of his duty only. If it is accepted that he is not answerable for acts of misconduct committed in his private capacity then it would mean that the Government would be powerless to dispense with his services, however reprehensible his conduct in private life may be until and unless he commits a criminal offence or an act which is specifically prohibited by the conduct Rules. The result would be to place the Government in a position worse than that of an ordinary employer. These Rules, therefore, rightly apply for all

acts of misconduct, misbehaviour or misdemeanor whether committed in the course of an official function or in private life. A public officer required to maintain integrity and to be devoted to duty, is merely asked to keep within the bounds of that administrative decency which goes by the name of civilised administration.
What constitute an 'unbecome' act, it is not possible to define. It is not possible to have an exhaustive list of actions when would be 'unbecoming' of a government servant. There are well understood norms of conduct, of morality, decency, decorum and propriety becoming of a government servant. A fall from such standard would render an act unbecoming. Like similar other laws on the statute back, the laxity in strict application of the Conduct Rules have lodged to a situation in which these have ceased to instil any fear in the hearts of the dishonest and corrupt. That is why today we see majority of the Government servants merrily acquiring assets disproportionate to their known sources of income, often, in league or connivance with the political superiors. Apart from pollution the environment what it has brutally pecimated is the respect and regard for 'work culture'.

By and large the Civil Servants have sufficient resources so they do not have to work hard to obtain food, clothing and so forth. But in the present day merely having enough to wear and sufficient to eat is not enough. They want something for more. They yearn for more and more. This clearly illustrates that unless satisfaction and contentment are brought about through transforming the mind, it is not possible to achieve lasting happiness through external means, however, favourable the external conditions may be. Happiness and discomfort are very much dependent on our mental attitude.

To conclude it will be worth to remember that all conflicts have their roots in ago, bias, partiality, favouritism and discrimination, which eventually lead to injustice. And the conflicts in administration arise due to irregularity, inefficiency, irresponsibility, irreverence and insincerity and harmony can come about not from the absence of conflicts but from the ability to cope with them.